D0845091

University Press of Florida

Gainesville · Tallahassee · Tampa · Boca Raton · Pensacola · Orlando · Miami · Jacksonville

JAMES O'ROURKE   Keats's Odes and
Contemporary
Criticism

Copyright 1998 by the Board of Regents of the State of Florida
Printed in the United States of America on acid-free paper

03 02 01 00 99 98 6 5 4 3 2 1

Library of Congress Cataloging-in-Publication Data

O'Rourke, James L.
Keats's odes and contemporary criticism / James O'Rourke.
p. cm.
Includes bibliographical references and index.
ISBN 0-8130-1590-1 (alk. paper)
1. Keats, John, 1795-1821—Criticism and interpretation—History—20th century. 2. Odes—History and criticism—Theory, etc.
I. Title.
PR4837.O75 1998
821'.7—dc21 98-6635

The University Press of Florida is the scholarly publishing agency
for the State University System of Florida, comprised of Florida
A & M University, Florida Atlantic University, Florida International University, Florida State University, University of Central
Florida, University of Florida, University of North Florida, University of South Florida, and University of West Florida.

University Press of Florida
15 Northwest 15th Street
Gainesville, FL 32611
http://nersp.nerdc.ufl.edu/~upf

CONTENTS

ode to a Nightingale

To Autumn

THIS STUDY OF FOUR of Keats's major odes seeks to show how these poems traverse, and often exceed, the range of our modern critical practices. My readings of the odes focus on how Keats's famed negative capability and his exceptional ear for language enabled him to use the literary exercise of writing odes as a vehicle for exploring how both one's beliefs and one's sense of self can be formed, displaced, and remade through the material base of words.

These readings are indebted to the deconstructive methods of reading that flourished in Romantic studies in the 1970s and 1980s. The status of deconstruction as a mode of literary criticism has ebbed in recent years; deconstructive criticism has, on one side, been denounced for its supposed deviation from a properly Derridean orthodoxy, and, from another, marginalized by the simplistic story of an institutional history, in which deconstruction reigned for a brief period in literary studies but has now been superseded by the New Historicism. In the field of Romanticism, the latter narrative has been given an unfortunate impetus by Jerome McGann's critique of deconstruction as the culmination of a "text-only" criticism that should be superseded by a properly historical criticism ("Keats," 988). McGann's antideconstructive polemics have obscured the degree to which deconstruction helped to inaugurate the present age of interdisciplinarity in literature departments in North America. Once Derrida began to argue that the prestige of philosophy as a master discipline depended upon a sleight of hand, through which philosophical texts concealed their essentially tropic natures, literary critics quickly realized that the same mode of deconstructive reading could be applied to any discipline—such as history or autobiography—that claimed to offer a transparent referentiality.

Literary criticism is itself one of the disciplines in which legitimacy rests heavily on its claims to a referential relation between its own words and the primary texts upon which it comments; thus the ways in which various critical paradigms have inscribed the cultural significance of these highly canonized poems tell a good deal about our recent critical history. I have taken the dominant critical paradigms of the present to be the New Criticism, whose continued viability in the American academy has no stronger proof than Helen Vendler's book on Keats's odes; de Manian deconstruction, which, for all its insight into the rhetorical determination of other critical approaches, has its own highly vulnerable linguistic assumptions; the New Historicism, whose most influential spokesperson in Romantic studies, Jerome McGann, has staked out the ode "To Autumn" as an exemplary test case for the hegemonic claims of a "socio-historical" method as the "governing context of literary investigations" (1025); and Freudian psychoanalysis. The point of the discussion of the critical histories of these poems and the theoretical contexts of those histories is not to score points against individual critics, but to illustrate, as clearly and as fundamentally as possible, why these poems have played such a significant role in our modern cultural history, and how they continue to be more than we thought we had bargained for.

Chapter 1, on the "Ode to a Nightingale," addresses New Critical and deconstructive readings of the poem in order to show the limits of these modes of formalist criticism in conveying the affective valence of literary language and goes on to argue for the value of the category of the Kristevan *semiotique* in capturing the aesthetic power of the poem. Chapter 2, on the "Ode on a Grecian Urn," challenges the claims of historicist critics to offer a genetic account of the coming into being of the literary text through its determination in the public sphere. Close study of the controversies over

Greek sculpture in Regency England shows that Keats engages precisely the same questions regarding the relation between the individual artwork and its cultural context that now inform the ode's most recent critical history, and that Keats addresses these questions more subtly than do the poem's modern critics. Chapter 3, on the "Ode on Melancholy," pursues the critique of genetic analysis, this time in the private realm, through a comparison of the exaggerated posturing of the ode with the explanatory power of psychoanalytic texts (particularly those of Freud) that treat the same topics that the poem engages, and suggests that Keats was well aware of the artifice behind the ode's turn to sensuous excess. Chapter 4, on "To Autumn," contends that the poem's own negative dialectic, between a nostalgic celebration of organic presence and an awareness of the unbridgeable gap between the unmoored activity of consciousness and the inexorable predictability of nature, is a more nuanced treatment of its central themes than is found in either the formalist celebrations of its perfection or the political critique of its supposedly reactionary intentions.

This book discusses the four poems in the order in which they are generally believed to have been written, though in doing so it makes no claims for seeing them as a sequence. The order in which the poems were composed is uncertain, and whatever their exact sequence, the brevity of the period within which they were written leaves me with little confidence that a narrative of Keats's emotional or intellectual development can reliably be drawn from such a limited body of evidence. I have not included either the "Ode to Psyche" or the "Ode on Indolence" in this study. In neither of these poems does an ongoing dialectic of linguistic displacement and condensation accelerate to the point of annihilating a stable and centered persona; thus, whatever the value of these two poems, it is fundamentally different from that of the subjects of this book.

In each of the four odes discussed here, there is at least one point where the initial premise of the poem's "I" is contradicted and deflected such that it would be misleading to attribute that deflection to the controlled strategy of a transcendent subject. In each case, the deflection occurs near the turn into the last stanza: in the reiteration of the word "forlorn" in "Nightingale," in the contemplation of the "desolate" "little town" in the "Grecian Urn," in the recognition of "Beauty that must die" in "Melancholy," and in the interrogative reaching toward the "songs of spring" in "To Autumn." But there are no such moments in the "Ode to Psyche" or the "Ode on Indolence." In "Psyche," there is a perfect continuity from the "I" who at the outset of the poem "wander[s] in a forest thoughtlessly" to the "I" who

will be Psyche's priest. The poem's conclusion suggests that his initial perplexity is resolved by this decision, and that his will be an entirely untroubled
vocation. The "Ode on Indolence" contains a bit more drift, especially in
the poem's second stanza; its language begins to sound like the opening of
"Nightingale" in the gliding alliteration of "How came ye muffled in so
hush a mask? / Was it a silent deep-disguised plot,"[2] but the speaker is soon
able to reclaim his control of the poem's agenda.

The deflections and decenterings in the "Nightingale," "Grecian Urn,"
"Melancholy," and "Autumn" odes represent Keats's most radical excur-
sions into the first half of the *fort-da* game that Freud describes in "Beyond
the Pleasure Principle"; they show Keats's ability to play "gone," to see how
far he can go, without the need to safeguard or recoup that expenditure. A
different Keats, a more earnest figure with a stronger sense of purpose and
of social responsibility, is more easily translated into critical terms and is
more often foregrounded in Keats criticism. The poetic career of this familiar figure begins in "Sleep and Poetry," in which Keats suggests that he
"must pass" the "joys" of a sensual poetry for "a nobler life / Where I may
find the agonies, the strife / Of human hearts" (122–25); it culminates in
"The Fall of Hyperion" when Moneta admonishes Keats's persona:

> The poet and the dreamer are distinct,
> Diverse, sheer opposite, antipodes.
> The one pours out a balm upon the world,
> The other vexes it. ("The Fall of Hyperion," 199–202)

In the most important recent study of Keats's odes, Helen Vendler has
brought this more respectable figure to the center. In doing so, she has
given us a highly polished account of Keats's craftsmanship in these poems,
but Vendler's study nonetheless diminishes the most powerful effects of the
odes. In addition to being the workmanlike and clear-sighted fellow of
Vendler's study, Keats was a very unlikely figure: a bohemian who was every
bit the genius he thought he was. He moved in a circle of like-minded
friends who were thoroughly contemptuous of the perceived philistinism of
their own culture. Keats's disdain for the prevailing tastes of his society, and
his complete confidence in his own, led to such howlers as his pronounce-
ments of the world-class importance of Haydon's paintings. It also led to his
belief that he would be "among the English Poets" when he died, and to his
cultivation of the gift that put him there despite his early death. Keats's
greatest gift was an uncanny ability to experience language materially—
"For awhile after you quit Keats," F. Scott Fitzgerald wrote, "all other po-

etry seems to be only whistling or humming" (88). In our contemporary critical vocabularies, we have learned that it is at the level of the material signifier that language begins to lose its stability and to go outside or in between what it was before. When Keats did this, he produced a poetry capable of moments of great beauty and of subtle critique of the common assumptions of his culture and, sometimes, of the shared terms in which he and his circle dissented from those assumptions. In recent criticism, Vendler and Marjorie Levinson have given us detailed, though very different, portraits of Keats as a thoroughly interpellated being. The Keats who emerges from this study is a more eccentric figure whose poetry moves into uncharted discursive spaces and who can end a text in a confession of his inability to distinguish waking from dreaming, a state of which Moneta could not approve. I hope to have conveyed here some sense of the play of this mind that sought to be a "thoroughfare for all thoughts" (*KL*, 2:213). In a critical era that has absorbed a Lacanian critique of ego psychology, the cultivation of what Keats called "negative capability" can acquire a good deal of critical force in helping to peel away the layers of habit that pass for knowledge and in effecting the transformation of "man" into a less predictable being.

ACKNOWLEDGMENTS

I want to thank those who read portions of this manuscript and offered support and advice during its long gestation: Hazard Adams, Hans Braendlin, Doug Collins, Ralph Freedman, Mona Modiano, and Evan Watkins. I also want to express my appreciation to my editors at the University Press of Florida, Alexandra Leader and Gillian Hillis, whose efficiency and enthusiasm for this project have been most helpful and gratifying. Institutional support from Florida State University has included two summer stipends from the Council on Faculty Research Support and the always cheerful and knowledgeable efforts of the Interlibrary Loan Department. Nicholas Clarke, the senior computer consultant to the English Department at Florida State University, was invaluable in making the manuscript technolegible.

This book was begun in one intellectual community and concluded in another, and to my erstwhile and present colleagues at the opposite ends of this country I owe great debts for friendships that have enriched my personal life and sustained my sense of the value of intellectual enterprise. I am deeply grateful to Allen Hibbard, John Murphy, Brian Richardson, David Robinson, June Rugh, Julie Shaffer, Lynn Thompson, and Caren Town for

The maker's rage to order words of the sea,
Words of the fragrant portals, dimly-starred,
And of ourselves and of our origins,
In ghostlier demarcations, keener sounds.

Stevens, "The Idea of Order at Key West"

ι

ι

ι

ι

ι

ι

ι

ι

ι

ι

ι

CHAPTER 1

Ghostlier Demarcations, Keener Sounds

ι

Intertextuality and Agency in

ι

the "Ode to a Nightingale"

ι

ι

ι

ι

ι

TO JUDGE FROM the volume, the variety, and the polemical force of the modern critical responses engendered, there have been few moments in English poetic history as baffling as Keats's repetition of the word "forlorn" in the "Ode to a Nightingale." The sense of spontaneity created by this repetition and the consequent effect of direct access to the raw material of the poet's thinking have led to extended discussions of both Keats's manner of composition and his autonomy as a creative subject. The critical questions that have arisen about the "Nightingale" ode have changed very little in their genesis since Robert Bridges judged it to be the greatest of Keats's odes even though he believed, regarding the transition from one "forlorn" to another, that "in the penultimate stanza the thought is fanciful or superficial," and the "introduction, too, of the last stanza is artificial" (130). While the ways in which this supposed artificiality and its implications for Keats's authorial status have been assessed have changed significantly from the New Critical era to the present day, the critical history of the "Ode to a Nightingale" is, nevertheless, in one sense foreshortened; this poem whose self-constructed history is primarily literary has not lent itself to cultural materialist analysis. Its modern critical history registers a shift from one formalism to another: from the New Criticism, which was coterminous in America with the dominance of the Harvard school of Keats criticism, to the very different style of Yale poststructuralist formalism.

The most recent discussions of the "Nightingale" ode have centered on questions arising from the poem's self-consciousness about its literary history and on the precise weight to be given to its various intertextual borrowings. These questions have repeatedly served as the staging ground for addressing the terms in which both this poem and Romanticism as a whole have been reinterpreted by Bloom, de Man, and Hartman as a rhetoric of self-consciousness and fragmentation. As the stakes of this argument have seemed to its participants to involve far more than the canonic status of the "Ode to a Nightingale," claims made about the poem have become increasingly broad even as they continue to originate in theses determined primarily by answering the poem's final, unanswered questions. Whether the "Nightingale" ode presents the "it" of its penultimate line as a vision or as a mere daydream, and whether the return to the everyday world at the poem's close is consequently a gain or a loss in perceptual clarity, have been the central concerns of the ode's reception history to the present day. What is of greatest value in the "Ode to a Nightingale," I want to suggest, lies not in more definitive answers than those the poem itself provides to its closing questions, but instead in the vehicle itself, in the access that the "Nightin-

gale" ode allows to a highly unstructured process of composition that enters
literary history as an echo chamber. In an 1816 sonnet, Keats writes of the
legacy of past poets as a "pleasing music" that "when I sit me down to rhyme
/ . . . will in throngs before my mind intrude":

> How many bards gild the lapses of time!
>   A few of them have ever been the food
>   Of my delighted fancy,—I could brood
> Over their beauties, earthly, or sublime:
> And often, when I sit me down to rhyme,
>   These will in throngs before my mind intrude:
>   But no confusion, no disturbance rude
> Do they occasion; 'tis a pleasing chime.
> So the unnumber'd sounds that evening store;
>   The songs of birds—the whisp'ring of the leaves—
>   The voice of waters—the great bell that heaves
> With solemn sound,—and thousand others more,
>   That distance of recognizance bereaves,
> Make pleasing music, and not wild uproar.

"How many bards" contains several foreshadowings of the imagery of the
"Nightingale" ode, and its wealth of aural imagery reflects an intertextuality
that is primarily phonetic rather than thematic. The synthetic "pleasing
chime" incorporates both "the songs of birds" and "the great bell that heaves
/ With solemn sound," thus anticipating both the initial birdsong and the
closing knell of the ode. The sonnet instances the intrusion of its poetic
precursors through a Shakespearean echo: Its "unnumber'd sounds" recall
the "unnumb'red idle pebble" of *King Lear* (4.6.21).[1] The echoes of past
bards lose their textual bindings and semantic weight to the imprecision of
memory as they become only a "pleasing music"; "distance of recognizance
bereaves," and the "beauties" of poetic phrases are opened to new "throngs"
of poetic associations. Such oblique borrowings populate the "Nightingale"
ode with a density that is unusual even for Keats, and the following discussion of the ode's intertextuality is meant to illuminate in an exemplary rather
than an exhaustive manner both the modern critical history of the ode and
its own construction of its literary history. The perception of the poem's
artificiality, which persists even to the present day in Vendler's characterization of the "Nightingale" ode as an early exercise in spontaneous aestheticism that "Keats abandons for good" (*Odes*, 109) in the later odes, is
grounded not in Keats's immaturity or his too hasty craftsmanship but in

the limits of our formalist practices in describing the signifying process of lyric poetry. As "How many bards" tells us and as the "Nightingale" ode shows, the most spontaneous poetry often mimics other poetry far more closely than it does anything in the natural world, yet its distance from birdsong does not necessarily entail any loss of the material presence of aurality. The signifying process of the "Ode to a Nightingale" involves not only what Keats borrowed but how he borrowed, and this essay is meant to suggest how he did so, as discrete moments of phonetic repetition lead to the rapid assimilation of broad networks of interwoven reference.

Although the "Nightingale" ode was particularly admired and repeat-edly singled out for extensive quotation by contemporary reviewers of the *Lamia* volume, Bridges's sense that there was a fundamental structural weak-ness in the poem began to gain ground in the early part of the twentieth century. Soon after H. W. Garrod and Albert Gerard amplified Bridges's complaint that Keats's fascination with "rhythm and words" had caused him to "lose hold of the main idea" of the poem (Garrod, 117; Gerard, 495), R. H. Fogle moved to defend the ode against what he saw as the "damaging charges" leveled against it by Bridges, Garrod, and Gerard. Worrying that Gerard's contention that "the movement of feeling is at the mercy of words evoked by chance" had served to "indict . . . the Ode for bad art and low-grade mental activity," Fogle acknowledged "the specific problem of asso-ciational transitions like 'fade away' and 'forlorn'," but, he argued, even if "the transitional links of the poem" seem "at first sight spontaneous and merely associational . . . they are too invariably happy, however, to be liter-ally unpremeditated." Of Garrod's contention that the ode is determined by its "rhythm and words," Fogle responds dryly, "One wonders who deter-mines the rhythm and words" (221–22). Fogle's distinction between an au-thor who functions as the detached creator of the poem and a lyric persona who is merely a dramatic character at the mercy of contingent relations within the text echoes Cleanth Brooks's classic New Critical defense of the thematic coherence of the "Nightingale" ode. Brooks accounts for the rep-etition of the word "forlorn" by separating a figure he calls "the poet"— whose place is "in the poem," where he "suddenly realizes" its shifting im-plications—from another figure, called "Keats," who resides outside the text as the fully conscious architect of the shift in meaning that is triggered by the repetition of the word. This distinction allows Brooks to contend that "Keats's repetition of 'forlorn'" becomes "a concentrated instance of the theme of the whole poem," wherein the world of actuality is rendered "more painful by contrast" when it is held up to the ideal "world of the imagination" (*Modern Poetry*, 31). The methodology of Brooks's interpretive practice as he explicates the repetition of the word "forlorn" contradicts the basic principles of his supposedly formalist theory. Despite the New Critical critique of the intentional fallacy, Brooks removes the level of action in the poem from the dramatic level of the persona "in the poem" to the level of "Keats" himself, and then, despite the "heresy of paraphrase," he identifies the value of the poem with a paraphrasable thematic statement made by "Keats" about the value of imaginative truth.

The common sense of this New Critical explication and of Fogle's rhetorical question about "who determines the rhythm and words" of the poem runs counter to the premise of "How many bards": that when Keats "sit[s] me down to rhyme," sounds, rather than thoughts, become the instigating presence for composition. This sensitivity to the material presence of words is the basis of Keats's distinction in the "negative capability" letter between "the sense of Beauty" attributed to Shakespeare and the activity of "consideration" that characterizes Coleridge's greater desire for "knowledge" (*KL*, 1:194). Cynthia Chase's citation of the parallel with the apostrophic sonnet beginning "O thou whose face," which is spoken by a nightingale and which ends with the paradox that "he's awake who thinks himself asleep" (224), shows how the "Nightingale" ode belongs to the genre of Keats's poems that can fall within the grip of the deepest uncertainties "without any irritable reaching after fact and reason." Keats's epistolary observation that "there is no such thing as time and space, which by the way came forcibly upon me on seeing for the first hour the Lake and Mountains of Winander" (*KL*, 1:298) even offers a biographical access to the poetic persona who is unable to decide whether his final perception of "near meadows" and a "still stream" means that he is awake or asleep. It may seem mere common sense to refer to the reality of empirical surroundings in order to distance oneself from this confusion, but it cannot be assumed that Keats himself would remain detached from the "Nightingale" ode's imaginative departure from the "sole self" of the poem's persona. Commonsense assumptions about the capacity for or the necessity of "premeditation" of such associations as that effected by the echo of "forlorn" in this poem are far from assured at any level of narration. "Keats" cannot be used as a metaphysical touchstone and should not be relied upon for a stability based on continuity of identity that he himself never espoused.

The critical imperative behind Fogle's defense of Keats may have owed something to its time. Fogle's essay was first published in 1953, when it seemed in some quarters that the Romantics still needed some defense of their cognitive respectability and craftsmanship, but the suspicion that this poem is a little too spontaneous and unstructured soon resurfaced in E. C. Pettet's reading of the poem. Pettet judges that the first occurrence of "forlorn" probably represents a lapse on Keats's part, and he suggests that

> even if the word in the seventh stanza is to be taken with the minimum of emotional tone, it is certainly a strange one to be attached to a dream and a sort of poetry that Keats had always regarded with such unqualified imaginative delight. Possibly—for even in 1819 rhyme sometimes ran away with him—the word slipped in without much consideration as an easy, sound-pleasing, alliterative rhyme to finish the stanza. (278)

Subsequently, David Perkins and Walter Jackson Bate offered succinct thematic explanations of the first occurrence of the word "forlorn," Perkins saying that "The faery lands are forlorn because man cannot live in them," and Bate that "Those impossible lands are 'forlorn' because they are not at all for man" (Perkins, 255; Bate, 509). Perkins and Bate describe Keats as a more realistic, less visionary thinker than Brooks does, but they share the New Critical assumption of the desirability of a poetics of metaphor, the controlled substitution of image for idea, over metonymy, which depends on linear and contiguous associations, in order to redeem Keats's poetic practice. As the New Critics entered the argument between the poem's defenders and its critics, they adhered to critical protocols which stipulate that meaning is a more proper determinant of word choice than are stylistic features such as "rhythm and words," and furthermore that the poet is responsible for remaining ever in control of the meanings his words are intended to convey. The only disagreement among New Critical readers of the poem is whether Keats lives up to this responsibility in the "Ode to a Nightingale." The New Critical debate over the ode thus evades the most difficult questions that the poem poses to the formation of a formalist critical vocabulary. Both the precise mode of intentionality of a literary text and the representation of that intentionality in the relation between the author and the speaker of a first-person lyric poem are oversimplified by the preemptive dismissal of intentionality as an interpretive category, and Brooks's resort to the category in practice reflects the impossibility of abandoning the concept entirely. To assume the extralinguistic autonomy of the author only oversimplifies the question in the opposite manner; the resulting thematic analyses inevitably transform the most spontaneous moments in the text into paraphrastic statements that belie such spontaneity.

Bate's and Perkins's explanations of the meaning of the word "forlorn" demonstrate, in their succinctness, the ease with which semantic determinism is commonly assumed in critical commentary, an assumption that has caused most critics to overlook or disregard the sonic features of the first appearance of the word "forlorn." Among the ode's New Critical readers, only Pettet makes even a glancing reference to the alliteration of the first appearance of "forlorn," and he mentions it only to express the hope that this alliteration is not the reason for Keats's use of the word. Yet balancing the lack of thematic preparation in the poem for this bleak description of "faery lands" there is an excess of phonic motivation; in order to finish the line, the final word needs to rhyme with *corn*, and its consonants—*f, r, l, n*— come directly, and in order, from "*faery lands*." The density of its phonetic constitution is the reason "forlorn" seems "like a bell" to the poem's speaker, but if the word is determined from within the sensory and contingent stylistic features of the poem, this metonymic operation is irrelevant to the thematic explanations offered by Bate and Perkins and contradictory to the defenses of Keats's conceptual authority constructed by Brooks and Fogle.

As Yale formalism came to displace a New Critical common sensibility as the primary source of a critical vocabulary for the study of Romanticism, there was a change in the methodology and contextual references used in describing the "Nightingale" ode's deflection from the clarity of the signified to the opaqueness of the signifier; however, the implicit opposition that privileges conceptual mastery over the drifting of the signifier remained intact, despite overt rhetorical challenges to its stability. Chase offers the most thorough articulation of the Yale critics' argument for the importance of Miltonic influence as the sonic motivation for the appearance of the word "forlorn," through the ode's echo of this plaint from Adam to Eve:

> How can I live without thee, how forgo
> Thy sweet Converse and Love so dearly join'd,
> To live again in these wild Woods forlorn? (*Paradise Lost*, hereafter
> cited as *PL*, 9.908–10)[2]

Chase tracks the precision with which Keats "reenacts the effect of Milton's syntax," showing that in each case the deferred adjective "forlorn" refers first to a place ("wild Woods," "faery lands") and then to the speaker's own condition (223). Chase thus finds Milton to be the "poetic father" of the ode, and she argues that "the power to pass from hearing to singing is one the ode ascribes not to the poet himself but to Milton, the 'immortal bird' to whose phrases Keats's ode 'listens,' 'darkling,' more than any other" (212–13). Although the theme of Bloomian influence is clearly present, Chase does not characterize Keats's dependence on Milton as a fully oedipal agon, but she nevertheless constructs a similar structure of inadequation that demonstrates the impossibility of recovering an imaginary priority of full presence. Shifting from a Bloomian to a de Manian framework, Chase locates Keats's humbling before a Miltonic image in the inevitable dependence of perception on rhetorical constructions that rob it of "particularity." "Understanding depends on the possibility of imagining a sign as a voice," Chase contends, but that "imagining" is really a "rhetorical moment, rather than a natural given" and hence the poem "does not celebrate perception but displays its dependence on prosopopoeia" (224). Despite the use of a more technical rhetorical vocabulary, "prosopopoeia" rather than "rhythm and words," Chase's conclusion about the poem is not very far from Garrod's. Chase's subordination of Keats to an imaginarily full Miltonic "power to pass from hearing to singing" rephrases but does not really abandon the belief that discourse must either be "premeditated" or else represent a failure of meaning, even if Chase's account of the ode never implies anything like "low-grade mental activity." Both Garrod and Chase conclude that the dominance of rhetorical features over deliberation and conceptual clarity compromises Keats's ability fully to claim the imaginative identity of a Miltonic poet.

In making Milton the single precursor of the ode, Chase follows in a line of Yale critics (Bloom, Brisman, Fry, and Hollander) who have made similar claims about this poem.[3] The nomination of Milton as the "poetic father" of the "Nightingale" ode has recently been called into question in a number of studies that not only cite a remarkable number of Shakespearean echoes in the text but that also challenge the thematics of Bloomian influence study as they argue for the importance of Keats's reliance on Shakespearean, rather than Miltonic, sources. The argument was first joined by Willard Spiegelman, who draws pervasive parallels between *A Midsummer Night's Dream* and the ode, hoping, he says, "to steer readers away from the Keats living under the iron hand of Milton, and toward a poet whose homage to at least one precursor is hardly anxious at all but delicately embellished and lovingly harmonized" (354). Jonathan Bate's *Shakespeare and the English Romantic Imagination* begins with a polemic against Bloom for overemphasizing the importance of both Milton and anxiety for Romantic writers, and Bate finds in the "Ode to a Nightingale" a diversity of sources but a predominance of Shakespeare; Bate hears "about fifty" "Shakespearean analogues" in the poem (192). The Shakespearean thesis advanced by Spiegelman and Bate has drawn significant empirical, though less polemical, support from the studies of R. S. White, who cites allusions from eleven of Shakespeare's plays in the ode to support his contention that "the omnipresent influence, hovering close behind every stanza, is Shakespeare" (227); from Eamon Grennan, who points out that Keats's "become a sod" echoes Claudio's fear in *Measure for Measure*, that at death he will "become / A kneaded clod" (3.1.121–22; Grennan, 276); and from Barry Gradman, who suggests that the difficulty in making sense of Keats's reference to "Ruth, sick for home," standing "in tears amid the alien corn" when, in fact, the biblical Ruth leaves home quite willingly and is never described as weeping in her adopted family's fields can be overcome if we follow this approach: imagine that the importance of *King Lear* to Keats "worked on his mind, shaped his aesthetic standards, [and] inevitably colored his expression" so that Keats conflated Ruth and Cordelia as examples of "filial piety" to arrive at the single image of the weeping daughter in the poem (21–22).

The argument over the shape of the ode's intertextuality and the accompanying disagreements over the degree of anxiety that accompanies Keats's poetic borrowings have initiated another round of the argument over the integrity of Keats as an autonomous poetic subject. The recent Shakespearean readings of the poem defend "Keats" in terms very similar to those employed by Brooks, Fogle, Walter Jackson Bate, and Perkins in an earlier era. Although the more recent version passes "Keats" through a Shakespearean intertextuality, Keats's creative autonomy is rescued through the contrast between his controlled borrowing from Shakespeare and the Bloomian story that would place the ode in a Miltonic shadow. Spiegelman describes Keats bringing Shakespearean images to fruition as he calls *A Midsummer Night's Dream* "the seasonable sweet that has flavored and ripened the later poem" (360), and White argues of the "Nightingale" ode that "The poem is richly saturated in Shakespeare, yet the assimilations are so profound that the Ode is finally original, and wholly Keatsian" (217–18). White's conclusion embodies a paradox in the Shakespearean readings of the poem; the content of White's study is the enumerating of Shakespearean influences, but his valorization of Keats's poetic autonomy demands the circumscription of the importance of those influences, so that the rhetorical value of terms like "finally original" and "wholly Keatsian" in White's conclusion bear little relation to the material cited throughout the essay. Jonathan Bate casts the Shakespeare-Keats relationship in terms even more protective of Keats's personal integrity when he argues that Keats is "left enriched by the voice of Shakespeare, the 'immortal bird'; as at the end of the *Lear* sonnet, the poet returns from Shakespeare to the world refreshed, given 'new phoenix wings'" (197). Shakespearean readers of the poem have taken to questioning even the most seemingly secure Miltonic allusions.

Jonathan Bate reminds us that the entirety of *The Passionate Pilgrim* was attributed to Shakespeare in Keats's time, including an allusion to a "forlorn" nightingale (193). White calls "darkling" a "striking Shakespearean word" and gives three citations, from *A Midsummer Night's Dream*, *King Lear*, and *Antony and Cleopatra*, all plays that are also echoed elsewhere in the ode.

This controversy has begun to generate its own internal irony, as the sheer volume and range of Shakespearean echoes that continue to be discovered in the poem threaten to jeopardize the thematics of controlled allusion promoted by the advocates of the thesis of Shakespearean influence. In Keats's image of the "emperor and clown," Mark Taylor hears an allusion to Alexander and Yorick from *Hamlet*'s grave-digger scene (25); Barry Gradman, who sees *Lear* as the Shakespearean play most important to Keats, hears Lear and his fool (22); and Spiegelman, who contends that *A Midsummer Night's Dream* is the "play that rings loudest within the poem" (353), suggests Theseus and Bottom (362). But even when Keats echoes several writers simultaneously, Jonathan Bate argues, the "sustained series of echoes" matters more than the "incidental parallel," and he finds that "a dozen or more" echoes of *Hamlet* make the "Ode to a Nightingale" "a poem haunted by the language of *Hamlet*" (195). Bate sees "Keats begin[ning] to play Hamlet in earnest" in the third stanza, and he contends, "If the third stanza has shown Keats to be Hamlet, we can now only assume that the nightingale is Shakespeare" (196). Bate means these personifications to be taken quite literally; when the bird's "plaintive anthem fades," Bate reads Shakespeare the nightingale leaving Keats just as the ghost leaves Hamlet, "to face the waking world . . . with the implied injunction 'Remember me'" (197).

The extravagance of Bate's desire to cast the ode as a coherent dialogue between Keats as Hamlet and the nightingale as Shakespeare may itself be the best argument for Chase's critique of the entire interpretive tradition of this poem. Chase argues that critics have evaded the problem raised by the ode's unresolved ending, which poses the "question of whether perception is not hallucination" (211), by treating the trope of prosopopoeia as a "natural given" rather than a "rhetorical moment," thereby enabling the assumption that one hears a "sign as a voice" (224). The discrepancies among what Taylor, Gradman, and Spiegelman hear in the allusive background to Keats's "emperor and clown," as well as Bate's and Spiegelman's discoveries of two different plots for the ode that closely track two different Shakespearean plays (Spiegelman finding the source in *A Midsummer Night's Dream*, Bate in *Hamlet*), amply illustrate the difficulty of reliably "*hearing* writing" (Chase's emphasis, 211). The Bloomian alternative to this defense of Keats's creative autonomy, however, only replaces it with an equally reductive structure, the identification of Keats with a single symptom: anxiety in the face of Miltonic power. Where Bate identifies the "immortal bird" as Shakespeare, Chase, even after her critique of such undeserved prosopopoeia, goes on to provide just as determinate a personification of the nightingale when she calls Milton "the 'immortal bird' to whose phrases Keats's ode 'listens,' 'darkling,' more than any other" (212–13).

The discovery of distinct intertextual patterns in the "Nightingale" ode has repeatedly been used as a basis for constructing not only the plot of the poem but its thematic intent. Spiegelman finds in a series of allusions to *A Midsummer Night's Dream* an analogy between Puck, who in Spiegelman's metaphor leads the lovers on a "wild bird chase," and Keats's nightingale as "Fancy, that feminine elf," who "has teased him only halfway" (350), and he is thus able to endorse Jack Stillinger's judgment that the poem's message is that "The nightingale has proved to be a 'deceiving elf,' the 'fancy' (=imagination) 'cheat[s]'" ("Imagination," 7). Spiegelman, like Stillinger, discovers in the poem a subject of unequivocal and frustrated desire rather than one whose discourse ends on a note of genuine perplexity, and the gendered inflections that Spiegelman adds to Stillinger's account finally warn all/male readers against such romantic illusions. This reading perfectly continues the interpretive tradition, of which Stillinger has been the most visible and unambiguous representative, that Chase describes as a "critical unanimity" that Keats's poetry is to be valued as it "anticipate[s] the undeceived modernist vision" (210). As Chase rightly argues, the closing imagery of the "Ode to a Nightingale" offers no secure resolution of the epistemological dilemma it propounds. Chase's question of "whether perception is not hallucination" is an apposite one to pose to an interpretive tradition that has not only heard the allusive moments of the "Ode to a Nightingale" but has also imagined that it has heard the voice of someone unproblematically named "Keats" who can tell us the meaning of those allusions. But even Chase's conclusion, that Keats cannot know this meaning but that he knows someone else (Milton) who does, only defers the moment of signification in which language always refers to a fullness of presence beyond its own meanderings.

The "Ode to a Nightingale" certainly questions "whether perception is not hallucination," but as Chase's analysis shows, the hallucinations in the interpretive tradition of the ode become most delusive when prosopopoeia is overburdened and signs are given univocality; the ode is said to respond to a single author or a single work, or else the poem's main characters, its persona and the nightingale, are turned into overly determinate personifications. But the aptness to "hear writing" is an experience that the "Nightingale" ode testifies to with great intensity, and even if some pruning of the excesses of critical overzealousness may be necessary in establishing the ode's literary backgrounds, a very large volume of poetry that is contacted through sonic memory remains to shape the voice of the poem. This habit of echo begins in the poem's naturalistic opening line, in which, as Anne Cluysenaar points out, the ode echoes a famous line from *Hamlet*. Keats's

My heart aches, and a drowsy numbness pains

involves a phonetic reshuffling of

The heart-ache, and the thousand natural shocks.

In Keats's echoes and alliterations of Shakespeare, he adopts Shakespeare's coinage "heart-ache" to avoid the cliché of "My heart breaks," but where Shakespeare uses a /k/ consonance in *ache/shocks*, Keats slides into the assonance of *aches/pains*, which in turn constitutes, even as it separates the terms of, another cliché. When "and a drows" mimics "and the thous," and the final three syllables of each line are framed by /n/ and /s/, the opening words of the ode seem to come from a half-conscious speaker who is repeating verbal patterns that he has heard before, without offering any surety that he intends anything in particular by the repetition. Cluysenaar's account of how she discovered this parallel demonstrates how productive it can be to enter into the spirit of the ode's most unpremeditated poetics. Cluysenaar writes that a colleague "remarked that Keats' line raised an echo in his mind which he had not yet traced. I was to lecture next day. During the intervening night, I found myself sitting up in bed with the solution presented here. It had come to me in sleep!" (156).

This skewed echo of *Hamlet* is only the first instance of the muddled texture of the entire first stanza, which overbalances its logical incongruities with a habit of phonetic repetition that provides a comforting sense of aural coherence. The speaker tells us, first, that his "heart aches," blending a poetic cliché (the heart as the seat of sensation) with a naturalistic sensory complaint. Keats, the physician-poet, could not be oblivious to the degree of poetic license taken here. Although "drowsy numbness" would be expected to relieve that pain (as "shade to shade . . . com[ing] too drowsily" does in "Melancholy"), it only augments it as, oxymoronically, "drowsy numbness pains"; the surprising verb gets some of its sharpness by beginning with the plosive /p/. "My sense" has no actual anatomical reference point, but the possessive adjective suggests that it must have a location somewhere, and in the wake of the misleading physical specificity of "My heart," the term contributes more than it can literally support toward giving the speaker's lament the sense of a physical grounding. The speaker then discloses that the cause of these physical sensations, these aches and pains, is not itself physical in nature but is an imaginative impression produced on him by the sound of the nightingale. Although the outcome of this impression is painful, the speaker alleges both that the source of this painful sensation is benign (the nightingale's "happiness") and that his own pain results not from an inability to participate in that happiness ("not through envy") but from an excess of participation: "being too happy in thine happiness." The oxymoronic "drowsy numbness pains"—where the effect greatly exceeds its cause—finds a complement in this painfully excessive happiness, itself a contradictory effect of an excessive cause, but neither state explains the other. In sum, the whole line of causality in the stanza claims that the emotion of happiness passes from the nightingale to the speaker but is then mysteriously transformed into a contrary state of physical pain.

The fragmented logic of the stanza is offset by its aural tightness. When Keats substitutes the assonance of *aches/pains* for Shakespeare's *ache/shock*, the solitary /k/ of "aches" drifts off to become active elsewhere, in the consonance of *hemlock/drunk/sunk*. The first rhyme word in the poem, "drains," not only rhymes the second half of the alliterative cliché "aches and pains," but it does so by further alliterating the intervening line ending "drunk," which was itself alliterative of "drowsy," an alliteration that resurfaces in the latter half of the stanza in "Dryad" and "trees." *Trees* also introduces the broad /ee/ that recurs in "beechen green" and then joins the sibilant esses of "shadows numberless," "singest," and "summer" to bring the stanza to phonetic closure in the synthetic "ease." The murky image of "shadows numberless" creates a near phonetic repetition of the initial "drowsy numbness." This aural repetition is put into the service of an imagistic logic that tries to make a persuasive case for the generation of a physical sensation from an imaginative idea through the simile of the second through fourth lines:

> as though of hemlock I had drunk,
> Or emptied some dull opiate to the drains
> One minute past, and Lethe-wards had sunk.

The simile is not actually of the state of drowsy numbness but of its cause, which is as yet unspecified. Thus by the time the sympathetic identification with the nightingale's happiness enters the poem as the reason for the speaker's condition, its ability to produce physical sensation has been established by this analogy to physical stimulants. The identification of the speaker with the nightingale is asserted in the iterative closure of "happy in thine happiness," in which the direct repetition seems to enclose a bond of complete identity. The syntax of the poem leads the reader to believe that the seventh line will begin "That I," rather than "That thou," and that some further description of the speaker's condition would follow. The shift from the speaker to the nightingale, from "I" to "thou," follows upon the assertion of the identity of the two, and effaces the border between the speaker and the nightingale as the nightingale replaces the speaker as the central subject of the stanza.

This union of the two figures in the poem lasts only for the brief duration of the first image of the nightingale "sing[ing] of summer in full-throated ease." By the outset of the second stanza the speaker is trying to reestablish a link to the nightingale, a connection that seems to have fallen away somewhere in the ellipsis between stanzas. That such a significant event in the poem's plot, namely, a separation of the nightingale from the speaker, should occur only elliptically establishes the ode's texture as a stylized stream of consciousness, in which involuntary events do not quite rise to the level of verbal representation. The loss of identification, brought about by forces contrary to the speaker's desire, occurs outside his conscious mental activity and exists in the poem only as a fait accompli to which he needs to respond. What was unavoidable in the first stanza is now nearly impossible to reclaim; the paradoxical state composed of happiness, numbness, aches, and pains, once as ineluctable as the consequence of drinking a poison or an opiate, now stands on the other side of an incomplete odal apostrophe: "O, for a draught of vintage." Unlike the "Ode to Psyche," in which the first three stanza openings could be direct addresses to the goddess herself ("O Goddess!"; "O latest born"; "O brightest"), here the opening "O" speaks to no one and leads only into a self-referential lament. The desired "draught of vintage" that would assuage the speaker's pain is derived from the imagined "dull opiate" of the first stanza, and "draught" has its phonetic inspiration in the most persistent alliteration of the first stanza, *drowsy/drunk/drains/Dryad/trees*. The mythological telos of sinking to Lethe is transformed into the naturalistic source of the vintage in the "deep-delved earth," as the line of causality of the second stanza reverses that of the first; in the first stanza an imaginative impression is said to generate physical sensation, while in the second stanza physical stimulants are imagined as the means of producing an ecstatic change in consciousness. As the speaker is fully invested in a desire to transcend a materiality he feels as a burden, that desire lends a hyperbolic color to expressions, either ecstatic or merely emphatic, of escape. The tone of "O, for a draught of vintage!" and "O for a beaker full of the warm south" recurs in the exclamations of the fourth stanza, "Away! away! for I will fly to thee" and "Already with thee!," but these exclamations are only momentarily forceful stirrings from the poem's already dominant entropic tendencies. The speaker revives himself from nodding into "shadows numberless" with his first shout—"O, for a draught of vintage"—which inaugurates the lively pageant of "Dance, and Provencal song, and sunburnt mirth," but the liveliness of that "warm South" remains at a distance from his own condition; even if he "might drink," he could only relapse into the "forest dim."

At the outset of the third stanza, echoes of *Hamlet*, drawn mostly from the first and third soliloquies and from Hamlet's conversations with the ghost of his father, begin to accumulate. In the first line of the stanza, "Fade far away, dissolve, and quite forget," "fade" suggests the fading of the ghost (1.1.163; noted by Vendler, 85, and Bate, 196), "dissolve" is made from "resolve itself into a dew" (1.2.129–30) through the trick of the displaced first consonant (*pains/drunk/drains*), and the desire to "forget" reaches into the play's theme of irrepressible memory: the ghost greets Hamlet at his second appearance with "Do not forget" (3.4.114), while his last words from his first appearance were "Remember me" (1.5.92); Hamlet laments over him in the first soliloquy, "Must I remember" (1.2.143). The "weariness, the fever and the fret" passes through "Tintern Abbey"'s "hours of weariness" and "fretful stir unprofitable, and the fever of the world" (27, 52–53) back to its origin in the melancholy catalog of the third soliloquy from *Hamlet*, which begins "How weary, stale, flat and unprofitable" is "this world" (1.2.133–34). "Where but to think is to be full of sorrow" draws on both "there is nothing either good or bad but thinking makes it so" (2.2.249–50) and the possibility that it is nobler "in the mind to suffer." As Keats rhymes "think" in this stanza off "drink" from line 19, framing the rhyme by placing both words in the same position at the fourth syllable, he returns to one of his own most aurally memorable rhymes, the *think/sink* closure of his Shakespearean sonnet "When I Have Fears." That poem begins with an echo of Hamlet's most famous words, "To be or not to be," which is turned into the sonnet's fear that one might "cease to be." Keats mixes his own puns and echoes with Shakespeare's; the sixth stanza of the "Nightingale" will echo, in "to die, to cease," both *Hamlet*'s "to die, to sleep" and Keats's own "cease to be." The ode's first stanza has already exploited a past-tense version of the *think/sink* rhyme: *drunk/sunk*. And as Jonathan Bate suggests, the repeated "Adieus" of the last stanza of the ode will echo the farewell of the ghost to Hamlet: "Adieu, adieu! Remember me" (1.5.112; Bate, 197). These adieus also echo, less solemnly, both Flute/Thisbe in *A Midsummer Night's Dream* ("And farewell, friends, / Thus Thisbe ends, / Adieu, adieu, adieu" [5.1.342–44]), and Shakespeare's pun in *Hamlet* on "a dew/Adieu." When the ghost says "Adieu" to Hamlet (and admonishes him, "Remember me"), he is just about to "melt, thaw and resolve" his seemingly solid flesh into a "dew" that vanishes at the first rays of the sun. One reason that Keats plays so freely with Shakespeare is that this same sort of phonic wordplay informs the passages from *Hamlet* that he incorporates into the ode. The passage from Hamlet's third soliloquy,

> The heart-ache, and the thousand natural shocks
> That flesh is heir to, (3.1.63–64)

which inspires the ode's opening, is joined, through the linking echo of "flesh," to the opening of the first soliloquy,

> That this too too sullied flesh would melt. (1.2.129)

That "flesh is heir"/*air* is a recurrent pun throughout *Hamlet*, one that Keats returns to in the sixth stanza of the ode in the image of "take into the air my quiet breath." Keats's Shakespearean intertextuality is a matter neither of single word echoes nor of commentary on the original sources; it involves phonetic and thematic networks of association that run through both Shakespeare's and Keats's texts. As the ode progresses, Shakespeare will not be the only source of such free association.

The third stanza closes with a series of images of eyes becoming impotent, losing their power both to see and to compel others to look at them:

> And leaden-eyed despairs,
> Where Beauty cannot keep her lustrous eyes,
> Or new Love pine at them beyond to-morrow.

As this image carries over into the fourth stanza, the loss of sight is given a different kind of power in the image of the "viewless wings of poetry." This reversal depends, in the internal imagistic logic of the poem, on recovering the power of the oxymoronic state of excessive happiness identified with images of darkness, the "shadows numberless" and "forest dim." Some of the critical commonplaces about this ode—that it makes an abrupt passage from "a sunlit day to a midnight scene" (a weakness, according to Vendler, that exposes "signs of improvisation" [96]), and that it differs from the "Ode on a Grecian Urn" in being about a natural object while the "Urn" is about an art object—are based on an overly literal reading of this scene, particularly of the line "But here there is no light." The darkness that begins to overpower the speaker in the poem's fourth stanza does not represent a naturalistic scene but shows the speaker's immersion in a densely overdetermined network of literary and artistic references. The choice of a new vehicle of escape, not drink but poetry,

> Not charioted by Bacchus and his pards,
> But on the viewless wings of Poesy

is a decisive statement of an opposition between ordinary material existence and a higher, more intense reality in art in more ways than one. The obvious literary reference, to Milton's image of "viewless wing" in his sonnet "The Passion," is reinforced by a Shakespearean echo; since Keats's "become a sod" is going to echo Claudio's fear in *Measure for Measure* that he might "become a kneaded clod," the image of the "viewless wing" clearly recalls for Keats Claudio's alternative fear that the afterlife might entail being "imprison'd in the viewless winds" (3.1.125). The "Queen-Moon . . . Cluster'd around by all her starry Fays" suggests Titania, who is referred to four times in the *Dream* as the "Fairy Queen" (2.1.8; 2.2.12; 3.1.73; 4.1.69). As Spiegelman points out, the image of "verdurous glooms" echoes Keats's own comment in the margin of his copy of Shakespeare that *A Midsummer Night's Dream* was "a piece of profound verdure." Spiegelman goes on to suggest that the seeming confusion of spring and midsummer flowers in the ode's fifth stanza shows that Keats has the "imaginative sense to honor Shakespeare's double frame" (355); presenting a garden in a second, midsummer bloom recreates the disorienting effect of the temporal duplicity of a play whose text sets it on May Day while its title places it in midsummer. Keats's ode sets out to accomplish what Shakespeare's actors regularly did in plays like *A Midsummer Night's Dream*: convincing an audience sitting in broad daylight that it is actually very dark. The "dull brain" is a flash echo from another play that performs the same trick: "My dull brain was wrought / With things forgotten" (*Macbeth*, 1.3.151–52).

The allusive background of this stanza is just as densely packed with references to the visual arts and their literary backgrounds as it is to Shakespeare. As Ian Jack points out, the image of "Bacchus and his pards" is derived from the Titian painting *Bacchus and Ariadne*, the same painting that occasioned the description of that pair in "Sleep and Poetry" (131). The painting was a favorite in the Keats circle; Hazlitt praised its "prodigious gusto" (10:72), and it inspired Leigh Hunt to publish his mini-epic "Bacchus and Ariadne" in 1819. The ode's citation of the painting is not limited to this single image. The lines "the Queen-Moon is on her throne, / Cluster'd around by all her starry Fays" refers not only to Shakespeare's Titania but also to the outcome of Ariadne's story as told by Catullus and Ovid and as represented in Titian's painting. In the original myth, which Keats would have known from his Latin studies at Clarke's school at Enfield and from Dryden's translations of Ovid, Bacchus marries Ariadne after her abandonment by Theseus, and then, at her death, makes a constellation either of her or of a crown he gave her at their marriage.[4] Titian depicts both the source of Ariadne's grief in the ships carrying Theseus away as he abandons her, and her eventual redemption into the constellation created by Bacchus, which Titian places in the upper left corner of his painting. The intertextual twinings of Keats's sources are pulled even tighter as Titania and Ariadne are connected by one of the quirkier passages in *A Midsummer Night's Dream;* Shakespeare's Theseus is Ariadne's faithless lover, and Oberon recalls Theseus's abandonment of Ariadne at the same time that he accuses Titania of being in love with Theseus (2.1.76–80).

Keats's capacity for absorption in works of art is well known—"He went again and again to see the Elgin Marbles," Severn reported, "and would sit for an hour at a time beside them rapt in revery" (Sharp, 32). The ode's allusions to Titian, its original appearance in the *Annals of the Fine Arts,* and its reference to the "viewless wings of Poesy" place it squarely within the ongoing discussion in the *Annals* of the relations between poetry and painting. This debate was formulated in the argument between Winckelmann and Lessing over the statue of the Laocoön and was pursued in Britain by Haydon, Hazlitt, Hunt, and many others. Those on the *ut pictura poesis* side of the argument (with Winckelmann) characteristically described both poetry and painting as vehicles of the same transcendent or cultural spirit, while those who sided with Lessing stressed formal distinctions between the visual and the "viewless" arts that entail differences in what each can represent. Keats addresses this debate more thoroughly and more analytically in the "Ode on a Grecian Urn," but in the ecstatic spirit of the "Ode to a Nightingale" the governing term is simply the "intensity" that he looked for in any art. Keats's axiom that "the excellence of every Art is its intensity" functions as the hinge of his comparison of a painting (West's *Death on the Pale Horse*) that he sees lacking such intensity and a play (*Lear*) that possesses it in such force that it is capable of "making all disagreeables evaporate" (*KL*, 1:192). The desire to make "disagreeables evaporate" through poetic intensity would enable the ode's speaker to reenact Titian's accomplishment in *Bacchus and Ariadne* of subsuming Ariadne's trials within a narrative of celestial transfiguration. As the "Ode to a Nightingale" echoes Shakespeare and Milton in its assertion of its own ability to soar "on the viewless wings of Poesy," it claims a power equivalent to Titian's to remove itself above the everyday sorrow of thought, a sorrow that, the poem fears, the "dull brain" cannot help but know.

This power cannot be achieved simply through the statement, however emphatic, of a desire, but it begins to make a more convincing appearance toward the end of the poem's fourth stanza, as the ode's previous alternation between forceful assertions of transcendence, whose very emphasis betrays the strain of their production, and their quick recapture by a miring materiality becomes distinctly more subdued. While the fourth stanza's first attempt at flight "on the viewless wings of Poesy" is arrested by the slow and heavy counterforce of "Though the dull brain perplexes and retards," the next invocation of an ethereal flight,

> Already with thee! tender is the night,
>> And haply the Queen-Moon is on her throne,
>>> Cluster'd around by all her starry Fays

receives only a momentary check in the brief relapse "But here there is no light"; this is itself immediately reversed by images that suggest an immersion in the richly aestheticized world of the nightingale:

> Save what from heaven is with the breezes blown,
>> Through verdurous glooms and winding mossy ways.

As the "verdurous glooms" recall the "shadows numberless" of the poem's opening, they place the speaker in the nightingale's locale, the "forest dim" that transcends earthly sorrow, not through an ascesis of sense but through a sensory richness that obliterates the distinction between the external, material world and the inner world of experience: The light from Ariadne's crown is given enough density to be carried on "breezes" from the constellation to the garden inhabited by the poem's speaker. The synesthesia through which this light becomes the odors of the fifth stanza has its own specific literary source; it is suggested by the description of Ariadne's crown in Spence's *Polymetis*, a compendium of mythology that Keats knew well. Spence notes that in the first reference to this constellation in Ovid, it is said to be constituted of "*gemmae,*" which Spence calls "a very unlucky word," since "It naturally signifies buds of flowers, or leaves; and by way of allusion, gems, or precious stones." Spence notes that as a result of this first meaning, "the persons born under Ariadne's crown, will delight in flower-gardens" (165). Titania's share in the image of the "Queen-Moon" also suggests in the ode's span from the heavens to the earthly garden the meeting of Titania and Bottom in the imaginary forest of Shakespeare's *Dream.*

The "Ode to a Nightingale" seems to naturalize its transition from celestial light to earthly odors as it plunges its speaker into "verdurous glooms and winding mossy ways," where the only available sensory phenomenon would be the smells, just material enough to be wind-borne, of hawthorn, eglantine, violets, and musk-rose. These particular smells, however, are borne on the winds of literary allusion; as Spiegelman points out, eglantine, violets, and musk-rose are all mentioned in a single passage (2.1.250–52) in *A Midsummer Night's Dream.* The flower added to the Shakespearean catalog, white hawthorn, and the blending of its smell with moonlight, drifts in even more interestingly from Keats's memory of Hazlitt's lecture "On Poetry in General." Hazlitt cites the "lunatic, lover, poet" passage from *A Midsummer Night's Dream* as an exemplary account of poetic imagination and advises "let the poet or the lover of poetry visit it at evening, when beneath the scented hawthorn and the crescent moon it has built itself a palace of emerald light" (*Complete Works,* 5:9).

The proliferation of literary echoes accompanies the poem's loss of cathexis toward the transcendent. Each of the first four stanzas begins on a melodramatic note ("My heart aches," "O, for a draught of vintage," "Fade far away," and "Away! Away!") and becomes progressively more subdued and reflective as it unfolds. The fifth stanza opens more quietly: "I cannot see what flowers are at my feet." The aspiration toward transcendence on the "viewless wings of Poesy" culminates in the fourth stanza in the mythic figures of the Queen-Moon and her starry Fays, but these figures are so far from any naturalistic ground that they do not carry the speaker across to an ideal but rather open up the distance between him and that imagined world. With the ideal beyond reach, the desire for transcendence of corporeality, which inspired the hyperbolic tone of the first four stanzas, is reconstituted at the poem's midpoint in a receptivity to aesthetic intensity. In contrast to the repugnance toward the material world in the third stanza, this world is, in the fifth stanza, described as a luxurious source of sensation, a transition that is accomplished in a movement away from visual imagery. The catalog of worldly ills in the third stanza was represented in a realistic visual imagery culminating in the allegory of lost sight, "Beauty" losing "her lustrous eyes," and Love losing its desire for them. The ode's fourth stanza imagines transcending such loss on the "viewless wings of Poesy," and as that image of blindness is carried into the opening of the fifth stanza ("I cannot see what flowers are at my feet"), Keats's invocation of the topos of the blind bard, deprived of sensory sight but privileged in insight, begins the next movement, from the mundane material world to an intensified poetic reality, leading to the allusion ("Darkling I listen") to Milton's invocation to absent light in *Paradise Lost*. The loss of sight effaces what Wordsworth called the "tyranny of the eye," the power of the visual sense to fix a gap of intransitivity between the perceiver and the object of perception. The image of light acquiring the density to be carried on breezes is the joining of the two worlds of the ode, the celestial and the "Here," as the earlier structure of polarity gives way to an imagery of continuity. The imagining of light borne on breezes is shaded into a description of a myriad of smells, which are truly, though barely, material enough to be carried by the wind. In the absence of light, the speaker is diverted from his binary opposition between the transcendent and the corporeal as the smells of the garden both reward and challenge him with perceptions that are sensorily richer, more subtle, and less easily defined than the objects of sight. His attention is entirely absorbed in the attempt to make the precise discriminations, and to savor the precise odors, of the surrounding garden.

The demands thus made on the speaker's concentration imbue the opening of the next stanza, "Darkling I listen," with a powerful dramatic tension. The use of the intransitive "listen" hovering over the semicolon pause suggests that, in the drama of the poem, the nightingale is now silent, and the speaker is poised in waiting for its song to resume. The Miltonic presence here is ineluctable; the "wakeful Bird" who "sings darkling" is the nightingale, but as Chase points out, Milton identifies his own "harmonious numbers" with the bird's song, while Keats only listens. What he hears, in the ensuing Hamlet-like meditation on death as a soft quietus, are the passages from Hamlet's soliloquies that had been incorporated into the ode's opening, now reverberating in other Shakespearean contexts. The most obvious echo in this stanza is the debt that Keats's

Now more than ever seems it rich to die,
    To cease upon the midnight with no pain

owes to Hamlet's

> *To die, to sleep—*
> *No more*—and by a sleep to say we end
> The heart-ache, and the thousand natural shocks
> That flesh is heir to. 'Tis a consummation
> Devoutly to be wished. (3.1.61–65)

The passage that had inspired the poem's opening lines ("The heart-ache . . .") is now joined to its surrounding context in the later part of Keats's poem. In addition, as R. S. White points out, Cleopatra prefigures Keats's "I have been half in love with easeful Death" when she describes "the stroke of death" as "a lover's pinch, / Which hurts, and is desired" (5.2.295–96). This last citation is the most elaborate of a series of allusions to the later acts of *Antony and Cleopatra* in the ode, and especially to Cleopatra's dying speech. As White notes, Antony addresses Cleopatra as "My nightingale,"(4.8.18), Cleopatra says that Antony's death should make "darkling stand / The varying shore o' the world" (4.15.11–12), and, where Keats can "in embalmed darkness guess each sweet," Cleopatra finds the asp "as sweet as balm" (5.2.311; White, 222–23). Cleopatra also calls the effect of the asp's bite as "soft as air" (311), echoing her flamboyant description of her own death:

> I am fire and air; my other elements
> I give to baser life. (5.2.289–90)

The image "soft as air" is central both to an associative linkage in Shakespeare and to Keats's absorption of that linkage into the ode. Cleopatra's "air" develops *Hamlet*'s pun that "flesh is heir" as Cleopatra's disdain for "baser life" fulfills Hamlet's desire to be done with "This too, too sullied flesh" and the ills that "flesh is heir to." Keats's romance with Death, during which he has

> Call'd him soft names in many a mused rhyme,
>   To take into the air my quiet breath

incorporates Shakespeare's liminal "air" imagery into the internal logic of the ode. Sliding "breath" into "air" reverses the direction of the incremental slide in the previous stanzas, from the immateriality of light to the odors that were just material enough to be carried on breezes; now, the slight materiality of the "breath" that keeps us in this life can easily be diffused into the slightly softer, more ethereal "air." The "soft names" addressed to Death echo the "soft incense" of the odors in the fifth stanza, as the liminal

Cleopatra, and the ode's speaker, who are contemplating its personal relevance. This opposition structures the imagistic contrast in this stanza between asking Death "To take into the air my quiet breath" and fearing that this only leaves one to "become a sod." Grennan's observation that "become a sod" echoes *Measure for Measure*'s "become a kneaded clod," when connected to the ode's earlier echo of Claudio's "viewless winds," subtends the opposition in this stanza between a dissolution into immateriality and an elemental materiality. Shakespeare's "winds," phonetically suppressed by the ode's previous revision of them into "wings," resurface in the "breezes" of the fourth stanza, and form the material ground for the liminal imagery of breath becoming air. The scope of Prospero's elegiac vision of our all becoming air confers a serenity on that vision, but such serenity is missing in the personal pathos of "Still wouldst thou sing, and I have ears in vain." This pathos, which emerges in the dramatic change in the speaker's attitude in the sixth stanza from "for many a time / I have been half in love with easeful death" to "Still wouldst thou sing, and I have ears in vain," is linked to a reappearance of the nightingale's song at the midpoint of the stanza. The poem's temporal markers tell us explicitly that the bird's song is a powerful presence for the speaker at lines 57–58, "While thou art pouring forth thy soul abroad / In such an ecstasy," though it seemed not to be so in the early part of the stanza, and seemed not to be present at all throughout the fifth stanza's intense focus on the odors of the garden. This suggests that the song is meant to begin again at the "Now" of line 55, and that it once again provokes the excessive response of the first stanza when the speaker's attempt to identify with the bird's ecstasy overflows into pain. Unlike the first stanza, however, in which the speaker claims an empathic identity with the nightingale's happiness, in this case a gap opens between the nightingale and the speaker, represented as a gap between "thy soul" and "I have ears in vain." This separation is enacted by the revision of possessive adjectives, which change from "my" to "the" to "thy," a series that culminates by leaving the speaker with no existence except the literal and the physical. In the poem's opening, the speaker could represent himself figuratively in the images of "My heart" and "my sense," but he soon found himself unable to identify with the mythic images of Titian, Shakespeare, and Ovid because "*the* [not "my"] dull brain perplexes and retards." When the nightingale becomes the sole possessor of an identity that outlives the body ("thy soul"), the "I" is left as nothing but a useless, material shell. The passages that narrate this displacement and the reduction of subject to object are also linked phonetically: When "no pain" echoes "pains," the opposition of "thy soul" and "I have ears in vain" completes the degradation of "my sense" into "the dull brain."

The seventh stanza of the poem is (pace Bridges) its greatest achievement, and is certainly its interpretive crux. When the poem asks, "Was it a vision, or a waking dream?" the word "it" refers most directly and profoundly to the state of mind represented in this stanza. This is the stanza over which some New Critics worried that Keats had gotten carried away by the rhythm and sounds of his own words, while others assured them that he had not; it is also the stanza in which Yale critics have seen Keats most overwhelmed by Miltonic power, and in which their critics have detected only deliberate and controlled allusion to Shakespeare. In the most recent controversy concerning this poem, and perhaps the one with the greatest scope, Murray Krieger has focused on the two final stanzas of the "Nightingale" ode as the basis for a challenge to de Man's revision of the terms of Romantic studies away from a symbolist aesthetics and into a rhetoric of "allegory" as that term is derived from Benjamin and Kierkegaard. Taking up de Man's identification of allegory with the mundane world of temporality and history, Krieger argues that as the symbol of the nightingale transcends time, it "creates for us a surrogate reality" in the world of imagination: "Humanity's individual lives are tied together by the bird once it has been turned into the all-unifying metonymic metaphor, so that history across the ages has been turned into the instantaneous vision of myth. Thanks to a repetition so complete that it achieves the identity of eternal recurrence (de Man's objections notwithstanding), time is redeemed" ("Waking Dream," 286). De Man's response to Krieger brings the modern critical treatment of this stanza into something of a full circle. De Man points out that as Krieger concentrates on the poem's penultimate query, "Was it a vision, or a waking dream?" in order to argue that this question encompasses both the "vision" of the seventh stanza and the "incompleteness of the vision" (288), he elides the poem's final and more perplexing question: "Do I wake or sleep?" Furthermore, de Man contends, this omission builds upon a previous elision in which Krieger overlooks the "assonance in the 'very word' *forlorn*" (de Man's emphasis), and in doing so evades "the thematically most important articulation or dramatic transition" in the poem. Whereas Krieger, like Brooks, sees the ode redeeming the ordinary into the mythic, de Man points out that this would have been very easy for Keats to do—awakening the speaker by "hav[ing] a fictional bell ring instead of the material, 'very,' word," de Man observes, would deploy a narrative cliché that signifies the difference between imaginative reverie and ev-

eryday life and so "epitomizes the banality of the quotidian." Instead of
preparing the ground for such an opposition between the imaginative and
the banal, de Man argues, Keats's ode confuses the terms of this potential
thematic opposition as it accomplishes its decisive articulation through the
"play of the letter," which, de Man points out, is "also the work of the dream,
accessible to us only within a system in which the difference between waking and dreaming cannot be decided and can, henceforth, not be assimilated
to a symbolic reconciliation of opposites" (*Rhetoric of Romanticism*, 186). A
reader with no stake in this argument might wish to observe in de Man's
emphasis on the assonance and "play of the letter" in the word "forlorn"
that the poem has not changed in the last hundred years but that its critical
reception is beginning to come to terms with its acoustic character.

This argument between Krieger and de Man has a specific psycholinguistic basis. Krieger's confidence that the nightingale functions as an "all-
unifying metonymic metaphor" depends upon an assertion that the poem
rises from the level of metonymy or contiguity, where the nightingale is first
identified with its song and then that song is identified with all previous
songs of all previous nightingales, to the metaphoric level of substitution
based on likeness, so that anyone in the presence of such a song can be
substituted for anyone else in that position and can see, in the "instantaneous vision of myth," the sameness of the human condition across the
fragmenting circumstances of history. In Freud's description of primary
process, this movement from metonymy to metaphor is the movement from
displacement to condensation. De Man contends that the "Ode to a Nightingale" does not in fact proceed from the level of metonymic displacement
to the reconstitution, through metaphor, of a "surrogate reality," but that
the poem only continues to regress to an even deeper level of displacement,
where the hinge between the visionary and the quotidian is controlled by
the "arbitrary sound" of the "play of the letter." The "very word," "forlorn,"
becomes not a sign at all but only a sound, and de Man concludes that "The
actual inclusion, in the texture of the lyric, of an alien piece of metalanguage
makes the 'Ode to a Nightingale' one of the very poems, the very allegory,
of the nonsymbolic, nonaesthetic character of poetic language" (187). Since
de Man has consistently used the term "aesthetic" to mean the belief in the
revelation of the intelligible in the sensible, his use of "nonaesthetic" is a
denial of the "surrogate reality" that Krieger posits, the existence of a transcendental, imaginative order that redeems material temporality.

The stakes of de Man's psycholinguistic objection to Krieger can be suc-
cinctly formulated through Lacan's distinction between *signification* and

signifiance. Signification, for Lacan, involves the "crossing of the bar" between the signifier and the signified in the formation of the "sign," which "represents something for someone" ("Position," 840). The sign thus constituted is the Saussurean sign, the dyad of sound and concept that is the basis of communication. This "someone" ("quelqu'un") is the same "who" to whom Fogle refers as a last resort in the rhetorical question "Who determines the rhythm and words?" but, as de Man always suggests, rhetoric has a way of opening more questions than it answers. The remaining question, which Lacan makes clear, is whether this "someone" is an extralinguistic agent or the effect of a signifying process ("mais ce quelqu'un, son statut est incertain" [840]), for it is entirely possible to describe *signification* as simply the temporary interruption of a more primary signifying process, that of *signifiance*, or the sliding of the signifier below the bar that separates it from the signified. *Signifiance*, for Lacan, designates this material slippage, the purely metonymic play of the letter. Left to itself, *signifiance* is a relay with no determinate or extralinguistic values; in its shuttling, "the signifier is that which represents the subject [*sujet*] for another signifier" (*Ecrits*, 316). This "subject" (as opposed to a "someone") exists only in the momentary allusion of one signifier to another. Thus for Krieger, as for Fogle, "Keats" is "someone," an exemplary figure who is able to comprehend the sameness of human destiny and communicate it intelligibly in the "instantaneous vision of myth." For de Man, "Keats" is only a linguistic subject, an epiphenomenal site constituted and deconstituted by the play of signifiers that signify nothing.

De Man's remarks on the ode, admittedly sketchy and composed as a response to Krieger and not as a thorough reading of the poem, in fact understate the degree of the "play of the letter" in the "very word" "forlorn." De Man identifies the word's material quality strictly with its assonance, yet consonance and rhyme are both also responsible for its appearance. In addition, de Man's focus on the materiality of the single word "forlorn," as if it interrupts an otherwise conventional text, overlooks the degree to which phonetic determination of word choice has been a prominent feature of the entire poem. The rhymes in the opening stanza—"drains" as a composite of "pains" and "drunk," and "ease" as a product of the dominant assonance (/ee/) and the dominant consonance (/s/) in the final lines of the first stanza—are composed very like "forlorn"; key passages in the poem are linked through the poem's internal rhymes (*drink/think, pains/brain/pain/vain*), and the habit of allusive echo (*sod/clod, air/heir, darkling, eglantine/hawthorn*) has kept the material signifier in the foreground throughout this text. But the associative chains that connect the poem's allusive contexts and ground its own wordplay do not reside only on the side of the signifier; the realms of the signified and the signifier, or the intelligible and the sensible, are not as clearly demarcated in this text as Lacan or de Man would suggest. The passages from Shakespeare that play on *air/heir*, for instance, are as closely linked thematically, as contemplations on suicide, as they are through the material agency of the letter. The ode's poetics are neither as transcendent of materiality as Krieger describes nor as dependent upon it as de Man insists.

"Forlorn," for all its intrinsic and intertextual resonance, is not even the oddest or the most "alien" word in the poem's seventh stanza. The honors here must go to "Ruth," which, though it has its own phonetic preparation (*path/through/Ruth*), has a serious problem with its referential status. For in the Book of Ruth, as many readers of the "Nightingale" ode have noted, Ruth never weeps; she never expresses regret for the home she has left behind. Barry Gradman's suggestion that "Ruth" came to Keats's mind as an image for Cordelia, and as part of a series of allusions to *King Lear*, is fairly persuasive. *Lear* is one of the plays that leaves its characters "darkling"; Edgar complains of being haunted "in the voice of a nightingale" (3.6.30); and the triumvirate of emperor, clown, and Ruth makes a nice fit with Lear, the Fool, and Cordelia. The confusion of Cordelia and the Fool ("My poor fool is hanged") even confers a bit of poetic license on the mingling of Ruth and Cordelia, and both women are connected to mentions of corn: Ruth sets out "to glean ears of corn" (Ruth 2:2) and meets Boaz as he "went to lie down at the end of the heap of corn" (Ruth 3:7), and Cordelia tells her soldiers to search for Lear "in our sustaining corn" (4.4.6). But even if one allows, as Gradman argues, that "the two women would become mingled in Keats's imagination, and that in writing of Ruth, memories of Cordelia's sadness would naturally intrude" (21), the commonsense objection to this conflation would invoke Keats's responsibility to a reader: Who is the *someone* who could be expected to see "Ruth" and hear "Cordelia"? One antithetical answer to this question is Chase's argument that this poem tests the "possibility of *hearing* writing" and raises, in its finally unresolved questions, the challenge that it cannot resolve—the "question of whether perception is not hallucination" (211)—precisely by testing the "continuity of perception with knowledge" (210). But by arguing that the intertextual or the intrinsic materiality of Keats's language subverts that continuity, Chase and de Man provide implicit answers, however ironic, to the ode's final questions. For them, the "it" of the seventh stanza can only be described as a "waking dream," a linguistic accident that reveals the arbitrary play of the letter. At the same time, the speaker's final condition in the poem, which leaves him unable to distinguish between perception and hallucination, is the equivalent of a "sleep."

The arrival at a stance of pure negation, as in de Man's characterization of the poem's language as "nonsymbolic, nonaesthetic," depends upon the initial premise, more fully articulated by Chase, that "the possibility of hearing writing" is a question of intelligibility. The "Ode to a Nightingale" offers abundant documentation, in the range of literary and artistic signs that are brought within its allusive field, of Keats hearing writing, even if it is not clear how, or if, its metonymic habits are finally brought into a unified metaphoric condensation. Its rules are loose but not arbitrary; even Keats's association of Ruth with Cordelia is not quite as idiosyncratic as it looks at first glance. Keats has heard Hazlitt, in "On Poetry on General" (the same essay that provides the "hawthorn" in the ode's fifth stanza), suggest that in "the story of Ruth," it "is as if all the depth of natural affection in the human race was involved in her breast" (*Complete Works*, 5:17), and "Ruth" in fact stands in for more than Cordelia in this stanza. The best-known verse from the Book of Ruth, "whither thou goest, I will go; and where thou lodgest, I will lodge; thy people shall be my people; and thy God my God" (1:16),[5] sounds like the inspiration for Eve's declaration in *Paradise Lost* that she would follow Adam into exile from paradise rather than live in the garden without him. Eve wakes from her last dream to tell Adam

> Whence thou return'st, and whither went'st, I know:
> For God is also in sleep, and Dreams advise . . .
>   but now lead on;
> In mee is no delay; with thee to go,
> Is to stay here; without thee here to stay,
> Is to go hence unwilling; thou to mee
> Art all things under Heaven, all places thou. (12.610–18)

This declaration mirrors Adam's decision that he would leave the garden with Eve rather than "live without thee . . . again in these wild Woods forlorn" (9.908–10), and both passages from *Paradise Lost* are also linked to the "Nightingale" ode through their proximity to dream imagery.

The allusive scope of the image of "Ruth" is extended even further through an association with Ariadne, an association that is carried out both thematically and through the "agency of the letter." Ariadne plays an exemplary role in the literary tradition of exile and subsequent redemption

Ariadne. From *Ovid's Epistles*, published by Jacob Tonson, Londoan, 1701.

through love that connects Ruth, Cordelia, and Eve; Ariadne betrays her family to aid Theseus, is abandoned by him far from home on Bacchus's island, and is then found and married by Bacchus. Keats could well have remembered from his days at Enfield translating the striking image from Ovid's *Heroides* that connects Ariadne, like Ruth and Cordelia, to "corn"; Ariadne laments that her abandonment by Theseus leaves her "body a-quiver like standing corn [*segetes*] struck by the northern blast" (*Heroides*, 131). He would certainly have been familiar with the simile from Dryden's loose translation of the *Ars Amatoria* as "Ovid's Art of Love," in which Ariadne "shook, like leaves of Corn, when Tempests blow" (line 621) while "Her briny Tears augment the briny Flood" (line 599). The ode's image of "perilous seas" registers Ariadne's view of the departing Theseus as noted by Dryden and as depicted both in Titian's painting and in a engraving of Ariadne that appears in an eighteenth-century translation of the *Heroides* as *Ovid's Epistles* by "Several Hands," including that of Dryden.[6] The association of a weeping woman and "perilous seas" would also remind Keats of Claude's painting *The Enchanted Castle*, which is alluded to in the "Epistle to Reynolds"; Claude's anonymous figure is yet another "Ruth." Keats's conflation of all of these female figures under a single name reflects Ariadne's place amid the repetitive similarity of the stories of Ovid's heroines (Penelope, Briseis, Phaedra, Dido, Medea) in the *Heroides;* opening the *Heroides* at random, a reader would be hard pressed to say who was speaking without checking the section title. Just as the ode's habit of association easily allows the stories of Ariadne and Titania to accrue to the conventional identification of the moon with the chaste Diana in the fourth stanza, the moment of sudden and cataclysmic loss experienced by Ruth, Eve, Ariadne, and Cordelia joins them to the traditional identification of the nightingale as the raped and mutilated Philomel.

To bring all of these stories into a single mythic vision in which, as Krieger asserts, "time is redeemed" is to participate in the most unproblematic way in what McGann calls "The Romantic Ideology"; imaginative unity simply subsumes all material reality and difference. The value accorded to this unitary vision depends upon a final, summary priority given to metaphoric condensation over the separate, contiguous parts of the vision, but the ambiguity of the opposition between one signifying process that produces thematic coherence and another that is barely structured by fleeting associations is familiar to Keats, and the ambiguous relation between these two discursive possibilities is at the heart of his unwillingness to commit this poem to a world of vision and myth as unambiguously as Krieger does. In

The Enchanted Castle, Claude Lorrain. Reproduced by permission of the National Gallery, London.

Adam's explanation to Eve of her first dream, in which she bites into a fruit and then flies, Adam identifies "Fancy" as a faculty that usurps the rule of "Reason" as we sleep:

> in the Soul
> Are many lesser Faculties that serve
> Reason as chief; among these *Fancy* next
> Her office holds; of all external things,
> Which the five watchful Senses represent,
> She forms *Imaginations, Aery shapes,*
> Which Reason joining or disjoining, frames
> All what we affirm or what deny, and call
> Our knowledge or opinion; then retires
> Into her private Cell when Nature rests.
> Oft in her absence mimic *Fancy* wakes
> To imitate her; but misjoining shapes,
> Wild work produces oft, and most in *dreams,*
> Ill matching words and deeds long past or late.
> (*PL*, 5.100–113; my emphases)

If we could depend upon Keats to agree with Adam here, we could distance ourselves from Krieger and join Jack Stillinger in the belief that the ode's message is perfectly expressed in the statement that "the fancy cannot cheat so well / As she is fam'd to do, deceiving elf," a passage that Stillinger identifies as "the end of the poem" (7). The conflation of Cordelia, Eve, Ariadne, and Claude's pensive figure at the level of the signifier in "Ruth" and at the level of the signified in Philomel could be written off as mere confusion, a "Wild work," "ill matching words and deeds long past and late." But the final indecision of the ode matches the paradoxical quality of its intertextual history. Even though the "Nightingale"'s "fancy" is indeed Milton's "Fancy," Keats's allusion to this passage from *Paradise Lost* only deepens the problematic of the poem's final questions. The ode's repeated echoes of *A Midsummer Night's Dream* make it impossible to overlook that Milton's account of "Fancy" echoes, whether or not Milton intended or knew it, Theseus's account of imagination as the common property of the lunatic, the lover, and the poet:

> as *imagination* bodies forth
> The forms of things unknown, the poet's pen
> Turns them to *shapes,* and gives to *aery* nothing
> A local habitation and a name. (5.1.13–17; my emphases)

Shakespeare's "Imaginations, Aery shapes" reappear, word for word, in Milton, but the Shakespearean text seems to honor what it calls "imagination" as strongly as the Miltonic text disparages what it calls "Fancy." The dream imagery of the ode is drawn from both sources, and as Eleanor Cook has pointed out, if the "Ode to a Nightingale" has a borrowed plot, the most precise source is not a Shakespearean play but Eve's first dream. In both Milton and Keats, Cook observes, there is the same sequence of "nightingale, moon, flight, fall, sleeping, waking" (429). The parallel is actually a little askew, since the exact sequence in the ode is "flight, moon," but the number of parallels is too extensive to be discounted. In comparing the different treatments of this sequence by Milton and Keats, Cook stresses the difference between Milton's confident opposition of truth to falsity and Keats's indecision: "If Keats were working with a Miltonic dialectic of true and false, he would know how to judge cheating fancy. But he is not. . . . What Keats implies through his echoes is that Milton's dialectic is itself an imagined thing. He must then ask the reader what imagination is, and what this poem is—a 'vision' or a 'waking dream'" (432). But while Keats's irresolution is clear in the ode's final questions, even Milton himself is an equivocal precursor on the status of dreams, fancy, and imagination. Eve dreams that she met an angel who offered her fruit of knowledge that she "could not but taste"; her dream is prophetic, whether or not (yet another open question) the consequences are fortunate. And *Paradise Lost* closes with an affirmation of the truth of Eve's second dream; she knows "Whence [Adam] return'st, and whither went'st" because, she says, "God is also in sleep, and dreams advise." Shakespeare makes an equally ambivalent source on the veracity of imagination if the poet's activity is comparable to that of the lunatic.

Krieger's attempt to stabilize the poem's conclusion in a manner that would maintain the privilege of imaginative vision over accidental association contests not only the de Manian deflection of Romantic poetics from symbol to allegory but also de Man's more explicit critique, in "Form and Intent in the American New Criticism," of an unexamined contradiction at the heart of the entire New Critical project. In that essay, de Man argued that there was a fundamental incompatibility between the New Critics' discovery of irony as the distinctive characteristic of poetic language and their insistence on the organic unity of texts (*Blindness*, 28–29). The disruptive force of irony, de Man argues, is incompatible with the premise of organic unity. When Krieger asserts that in Keats's image of a "a vision, or a waking dream," the "second of these alternatives is not wholly a denial of the first," he limits the potential power of irony in the ode through a metaphor of containment: "Whatever the incompleteness of the vision . . . the poem that contains it contains also the vision of that incompleteness" (288).

The "vision" of the poem, in Krieger's summary, "at its most critically aware, its most self-conscious," reasserts control over the doubt that its most imaginative work might be only a mistake. Krieger's "all-unifying metonymic metaphor" becomes an all-unifying, critically conscious agent through a personification of the poem as a containing consciousness that encompasses and subsumes, and is in fact enriched by, its capacity for ironic skepticism. While Chase's critique of the inevitable resort to prosopopoeia in establishing the coherence of the "Nightingale" ode is borne out in Krieger's personification of the text itself, the rhetorical gesture of personifying a text is not necessarily a misrepresentation if it simply acknowledges that a text is the reflection of an act of mind. The problem arises, as de Man demonstrates in Krieger's case, when the personification is constructed through elisions of those rhetorical features that would change the outlines of the portrait. The stability of Krieger's metaphor of containment is jeopardized by the ode's construction of a literary history that asks not only whether imaginative flight is a mistake but also whether it is only the random, possibly lunatic, free associations of fancy. Yale poststructuralism, as exemplified by Chase's and de Man's readings of this poem, simply pursues the other side of this dialectic. Chase takes the ode's unresolved questions— "Was it a vision, or a waking dream?" and "Do I wake or sleep"—to the point of Socratic irony. Asking "whether perception is not hallucination," and giving as the poem's answer that "the power to pass from hearing to singing is one the ode ascribes not to the poet himself but to Milton," Chase confronts poets with the same terms that Socrates offers Ion: If only the divinely inspired Milton is exempt from hallucination, it seems that a poet's only excuse for not knowing what he is saying is that he is possessed by a god. "Hallucination" becomes not just a possibility but a Socratically logical inevitability for Keats, and the activity of the poet becomes entirely comparable to that of the lunatic, or, as de Man has it, the dreamer.

While both Krieger's defense of a symbolist aesthetics and the deconstruction of that aesthetics by Chase and de Man situate themselves at the poles of the opposition that the "Ode to a Nightingale" explores, the poem's ability to switch from structures of binary opposition to a synthetic imagery that slides across the most thematically polarized terms (*self/other, subject/ object, material/immaterial, sound/sense*) indicates that the poetics of the ode do not exactly correspond to the terms of the discussion as formulated by

Krieger and de Man. That is to say, they are outside the terms of formalist critique as it has been constructed in Anglo-American literary study from the New Criticism to Yale poststructuralism. The difference between these approaches, in purely linguistic terms, depends upon the priority given to metaphor by the New Critics and to metonymy by de Manian deconstruction; their common denominator is their reliance on the irreducibility of the Saussurean sign. For Krieger and the New Criticism, the entire text of the "Ode to a Nightingale" functions metaphorically as a sign that "represents something for someone"; when Krieger promises that "the symbol creates for us a surrogate reality," he allows "us" to become that "someone." The emphasis placed by Chase and de Man on metonymic slippage enables them to describe the autonomous activity of the material signifier in the text, but it allows for only an arbitrary connection between the activity of the signifier and referential signification. The perception of a nonarbitrary link between signifier and signified can only be, as Chase puts it, a "hallucination."

While the New Critical approach to the poem overlooks or denies its strange habits of phonetic association and too easily domesticates its finally unanswered skepticism, de Manian deconstruction robs the poem of its affective power when it presents the assonance or the Miltonic intertextuality of the word "forlorn" as a more important rhetorical feature of the text than the conflation of Ruth, Cordelia, Eve, Ariadne, and Philomel because the former is more demonstrably "material." Neither Lacan's interest in metonymic slippage nor de Man's demonstration of the thematic instability of the linguistic play of the poem can account for its affective charge, which exists in an attenuated form even for the reader, and apparently in a highly potent configuration for the poetic persona. Yet the Lacanian definition of *signifiance* is not the only theory of the play of the signifier. Kristeva contests Lacan's definition of *signifiance* when she warns that the "discontinuities" of "a modality of *signifiance* in which the linguistic sign is not yet articulated" (*Revolution*, 26) are lost when analysis remains within the purely cognitive terrain of the Saussurean sign. In order, as Kristeva puts it, "to give status to affect and to the heterogeneity it introduces into the discursive order," she urges a return to the Freudian definition of the sign:

> We should keep in mind the incredible complexity of Freud's notion of a "sign," which is exorbitant compared with the closure imposed on the sign by Saussure's stoicism. The Freudian "sign" is outlined in *On Aphasia: visual, tactile,* and *acoustic* images linked to object associations

which refer, principally through an auditory connection, to the *word* itself, composed of an *acoustic* and *kinesthetic* image, of *reading* and *writing*. ("Microcosm," 37; Kristeva's emphases)

The asceticism of de Man's work clearly places it within the tradition of Saussurean stoicism, to which Kristeva would oppose an expanded definition of representation that would incorporate a somatic dimension. The linguistic terms of the argument between Krieger and de Man are resituated by this redefinition of the sign; instead of condensation occurring (as Krieger claims) or not occurring (as de Man contends) in the Saussurean sign as a joining of sound and concept that arrests metonymic slippage, in the Freudian sign we see the formation of the auditory and graphic "very word" not simply as a univocal linkage of sound and concept but as a condensation of a series of associations bound by mnemonic links. A scientific or a theological discourse—or any discourse that would constitute itself as a Saussurean *langue*—privileges denotation by repressing or marginalizing the variety of "object associations" (different for each speaker) that cluster around "the very word," while poetic discourse enriches itself by multiplying these associations. While all three of these formalist discourses—the American New Criticism, Yale poststructuralism, and Kristevan psycholinguistics—privilege literary language over the denotative tendencies of the langue of ordinary communication, the New Criticism and Yale poststructuralism resort too quickly in their practice to, respectively, theological and scientific discursive values. Only the Kristevan semiotic values literary language primarily for its motility and its verbal texture, and Kristeva's emphasis on the exorbitant power of the Freudian sign offers an alternative to the polarized choices at which de Man's work repeatedly arrives—either a randomness of metonymic displacements or a "tyranny of reference" that is "anti-poetic" (*Allegories*, 47). In order to capture the materially associative textures of Keats's odes, de Man's premise of the fundamentally unpredictable nature of poetic language should be supplemented by Kristeva's account of condensation occurring in a surfeit of imagistic associations rather than in the binary structure of the signifier/signified. The odes are neither a series of random associations, nor are they organized by a unitary thesis or subject position; their richness depends upon the wealth of associations (of objects, images, signs, and emotions) that cluster in their words.

When the "Ode to a Nightingale" is viewed in terms of the Kristevan semiotic, the paraphrastic similarity between the poem's third and seventh stanzas, where in each case the speaker laments the distance between the

world he inhabits and the far more desirable, imaginary realm of the nightingale, is overshadowed by the difference in the language of the two stanzas.
The language of the third stanza is clipped and flat, monosyllabic and full of
short vowels and common words: "quite forget," "fever and fret," "few, sad,
last, gray hairs." There is a thematic, and even an oblique imagistic, continuity between "Where youth grows pale, and spectre-thin, and dies" and
"No hungry generations tread thee down," but the degree of resonance in
the language has changed dramatically in the latter line. *Generation(s)* is one
of the most resonant words in the English language, largely because of its
prominence in the English Bible. Its best-known appearance, in the opening to the Book of Ecclesiastes, "One generation passeth away, and another
generation cometh; but the earth abideth forever," could be somewhere in
the thematic background of this stanza, but the more direct echo of a passage from the Book of Isaiah, "awake, as in the ancient days, in the generations of old" (51:9), is certainly a reason that the ode veers into a recollection of the biblical Ruth. The ode's entire seventh stanza is full of exotic
word choices that represent a literary landscape rather than the "here" of
the speaker: "alien corn," "magic casements," "perilous seas," "faery lands."
The resonance of the stanza also depends upon its phonic resources; it is full
of alliteration, sibilance, polysyllabic words, long vowels, and diphthongs.
Thorough prosodic analysis can only confirm what is immediately apparent
to the ear, a powerful aural presence that surprises the poem's persona and
that has disturbed generations of its critics.

　　The moment of return "from thee to my sole self" carries its own echoes.
Spiegelman points out that Theseus in *A Midsummer Night's Dream* ends
the play's revels by alluding to the sound of a midnight bell: "The iron
tongue of midnight hath told twelve" (5.1.352; Spiegelman, 358). The absence of a direct verbal echo in the ode is offset by the proximity of this
image to the vision/dream imagery with which both the *Dream* and the
"Nightingale" ode will conclude. The more significant echo at the outset of
the ode's final stanza is of Donne's "Ask not for whom the bell tolls"; Keats
reverses Donne's theme "No man is an island" as the ode's persona returns
to his "sole self." The image of "my sole self" completes a cycle that began
with the identification of the self as "My heart," distanced the self from "the
dull brain," lamented the distance from "thy soul" of the nightingale, and
now finishes with a divisive pun (*thy soul/my sole*) that leaves the self divested
of spirit. The loneliness that was the defining property of the archetypal
female figure (Ruth/Cordelia/Ariadne) now becomes the lot of the heart-
broken speaker.

The collapse of the imaginary representation of the self is accompanied by noticeable changes in the structures of images and the sounds of words. The words are once again common and monosyllabic, but the flatness is not entirely prosaic; the consonantal repetition in *like/bell/back* helps to enact the circularity of the process being described, and the internal rhyme on the one broad vowel (*toll/sole*) suggests the sound of the bell and connects it to the line's central idea, the speaker's sense of isolation. The poem no longer merges proximal variations on a "self-same song"; it now begins to use analogies and, finally, disjunctions. When the word "forlorn" is said to toll "like a bell," this is the first use of simile since the first stanza ("as though of hemlock"). The sound of "sole self" reawakens the alliterative memory of the "self-same song," but the "sole self" is unable to identify anything with or like itself.

The distance between this "sole self" and the place from which it has returned is registered in the difference between the two appearances of the word "forlorn," the first of which appears as the culmination of a series of phonetic and affective events that happen to the poem's speaker, and the second as the reflective act of a self-conscious, judging agent. Keats's own account, as related by Woodhouse, of his process of composition, that "thoughts come about him in troops, as tho' soliciting to be acc[epte]d & he selects," suggests, contrary to the evidence of this poem, that the two states are entirely compatible. Woodhouse's report that "he is generally more troubled by a redundancy than by a poverty of images" is borne out by the superfluity of allusion to Ruth, Cordelia, Eve, Ariadne, and Philomel, but the further claim that "he culls what appears to him at the time the best" does not occur in the "Nightingale" ode. In the case of "Ruth," the redundancy is not culled, and the result is a word whose excessive richness is not likely to be available to the reader. There is little reason to doubt the fidelity of Woodhouse's report as an accurate description of what Keats told him, but the happy coincidence of the faculties that Milton calls "Fancy" and "Reason," and that Keats calls "imagination" and "judgment," is asserted by one passage in Woodhouse's account and is called into question only a moment later. Keats was, Woodhouse says,

impatient of correcting, & says he would rather burn the piece in question & write ano[ther] or something else—"My judgment, (he says,) is as active while I am actually writing as my imagin[ation] In fact all my faculties are strongly excited, & in their full play—And shall I afterwards, when my imagination is idle, & the heat in which I wrote, has gone off, sit down coldly to criticise when in Poss[ession] of only one faculty, what I have written, when almost inspired."

But it is doubtful whether "judgment" is fully, or at all, present, in the "almost inspired" mode of composition if it is also true that

> He has said, that he has often not been aware of the beauty of some thought or expr[ession] until after he has composed and written it down—It has then struck him with astonish[ment]—& seemed rather the prod[uction] of another person than his own—He has wondered how he came to hit upon it. (*Keats Circle*, 1:128–29)

While both this report and the "How many bards" sonnet insist that there is "no confusion" between the "wild work" that produces redundant associations and the sorting out of the best matches of sound and sense, the "Ode to a Nightingale" ends with a confession of its inability to make sense of a discrepancy between an imaginative act that seems to belong to "another person" and the verbal resources of a "sole self" that are impoverished by comparison.

The association in Keats studies of a purely benign feeling of empathy with the state of "negative capability" can obscure the real difficulties presented by this discrepancy between an inspired compositional state and reflective judgment. The return "from thee to my sole self" reverses the direction of the passage in Keats's letters in which he says that "if a Sparrow come before my Window I take part in its existence and pick about the Gravel" (*KL*, 1:186), and the disjunctive force of the return "from thee" to a thoroughly different identity suggests the discontinuity between "negative capability" and the "someone" who is a social being. The literary history of the "Nightingale" ode demonstrates the rightness of Chase's rejection of a particular strain in Keats criticism that valorizes "the familiar proposal of a negative capability, or a poetry of sensations rather than thoughts" (224) as a vehicle for turning Keats's work into a "poetry of earth," but the equation of negative capability with a comfortable naturalism is more a product of New Critical principles than the effect of a careful reading of either Keats's poetry or his comments on poetic composition. For the New Critics, the ambiguities, ironies, and paradoxes of literary language were the means of conveying "a sense of the real density and contingency of the world" (Ransom, 885) as something more than "a mere abstraction from experience" (Brooks, *Urn*, 213), but while the New Critics believed that the escape from abstractions would set us comfortably at home in the natural world, Kristeva contends that the very notion of the "knowledge of a real object" is not a natural truth but the product of a psycholinguistic structure she calls the "thetic."

The more unsettling implications of Keats's statement that the poet is so without personal identity that "the identity of every one in the room begins to [s]o press upon me that, I am in a very little time annihilated—not only among Men; it would be the same in a Nursery of children" (*KL*, 1:387) are brought out in Kristeva's description of the dependence of a stable subjectivity on the "thetic" act of the "transcendental ego." To perform the ordinary act of signification that drives "the thin sheath of the sign (signifier/ signified)" through "material multiplicities" in order to identify "an object once and for all signified as real" ("Identity," 29), Kristeva contends, "the unshakable consciousness rests its position on transcendental laws, which it places outside itself in the natural sphere" (*Revolution*, 34). Mistaking the linguistic laws of its culture for transcendental laws that govern the existence of the material world, the Saussurean subject finds a confirmation of its own identity in the reception of its repetitive acts of signification.

The loss of identity that is celebrated in Keats studies as "negative capability" is rightly given the credit for Keats's ability to entertain an exceptionally fluid sense of the relation between signifiers and their assigned signifieds, but the loss of Saussurean subjectivity also carries a price. Acceptance of the discursive law is the condition of entry into a linguistic community; as Saussure asserts, "The arbitrary nature of the sign explains in turn why the social fact alone can create a linguistic system. The community is necessary if values that owe their existence solely to usage and general acceptance are to be set up; by himself the individual is incapable of fixing a single value" (113). Leaving behind the common currency of the Saussurean sign for the Freudian sign enables a poet to construct a discursive coherence that exceeds the denotative efficiency of the ordinary langue, but it simultaneously problematizes a reader's access to that richness. Saussure posits all members of a language group as equal sharers of the langue; the model allows for sociocultural modification without changing its basic structure, so that only the more literate or religious members of an English-speaking culture may recognize even the first level of allusion to "Ruth." This presumption of a shared langue allows Krieger to posit a common subjectivity in the premise that the "Nightingale" ode "creates for us a surrogate reality," but Krieger's assertion presumes an efficiency of communication that the "Ode to a Nightingale" does not produce. If it is difficult to imagine the reader who could see Ruth and hear Cordelia—one could try, by imagining someone whose literacy most closely matches Keats's, such as Hazlitt—it is impossible to imagine anyone who sees Ruth and hears Cordelia, Eve, Ariadne, and Philomel, and who sees Titian's Ariadne and Claude's figure from *The Enchanted Castle*, at the speed at which this happens for Keats. What the "Ode to a Nightingale" shows is not how Keats was sensibly like us, or ideally exemplary for us, but how strangely different he was from us. The "sole self" of the poem realizes this difference and feels himself to be not a piece of Donne's continent but an island unto himself.

Without the confirmation of the social consensus that transforms perception into reality, the ode's speaker is left in the grip of two banal but insurmountable epistemological quandaries: Is what I see "real," and is it what you see? The "near meadows" and the "still stream" are the speaker's final perception of the "alien corn" and the "perilous seas" of the seventh stanza, but the speaker is unable to decide which of these sets of terms more legitimately describes the phenomena before him. De Man invokes the impossibility, pondered by Descartes and Pascal among others, of knowing the difference between waking and sleeping, since "we always dream that we are awake" ("Waking Dream," 185). Keats's use of the imagery of "vision" and "dream" to construct the metalanguage that will determine which values adhere to which perceptions shows that his inheritance of this question passes through Shakespeare, and specifically through Prospero's insight that from the perspective of old age, in our mutability we are "like the baseless fabric of this vision," "such stuff as dreams are made on." The purely epistemological form of the question is set by *A Midsummer Night's Dream*, whose epilogue asks the audience to think

> That you have but slumb'red here
> While these visions did appear.
> And this weak and idle theme,
> No more yielding but a dream. (5.1.420–23)

The possibility that material perception is only the product of linguistic forces, no more real than a play and no more stable than a dream, is the poem's final epistemological dilemma. When I say "stream" and point, and you seem to know what I am pointing at, I believe not only that you see what I see but that what we see is in fact a stream and not a river, or a dream, or "the foam / Of perilous seas, in faery lands forlorn." That this seemingly material reality may be only the effect of the limits of both "the dull brain" and linguistic consensus opens the possibility that the product of a different psychic faculty, "fancy" or "imagination," and other linguistic forces, primarily the texts of Shakespeare and Milton, is not simply an illusion but something truer than the quotidian reality of linguistic exchange. Modern criticism that contends that Keats's capacity for common sense would protect him from such Romantic flights of fancy has to consign Hazlitt to the same flighty camp; Hazlitt contends (again, in "On Poetry in General") that "If poetry is a dream, the business of life is much the same. If it is a fiction, made up of what we wish things to be, and fancy that they are, because we wish them to be so, there is no other nor better reality" (*CW,* 5:3).

While the passages from *A Midsummer Night's Dream* and *The Tempest* that are echoed in the conclusion to the "Nightingale" ode are themselves indifferent to the potential disparity between a "vision" and a "dream," in the return of "judgment" or "Reason" in the reflective moment at the outset of the "Nightingale"'s final stanza the transcendental ego reconstructs the known, that is, the consensual boundaries that divide vision from dream, wake from sleep, and the near meadows and still stream from alien corn and perilous seas. If the involuntary quality of the imaginative trip seemed, in its time, to be an indication of its objective reality, the inability to return to that "almost inspired" state at will gives it an alien quality from the perspective of the judging consciousness, which now refers to that state as "it." The loss of the nightingale's music is the persona's loss of contact with the acoustic presence of the voices encountered in that departure. When Fitzgerald said, "For awhile after you quit Keats all other poetry seems to be only whistling or humming" (88), what he heard in Keats was the result of what Keats heard when he read Shakespeare and Milton. It was not what we hear. The "Ode to a Nightingale" does not adhere to the Saussurean principle that "the social fact alone can create a linguistic system . . . by himself the individual is incapable of fixing a single value" (113); the poem does not subscribe to the belief that the English language would be exactly as it is now if Shakespeare and Milton had never written. The materiality of language, which makes it mean more than one thing at a time, interferes with its efficiency but also multiplies the paths that it can take at any given moment. In presenting the exceptionally fluid yet barely structured language of this ode, Keats offers the best access a reader is likely to get to a sense of Keats's receptivity to poetry, a largely involuntary activity and one that does not translate into the common currency of Saussurean signs. The sonic character of the "Ode to a Nightingale" holds out to us the tenuous possibility of being submerged in a wild joining and disjoining of our cultural legacy, proferring an epistemological risk that pays off in the ambiguous capital of moments of imaginative transport that arrive only at greater uncertainties.

I think that one cannot read without trying to reconstruct the historical context, but history is not the last word, the final key, of reading.

Derrida, *Interview*

The true, the beautiful and the good—the ideals of a philistine culture.

Adorno, *Aesthetic Theory*

ℓ

ℓ

ℓ

ℓ

ℓ

ℓ

ℓ

ℓ

ℓ

ℓ

CHAPTER 2   ℓ

Antiquity, Romanticism, and Modernity

"Ode on a Grecian Urn"

ℓ

ℓ

ℓ

ℓ

ℓ

ℓ

ℓ

THE ASSERTIVE RHETORIC of the conclusion of the "Ode on a Grecian Urn" admits none of the uncertainty registered by the interrogative ending of the "Ode to a Nightingale." Whereas the "Nightingale" ode stops at a point of irresolution that exemplifies the impossibility of solving the epistemological dilemma it propounds, the final lines of the "Urn" display a confident authority that, considering the tenor of the poem, might justly be called Olympian. Nevertheless, these lines,

> "Beauty is truth, truth beauty,"—that is all
>   Ye know on earth, and all ye need to know,

famously judged by T. S. Eliot as "a serious blemish on a beautiful poem" (270), have generated at least as much critical dissension as the more obviously unresolved conclusion of the "Ode to a Nightingale." Apart from those few critics who have been willing both to identify Keats with a neoplatonic aesthetic creed and to argue for the higher truth of Platonic values, most of the attention paid to these lines has been devoted to finding some means of qualifying their unequivocal rhetoric, usually by distancing Keats himself from their sweeping assertions. While the repeated valorizations of the sensory over the ideal in Keats's letters ("O for a life of sensations rather than of Thoughts," "axioms in philosophy are not axioms until they are proved upon our pulses" [*KL*, 1:185, 279] should indicate the unlikelihood of Keats's Platonism, it is a curious fate for a poem to become as canonized as the "Ode on a Grecian Urn" through a critical history whose primary goal has been to dissuade the reader from believing what the poem seems to say.

The interpretive framing of the ode's final lines as something other than an unqualified expression of aestheticism has been sustained by an artificial controversy over their punctuation. The three extant variants from Keats's lifetime are

> Beauty is Truth,—Truth Beauty,—that is all
>   Ye know on earth, and all ye need to know.
> (Charles Brown's transcript)

> Beauty is Truth, Truth Beauty.—That is all
>   Ye know on Earth, and all ye need to know.
> (*Annals of the Fine Arts* 4 (January 1820)

> "Beauty is truth, truth beauty,"—that is all
>   Ye know on earth, and all ye need to know.
> (*Lamia and Other Poems*, 1820)[1]

To those who are inclined to accept a continuity between the statements made in these lines and similar declarations in Keats's letters ("What the imagination seizes as Beauty must be truth" [*KL*, 1:184]; "the excellence of every Art is its intensity, capable of making all disagreeables evaporate, from their being in close relationship with Beauty & Truth" [1:192]; "I can never feel certain of any truth but from a clear perception of its Beauty" [2:19]), looking at the variants in sequence suggests, as Earl Wasserman has noted, that Keats's revisions were designed to make clearer the distinction between the words attributed to the urn ("Beauty is truth, truth beauty," set off first by a comma, then by a period, then by closed quotation marks), and the broader claims made by the poem's speaker as he joins with and amplifies the urn's message (60). But this distinction was entirely effaced in 1959 by Douglas Bush in his edition of Keats's poems; Bush moved the closing quotation marks to the end of the poem, thus causing the lines to read

"Beauty is truth, truth beauty,—that is all
    Ye know on earth, and all ye need to know." (*Selected Poems*, 208)

Bush's punctuation of the poem was then adopted by David Perkins in the anthology *English Romantic Writers* (1251) and by Walter Jackson Bate in his biography of Keats (517), as a way of putting to rest the question of, in Stillinger's words, "Who Says What to Whom at the End of the 'Ode on a Grecian Urn'?" (113). By placing quotation marks around the entire final two lines of the poem, the Harvard school of Keats criticism has tried to leave no doubt that the lines are spoken by the urn, not by the poet.

There is, however, no legitimate editorial warrant for this repunctuation of the poem. Bush's argument, that the *Lamia* text could be altered because "we do not know . . . that Keats read proof of this poem" (*Selected Poems*, 350), was supported by Bate on the grounds that Keats was "probably too ill to oversee the publication of the 1820 volume" (*Keats*, 516). Bush and Bate, however, along with all other editors of the poem, accept all of the *Lamia* variants from the transcripts and the *Annals* version, including the change in line 9 from "What love? what dance?" to "What mad pursuit?" The punctuation of the poem's final lines has too often depended not on traditional editorial procedures but on a preferred interpretation of the poem. The rationale behind Bush's alteration of the text is candidly acknowledged by Michael Hinden, who adopts Bush's punctuation on the basis that "the editor a critic chooses to follow will be determined by the critic's sense of the overall meaning of the poem" (Hinden, 30). The attempt to create a text consonant with a belief in Keats's "robust realism, his sense of proportion" (Bate, 519), and the resulting surety that Keats would never endorse such

Wildean art-for-art's-sakeism as the closing words of the ode seem to express, should now have been definitively reversed by Stillinger's edition of the poems, which restores the *Lamia* punctuation. The *Lamia* text was the last to appear in Keats's lifetime, and the only one to appear under his name and in a collection of his work. (The *Annals* printings of the odes were signed only with a dagger.)

Despite the editorial untenability of Bush's repunctuation of the poem, the anti-aestheticist interpretation that the Bush text was created to serve has not been easily relinquished. Helen Vendler follows Stillinger in printing the text of the ode with the *Lamia* quotation marks, but she continues to maintain that "the *consensus gentium* seems to be that the last two lines are spoken by the urn to men." Vendler alludes to Stillinger's analysis of the various interpretations of these lines as if his comment that "Urn to reader" is the "commonest view of the conclusion of the ode" means that, by *consensus gentium*, "This crux now seems settled" (*Odes*, 312). Vendler does not mention Stillinger's observation that "The principal obstacle" to seeing the lines as addressed by the urn to the reader is "the printing of the text in the *Lamia* volume" (114). There remains the problem of how to adapt the *Lamia* text to the Harvard interpretation, and Bush's deviation from standard editorial practice in this matter indicates the difficulty of reconciling the two. That Bush should have felt the need to alter the text of the poem in order to qualify the poem's statement of aesthetic sufficiency indicates the difficulty of reading the sweeping and unconditional rhetoric of these lines in a spirit of ironic qualification.

The spirit of Vendler's judgment that "The language of the close of 'Urn' cannot be entirely assimilated to the language used earlier in the ode, and this is a flaw" (145), with its echo of Eliot's account of the final lines of the poem as a "blemish," continues to inform readings of the poem in which vocabulary and methodology are more au courant than Vendler's New Critical approach. Recent essays on the poem by Paul Fry, Michael Hinden, Douglas Wilson, Susan Wolfson, and Theresa Kelley that focus on the formal structure of the poem have all found the "Urn" internally fissured by formal and thematic discontinuities that stretch New Critical irony to the point where, as Wolfson puts it, the poem's conclusion "unsettles its performance of meaning."[2] Wilson connects this textual instability to a historical theme that has become common in recent readings of the poem, one that creates a different sort of critical distance from anything that smacks of art-for-art's-sake. "Part of the indeterminacy encountered by the reader," Wilson contends, "comes from the historic gap between Keats and the Hellenic culture when such urns were made" (829).

This historicist theme has informed another cluster of recent essays on the "Urn" by Philip Fisher, Stuart Peterfreund, Martin Aske, A. W. Phinney, and Daniel Watkins, all of whom have closely followed the terms of McGann's critique of Romanticism as an ideological evasion of history. McGann's brief comments on the "Grecian Urn" in "Keats and the Historical Method in Literary Criticism," which consist of little more than a recommendation that the reader consult Ian Jack's valuable account of Keats's familiarity with the visual arts, have had less influence on historicist readings of this poem than has McGann's citation in that essay of Marx's statements on the childlike normativity of the Greeks and his commendation of "Marx's profound sense of the pastness of the past, and of the importance which this differential has for all aesthetic experience" (1026). Historicist studies of the "Urn," adopting this premise of an ineluctable epistemic "differential," have situated Keats's work within the progressive, Hegelian narrative that underlies Marx's vision of history. Historicizing Keats's "Urn" has come to mean locating it within a "Romantic period" that stands midway between a preindustrial society of organic community and immanent social meaning and the modern era, in which our critical intelligence can identify the illusions of such residual formations as "Romanticism" and "art." Within this middle ground, the strain of Keats's emphatic rhetoric in the ode's conclusion is seen as exposing the distance between his own historical situation and "the golden and enchanted place known as Attic Greece" (Peterfreund, 65). Keats himself becomes capable only of feeling the effects of this difference, while its meaning becomes available to our more fully modern, historicizing critical consciousness.

This historicist narrative has the advantage of transforming the perceived blemish of the ode's final lines into a historical inevitability rather than a momentary lapse by a young poet. Fisher sees the poem itself as a kind of "museum" defining its "cultural lateness" in the contrast between its own modernity and an object that "must be from Greece, the culture in which a serene triumph, an almost effortless ease about art existed" (90). Fisher's depiction is made by Phinney into more than an image; reminding us that Keats's encounter with Greek art always occurred in some form of museum which separates the artwork from its "original context," and citing Gadamer's observation of the "similarity between the isolation of the artwork as an aesthetic object in the museum and the alienation of the artist in

modern society," Phinney argues that "the urn is, finally, a 'Cold Pastoral'"
(217). "Warm and inviting as it may appear," Phinney argues, the urn "must
remain a kind of 'cold beauty' for him, since he cannot, in the world and
time in which he lives, relish the 'real of beauty'" (224). This historicist
argument describes an aestheticized reading of the "Urn" as nothing but a
mystified repetition of an ideological illusion of the time of the poem's production.

The modern framing of the poem within an opposition that sets "the
cultural situation that had given purpose and meaning to the original work"
against the impossibility of "re-creating the Greek ideal in the modern
world" (Phinney, 213–14) itself recapitulates a particular mythography of
Greece that was current in the antiquarian revival of Regency England, and
that was entirely familiar to Keats. Hazlitt's sympathetic response to
Friedrich Schlegel's distinction between "classical" and "romantic" art illustrates the common theme of lost harmony and meaning:

> The natural organization of the Greeks seems to have been more perfect,
> more susceptible of external impressions, and more in harmony with
> external nature than ours, who have not the same advantages of climate
> and constitution.

> The mere lapse of time then, aided by the art of printing, has served to
> accumulate for us an endless mass of mixed and contradictory materials;
> and by extending our knowledge to a greater number of things, has made
> our particular ideas less perfect and distinct. The constant reference to a
> former state of manners and literature, is a marked feature in modern
> poetry. We are always talking of the Greeks and Romans;—*they* never
> said any thing of us. (*Complete Works*, 16:64, 66; Hazlitt's emphasis)

Although the narrative of an inevitable movement from an age of natural
and cultural harmony to a "mixed and contradictory" modernity can be told
in nostalgic terms, this is not the note on which Keats's poem concludes. Its
final lines, "'Beauty is truth, truth beauty,'—that is all / Ye know on earth,
and all ye need to know," are expressed entirely in the present tense, and the
final phrase rises from the level set by the penultimate statement; the lines
do not lament the loss of a harmony that existed only in a distant and irrecoverable past. Although the ode's gradual presentation of the urn itself as a
funerary object clearly warrants attention to the poem's shift from a nostalgia for Greek antiquity into a meditation on personal mortality, there is still
a great difference in tone between the mostly celebratory conclusion of

Keats's poem and the nostalgia that leads Fisher to conclude his essay by calling up, in opposition to the ode's supposed valorization of "sweetness," the historical inevitability of the "bitter taste of ashes, death, loss, absence and time" (102). Phinney's judgment that "the urn is, finally, a 'Cold Pastoral'" (224) resembles Stillinger's foreshortening of the "Nightingale" ode in the assertion that the perception of the nightingale as a "deceiving elf" is "the end of the poem" (7); Phinney offers, as a final perspective on the poem, a perception that the poem itself situates only as a moment in its unfolding narrative.

This historicist reading of the "Urn" achieves its deterministic explanatory power by depriving Keats of the ability to reflect upon and distance himself from a particular historical narrative that has been implicitly incorporated into the poem. The story of the inevitable decline of poetic power in the "modern" era was, however, only one of two very different narratives familiar to Keats that sought to define a historical relation between modern Britain and ancient Greece. The nostalgic narrative unfolds in its starkest form in Hazlitt's 1817 essay "Why the Arts Are Not Progressive" when Hazlitt contends that "The greatest poets, the ablest orators, the best painters, and the finest sculptors that the world ever saw, appeared soon after the birth of these arts, and lived in a state of society which was, in other respects, comparatively barbarous. Those arts, which depend on individual genius and incommunicable power, have always leaped at once from infancy to manhood, from the first rude dawn of invention to their meridian height and dazzling lustre, and have in general declined ever since" (*Complete Works*, 18:6). The story of an irrecoverable golden age of "noble simplicity and sedate grandeur" originates in Johann Joachim Winckelmann's *Reflections on the Imitation of the Painting and Sculpture of the Greeks* (2), translated into English by Fuseli in 1765, in which Winckelmann proclaimed that "Taste was not only original among the Greeks, but seemed also quite peculiar to their country; it seldom went abroad without loss" (34). But Keats would have been equally familiar with a counternarrative of renaissance that the *Annals of the Fine Arts*, under Haydon's influence, had adopted as its guiding theme. Haydon, a fervent champion of the Elgin Marbles, saw their arrival in Britain as a harbinger of artistic revival, exclaiming that "the genius of Greece still hovers near them: may she, with her inspiring touch, give new vigour to British Art, and cause new beauties to spring from British exertions!" (*Annals* 1:284–85). The first volume of the *Annals*, published in 1817, opened with Thomson's paean to Greece for having "led the way" in both "Science" and "Fancy." On the following page, that volume was dedicated to "The Select Committee of the Honourable House of Commons who by duly Estimating The Value and Recommending the Purchase of the Elgin Marbles to the British Legislature Have Created An Epoch In The History Of Their Country." Beginning with volume 2, each issue of the *Annals* contained as its initial epigraph Jonathan Richardson's claim, "I am no prophet, nor the son of a prophet; but I will venture to predict, that if ever the ancient, great and beautiful taste in painting revives, it will be in England."[3]

Fisher and Phinney confidently place Keats within an era that knew of its own inexorable loss of poetic power as they offer precise and nearly identical identifications both of the period of this loss—"after the French Revolution," according to Fisher (87) and "By the Romantic period" (Phinney, 209)—and of its cause. "It is only in modern art that the problem of an audience occurs," says Fisher. "Earlier art, produced for an occasion within a community, has no 'audience'" (88). Phinney, settling on the same theme, offers a recognizably McGannite disparagement of Cleanth Brooks's aestheticist reading of the "Urn": "The transhistorical nature of art can be shown to be itself historically conditioned. By the Romantic period, art has become an ornamental commodity whose value must be justified in a utilitarian society" (209).

The precise, though fictional, identification of the onset of modernity and the awareness of "cultural lateness" as something that occurred "after the French Revolution" or "by the Romantic period" reflects one of the most fictionally coherent narratives of literary history: Lukacs's story that connects the loss of organic culture with the era of "Romantic disillusionment." This Lukacsian literary history vastly oversimplifies not only the Romantic period and the terms of our "modern" alienation but also the epic consciousness to which they are opposed. Lukacs's Golden Age mythology, which contends that "in Homer's organic world, life and meaning were present with perfect immanence in every manifestation of life" (80), is easily belied by a reading of Homer's work. The *Iliad* itself is an account of an already bygone era, and its characters speak nostalgically of an earlier time in which one man could easily lift a boulder that in their own day could barely be budged by six men. Modern critics (from Winckelmann and Hazlitt to Lukacs, Gadamer, Fisher, and Phinney) seem to take quite literally a nostalgic fantasy of an organically unified past, which Homer was able to portray with some irony.

The opening lines of the "Ode on a Grecian Urn," in which ancient Greece is represented as a feminized urn, exploit the overdeterminations inherent in the neohellenic mythography of "Greece." The opacity of the initial image of a cultural icon that arouses, in the poem's speaker, both a desire for intimacy ("Thou still unravish'd bride") and a sense of pity ("Thou foster-child"), derives from the ode's simultaneous deployment and deconstruction of the symbols of an idealized Hellenic past. The paradoxically feminine gender identification imposed on ancient Greece arises from the duality of the idea of the "natural," which is both a historical term associated with Greece and a purely aesthetic, transhistorical valorization. The nostalgic historical narrative inspired by the Hellenic revival of the late eighteenth and early nineteenth centuries told of a teleological movement from the natural naïveté of antiquity to the self-consciousness of modernity; to the degree that a similar narrative now informs the most popular accounts of our relation to the authors of the Romantic period, Keats's poem is able to address some of the most common assumptions and valorizations in the study of Romantic poetry, such as the opposition between "organic culture" and the alienation of modernity.

The vocabulary in which the "Urn" enters this discussion emerges from a particular cultural context: the controversies that swirled through the art world of London in the wake of the arrival of the Elgin Marbles, debates in which the *Annals of the Fine Arts* played an important, though belated, role. When the poem intervened in the contemporary debate, it took the ideology of the *Annals* to its breaking point, and out of the collapse of that ideology the poem constructs its own perspective on the relation between ancient art and its modern reception. While reconstructing the historical context is a necessary prelude to understanding the poem, the "Ode on a Grecian Urn" becomes far more than a reflection of this local controversy.

The vocabulary of the "Urn" reflects the specific context of its initial publication in the *Annals*. Despite Eliot's assertion that Keats's use of the words "beauty" and "truth" is "remote" from the "ordinary use" of the words (270), the paired use of these words was a commonplace in Keats's circle, particularly in relation to the Greeks. To cite just a few of the most relevant examples, Haydon praises the more reformist members of the Royal Academy who were "alive to the beauty and truth" (*Autobiography*, 307) of the Marbles, and he censures the primary critic of the Marbles, Richard Payne Knight, for showing a "distaste for beauty, a doubt of truth" (315). Hazlitt says that "to the genuine artist, truth, nature, beauty are almost different names for the same thing" (*Complete Works*, 4:75), praises the "truth and beauty of the ancient mythology" (*CW*, 17:265), and, in a slight variation that suggests the agency of the letter in keeping the terms joined, he writes of "Greek statues" that they "flourish in immortal youth and beauty" (*CW,* 12:254–55). In 1822, continuing the argument on behalf of the Marbles, Hazlitt castigated Sir Joshua Reynolds, the former President of the Royal Academy, for having promoted an aesthetic idealism that taught that "a more refined idea, borrowed from the observation of a number of particulars, but unlike any of them, was the standard of truth and beauty."[4] Despite Eliot's demurrals, "beauty" and "truth" are not metaphysical terms until they have been estranged from a more ordinary use. "Truth," in particular, is not a Platonic term in Hazlitt's vocabulary, but the word he uses to oppose an aesthetic realism to the representation of imaginary ideals.

The conjunction of the terms "truth" and "beauty," with the sometimes addition of "nature," served a specific polemical purpose for Grecophile Britons of Regency London, who were also the ideological foes of the art establishment represented by the Royal Academy. In a series of essays on Reynolds's *Discourses* that were written in 1814 and reprinted in the *Annals of the Fine Arts* in 1819, Hazlitt criticized Reynolds's belief in a "decompounded, disembodied, vague, ideal nature . . . seen through the misty veil of metaphysics," and he insisted that "The concrete, and not the abstract, is the object of painting, and of all works of imagination."[5] The argument made by the partisans of the Marbles for a greater naturalism in artistic representation informs Keats's equation of the terms "beauty" and "truth" at the conclusion of the "Ode on a Grecian Urn." Readers of the *Annals* would not have found the conclusion of the "Urn" an unsatisfying, paradoxical or unfamiliar proposition. Keats's declaration that "Beauty is truth, truth beauty" is neither metaphysical nor ironic. It is Keats's contribution to a critique of a beau ideal, or grand style, in art; it is consistent with the valorization of the sensory over the intelligible in Keats's letters; and it is entirely in accord with the aesthetic naturalism of his intellectual circle and of the *Annals of the Fine Arts,* a periodical that had as its primary purpose the advancement of Haydon's side in his battle with the Royal Academy.

While the meanings of the words "beauty" and "truth" in the "Urn" are hardly remote from their most familiar usage, the beliefs valorized by those terms are apt to seem at least as dubious to contemporary critical scrutiny as they were to Eliot. Even Eliot's historicism, which consists of an emphasis on the continuity of tradition, distances him from Hazlitt's belief that the greatest art arises from the meeting of "individual genius" and "nature" (*CW,* 18:6). Running directly counter to Eliot's description of the incremental growth of a tradition is Hazlitt's identification of imaginative power with an original plenitude: "The arts hold immediate communication with nature, and are only derived from that source. When that original impulse no longer exists, when the inspiration of genius is fled, all the attempts to recal [*sic*] it are no better than the tricks of galvanism to restore the dead to life" (*CW*, 18:5). Hazlitt's belief in a transhistorical "genius" whose artistic manifestation is a "deep and innate sensibility to truth and beauty" (*CW*, 4:163) violates a modern sense of the cultural and epistemic determination of aesthetic standards, but, contrary to McGann's account of "the Romantic ideology," Hazlitt does not see himself as expressing the dominant belief of his time. In "On Beauty," written in 1816, Hazlitt writes, "It is about sixty years ago that Sir Joshua Reynolds . . . advanced the notion, which has prevailed very much ever since, that Beauty was entirely dependent on custom." Hazlitt wishes, on the contrary, to show that "beauty" is "in some way inherent in the object, and that if custom is a second nature, there is another nature which ranks before it" (*CW*, 4:68).

This confidence in an "innate sensibility to truth and beauty" informs all of Hazlitt's art criticism, in which Hazlitt roams from gallery to museum describing the "gusto" of Titian's flesh colors, the limited perfection of Claude, or the greatness of Raphael, which "is instantly communicated to all eyes that behold, and all hearts that can feel them" (*CW*, 4:144). Hazlitt sometimes admits the impossibility of defining beauty (*CW*, 4:68; 18:83–84), but not of recognizing it, even without any training in a particular art. He writes of a Frenchman who was "the only graceful dancer we ever saw" that "It was not necessary to have seen good dancing before to know that this was really fine. Whoever has seen the sea in motion, the branches of a tree waving in the air, would instantly perceive the resemblance" (4:72). Hazlitt's confidence was not idiosyncratic in Keats's circle. When Haydon wanted to convince Fuseli of the greatness and the authenticity of the Elgin Marbles, he simply took Fuseli to the Marbles. In Haydon's account, Fuseli's immediate reaction was "The Greeks were gods—they were gods" (*Memoirs*, 308).

Although Hazlitt identifies Attic Greece as a culture uniquely "in harmony with external nature," and although he laments the decline of that sensibility in the modern age, he nevertheless uses, with seemingly complete unselfconsciousness, natural analogies to describe the present, modern beauty of a French dancer. Another version of this paradox was initiated by Winckelmann when he urged German artists, "There is but one way for the moderns to become great, and perhaps unequalled; I mean, by imitating the ancients" (*Reflections*, 2). Knight's double charge against the Elgin Marbles, "You have lost your labour, my Lord Elgin; your marbles are overrated; they are not Greek, they are Roman of the time of Hadrian" (Haydon, *Memoirs*, 183), depends on the same paradox. The statues are not that good, Knight argued, and they are not that old, but the curious fact is that the two objections become indistinguishable. If aesthetic value depends upon the ability to arouse an "innate sensibility to truth and beauty," then a matter of a few hundred years' difference in the creation of the statues should not really matter. But once "Greece" has become the signifier of a Golden Age of an art born of a harmony with nature, questions of value and provenance become inextricably joined.

Complicating the paradoxical valorization of Greece as the organic source of the greatest of cultural artifacts is the simultaneous valorization of individual genius. When Haydon took Fuseli to see the Elgin Marbles, he looked for Fuseli's assent that they were not only great and Greek, but that they were also entirely from the hand of Phidias. The conjunction of the terms *Greece, nature,* and *genius* in a single essence was a powerfully held belief throughout the Hellenic revival, but their joining is nevertheless contingent and unstable. The potential dissociation of the term *nature* from *Greece* allows Hazlitt to find a present "harmony with external nature" in a comparison between a modern dancer and the waves of the sea, and it allows Keats to say that "if Poetry comes not as naturally as the Leaves to a tree it had better not come at all" (*KL*, 1:238–39). But within the intellectual circle of the *Annals, Greece* continued to function as a transcendental signifier, an image of the inimitable, which is able to focus all desire on itself as the totality of all that is worth having or being.

Keats's treatment of the simultaneous valorization of beauty as a natural, transhistorical phenomenon and as the cultural property of the Hellenic period passes this paradox through a gendered narrative; the story begins with the parallel in the opening stanza between the poet-speaker's desire to unlock the secrets of an urn represented as an "unravish'd bride" and the "mad pursuit" by the male figures within the text, "men or gods," of the "maidens loth." The gendered narrative that ensues has been denounced in the most unequivocal terms by Daniel Watkins and critiqued in more nuanced readings by Froma Zeitlin and Geraldine Friedman, all of whom locate the distance between the poem's speaker and the urn not in an unbridgeable gap between antiquity and modernity but in gendered stereotypes that persist across Western patriarchal history. Watkins describes the "Urn" as a straightforward "articulation" of "patriarchal morality as it existed in Keats's day" (246), and he sees the progression from one-sided ecstatic pursuit to the imminent sacrifice of the heifer in the fourth stanza as a "conquest" of a "'femaleness'" associated "'with lower material nature'" as "the poem *appropriates* the urn" (249; Watkins's emphasis). This gender polarity also initiates Zeitlin's and Friedman's readings of the poem, although they both see the ode coming to a more ambiguous conclusion, and they ascribe the ode's ambivalent critical history to the poem's straying from the expected narrative of conquest. Zeitlin connects the persistent critical dissatisfaction with the ode's ending to the collapse of that narrative of desire, proposing that between its overheated opening and the final "drastic shift from the poetic to the philosophical, the imagistic to the propositional," that the poem creates in the male reader "a sexual excitement that is never quite discharged in a gratifying lyric conclusion" (279–80). While "the effort at violent seizure was the poet's ecstasy," Zeitlin argues, this attempt at ecstasy fades, and "truth and beauty" become "his consolation prize" (293).

Even Friedman's deconstructive reading, which concludes that the poem finally undoes the stability of the "polarization of head and body according to gender" (235), presumes that the "Urn" begins in that polarity; this distinctly gendered story, as it identifies the desire of the poem with an unequivocally male desire on Keats's part, once again produces his "romanticism" as the embodiment of a purer and simpler force than our modern self-consciousness, and it understates the poem's own capacity for self-questioning. Watkins's magnanimous concessions of Keats's "sincere utopian impulses" (242) and the "sincerity of Keats's desire" (253) in the "Urn" identify a subject-position that appears in the poem, but it is one that is finally surpassed in the unfolding of the profoundly ambivalent relation between the ode's speaker and the Greek urn. As Watkins describes Keats's "sincerity," he assigns Keats to the realm of the natural; "Keats" becomes analogous to a material object, identical to himself and to his own desire, and entirely different from a self-conscious being capable of reflecting upon his or her own actions and beliefs. Watkins has thus "feminized" Keats by assimilating him into the world of the "body" and not the "head"; identifying this structure of feminization can serve as a prelude to an analysis of the paradoxical cultural codings of "masculine" and "feminine" that inform the histories of both the production and the reception of Keats's "Urn."

In distinguishing Keats's "sincerity" from our own potential for self-critical awareness, Watkins employs the same distinction used in Keats's time to distinguish the "classical" past from the "romantic" present, or—in

Schiller's terms—the "naive" from the "sentimental." When this identification of the archaic with the "naive" is pursued, as it is in a representative
fashion by Hazlitt, to suggest that the Greeks "were more in harmony with
external nature" than are we moderns, the cultural code that identifies
"Greece" with "nature" produces a curious paradox. Even though for the
Grecophile Briton of the early nineteenth century the exemplary figure for
Greece was Homer, and the exemplary Homeric text was the *Iliad*, the simultaneous, though discrete, identifications of ancient Greece and of femininity with nature produce a paradoxical coding of Greece as feminine.
"Greece" thus holds the exorbitant status in the cultural code of Keats's
circle that "Keats" holds in historicist analysis of the "Urn": fully masculine
in its active productive power, fully feminine as raw material for modern
reflective scrutiny. "We" can talk about the Greeks, or the Romantics, all we
like, and there seems to be no danger of their saying anything about us.

If the opening invocation of the "Urn" is, as Friedman argues, not quite
a conversation, it nevertheless presents a reciprocal and not a unidirectional
relation between the figured voice of the poem and the described urn:

> Thou still unravish'd bride of quietness,
>   Thou foster-child of silence and slow time.

Watkins's contention that these "opening two lines . . . establish the patriarchal voice controlling the remainder of the poem" (252) and Zeitlin's assertion that "the poet (and the poem) are judged by the success or failure of the
masculine drive to seize, possess, and consummate desire in the enterprise
that is deemed the most potent sign of manliness" (279) greatly underesti-
mate the fragmentation of the voice of the ode. In even its earliest moments,
the speaker's relation to the urn changes in nearly every word of these lines.
The initial apostrophe to the urn ("Thou") and its implicit personification
suggest a desire on the part of the speaker, but given the paradoxical coding
of Greece as both ideal and as natural, hence feminine, it is not immediately
clear whether the speaker's desire is for identification (with the Hellenic
ideal) or for possession (of the feminine). The ambiguity of the poem's second word, "still," derives from this undecidability. "Still" can suggest either
(adverbially) an admiration for the urn's durability or (adjectivally) the im-
mobilizing of the urn for the sake of possessing it; the adverbial connotation
emphasizes the urn's antiquity, its historical Greekness, and the adjectival
reading its materiality and its femininity. "Unravish'd" tips the scale toward
possession, but the rest of the line drifts away from the fulfillment of that

desire; if "Thou," or the "Urn" of the title, is already a "bride," she cannot be the speaker's bride, and as the "bride of quietness" she slides away from a human identity altogether.

The second line introduces a second attempt at personification in the image of "Thou foster-child." This personification seems to express a desire for an intimacy that is neither possession nor identification, but even this desire is barely expressed before the distance opens once more between the speaker and the urn. "Thou foster-child" is a figure on the margins of the cycle of human generation, and the long vowel of "child" reechoes the soft assonance that accompanies the urn's first evasion of the speaker's mundane humanity; in its phonic reiteration, the phrase "child of silence" balances and displaces the initial image of the "bride of quietness." While the most unequivocally gendered account of the poem produces a narrative of patriarchal conquest, which transforms women into "wives and daughters, into so much property to be tended and shaped by masculine desire" (Watkins, 252), the opening lines of the "Urn" are unable to maintain a securely sexualized identification of this uncertainly personified figure. The loose multiplicities of these two discrete personifications, "unravish'd bride" and "foster-child"—each embodying its own paradoxes and, when taken together, producing no synthesis into a single figure—ensure that the urn will have only an ambiguously figurative relation to our human reality. The potentially alienating resonance of "foster-child" would be particularly apparent to Keats from Fanny Keats's situation with a mean-spirited guardian. This poem, however, which begins in the Grecian key of "noble simplicity and serene grandeur," adopts a benign view of the passage of this artifact through its adoptive cultures.

The initial serenity of the "Urn" depends upon such suppression of the personal and, in a larger sense, the human. While apostrophe and personification suggest the possibility of a personal relation between the speaker and the urn, the fading of both speaker and urn into shadows cast by the expanse of an imperturbably silent temporality draws a nearly invisible border between the central presence of the urn and a human world whose most overt images, a bride and a child, represent a world of generation. The vowel play of the opening lines reinforces the effect of a gentle, untroubled durability. The poem first balances its broad vowels and then prolongs their resonance; the word "silence" seems, phonetically and semantically, to reenact the completeness reached in the "quietness" of the first line, but metrical balance demands that the line be extended. When it is, its concluding phrase, "and slow time," reaches to yet another long /i/ by wrapping around an even broader /o/, and the phrase "and slow time" suggests the temporal scope acquired by this frail artifact, which dwarfs the speaker's imagination.

The speaker's awe informs the confession of the urn's greater power in the poem's next lines:

> Sylvan historian, who canst thus express
>   A flowery tale more sweetly than our rhyme.

The exact meaning of "thus" is not initially clear; the primary antecedent for the word seems to be "Sylvan" which—particularly if one hears an etymologically incorrect pun on "sylph"—suggests the urn's feminine "sweetness." However, the urn's status as a "historian" supposedly capable of relating a "tale," or, as the next line has it, a "legend," takes the poem into another issue regularly explored in the pages of the *Annals of the Fine Arts:* the relation between poetry and the visual arts. The topic was something of an obsession with Haydon, and by 1820 Keats could list among the predictable conversations in his circle of friends that the talk at Haydon's was "like an acted play, from the first to the last Act" of "worn out discourses of poetry and painting" (*KL*, 2:244). The first essay ever printed in the *Annals* was titled "On the Affinity between Painting and Writing, in point of Composition"; its author, the Lord Viscount Sidmouth, was commended by James Elmes, the editor of the *Annals* and a friend of Haydon, for an argument that Elmes claimed demonstrated "the affinity between the higher branches of the FINE ARTS AND LITERATURE, which, though doubted by few, has seldom been more ably argued and balanced" (*Annals*, 1:1). In fact, although Sidmouth expresses his sympathy for Haydon's campaign for an artistic revival ("Nor is the strength of genius yet exhausted: men may yet arise equal, if not superior to their predecessors" [1:20]), much of his essay dwells not on the "affinity" of the two arts but on their differences, and it argues for the superiority of poetry. Poetry, Sidmouth writes,

> will incontestibly claim a preference, on account of the greater extent of its power. It is not confined to the instant; it has not only "one sentence to utter, one moment to exhibit," but can describe subjects of a lengthened duration, and can avail itself of that progressive and increasing energy, which a succession of images never fails to produce. . . . The beauties arising from comparison are also beyond the reach of the pencil; incapable of describing the progress of thought, what idea can it give of the rapidity ascribed to it by Homer, from its similitude to lightning?

As words are expressive of all ideas, Poetry seems to comprise every possible subject of imitative excellence; and if we add to this the auxiliary
graces which it borrows from music, and the powerful assistance which it
derives from declamation and action, its superiority will be manifest,
both in point of dignity and utility, over the more confined powers of its
sister art. (*Annals*, 1:17–19)

Sidmouth thus distills a number of points made in the *ut pictura poesis* debate
of the eighteenth century about the technical resources available to poetry—sequence, comparison, and sound—that distinguish it from visual
representation. The "Ode on a Grecian Urn" exhibits, from its opening
syllables, a close attention to the "auxiliary graces which [poetry] borrows
from music," and commentary on the poem that has assimilated it into the
ekphrastic tradition has, like Elmes, slipped too quickly past the distinctions
drawn in Keats's immediate intellectual circle between the two arts. The
idea that a painting, which has only "one moment to exhibit," could perform the narrative function of telling a "tale" was much debated in the circle
of the *Annals*, and the "Ode on a Grecian Urn" is one of the most nuanced
contributions to that discussion.

Sidmouth's essay weighs in on Lessing's side of his argument with Winckelmann over the relation between the visual arts and poetry; whereas
Winckelmann emphasized the importance of a cultural spirit informing an
artwork, regardless of its medium, Lessing argued for the importance of the
formal differences between the visual and verbal arts. In its original form,
this argument focused on the statue of the Laocoön, and Fuseli served as a
central conduit in bringing the terms of both sides of this discussion to
England. Winckelmann argues, in the *Reflections*, that the sculpted Laocoön
shows a greater stoicism during his strangulation by snakes than does
Laocoön as described by Virgil, and that the greater heroism depicted by
the statue proves that it was produced by Greeks, they being the people with
the higher, more stoic moral characters. Lessing argues that the difference
between the two representations is due to the differing demands and resources of the two arts. He asserts that a sculptor cannot show a figure
emitting a cry because that would require an open mouth, which would
violate aesthetic decorum, but, he asks, "When Virgil's Laocoön screams,
who stops to think that a scream necessitates an open mouth, and that an
open mouth is ugly?" (20). Lessing goes on to argue against the notion that
poetry should operate *ut pictura poesis*, contending that "poetry has the wider
sphere, that beauties are within her reach which painting can never attain,

that she may often see reason to prefer unpicturesque beauties to pictur-esque ones" (55). In the most famous passage from his essay, Lessing bases the distinction between the two arts finally on their formal difference, "that succession in time is the province of the poet, co-existence in space that of the artist" (109); as a result, "the artist can use but a single moment of ever-changing nature" (16).

Winckelmann's *Reflections* were first translated into English by Fuseli in 1765, and Fuseli's advocacy of a "grand style" in painting found support in Winckelmann's characterization of Greek art: "It is not only Nature which the votaries of the Greeks find in their works, but still more, something superior to nature; ideal beauties, brain-born images" (*Reflections*, 4). But as Fuseli became familiar with Lessing's side of the argument he cited Lessing's essay on the *Laocoön* and paraphrased the central distinction of that essay at the outset of his third Lecture to the Royal Academy, delivered in 1801 and republished in 1820. Fuseli had thus been converted to the principle that "Successive action communicated by sounds, and *time*, are the medium of poetry; *form* displayed in *space*, and momentaneous energy, are the element of painting" (*Lectures*, 407). This principle is restated in various forms by English authors, as in Sidmouth's essay in the *Annals* and in Hazlitt's obser-vations that "The Art of Painting" is "inferior to poetry in magnitude of extent and succession of detail—but its power over any one point is far superior" (*CW,* 18:184), and that "painting gives the event, poetry the progress of events" (*CW,* 5:10). As Keeper of the Royal Academy beginning in 1804, Fuseli became Haydon's teacher in 1805, and he was Severn's teacher when Severn and Keats were visiting galleries regularly from 1816 through 1819.

Although it is unclear how much German aesthetic theory was absorbed by Keats, either from Hazlitt or through Haydon and Severn from Fuseli, Keats would surely have known that the analogy between the visual and verbal arts was contested on a number of fronts, and that a rivalry over which art was superior formed part of the debate. Some critical com-monplaces about this poem—that it is unproblematically ekphrastic, or that the poem attempts to mirror the urn—greatly oversimplify the terms of a complex discussion that was central in Keats's intellectual development. Keats would certainly have read the discussions of the relation between poetry and painting in Haydon's essays on Raphael's cartoons in the *Annals* of 1818 and 1819. In the first of these essays, Haydon quotes *Endymion* to illustrate a point, and several details from the later essay appear in Keats's "Urn"; Haydon refers to Raphael's portrayal, in *The Sacrifice at Lystra*, of "a heifer a year old," a "white bull with gilt horns and garlands" and a "boy flute-player," and he quotes a Renaissance antiquarian to the effect that "the flute seems to have been most used at sacrifice." The most important point that Keats takes from Haydon's essay is the observation that

> Poets can make their characters speak their thoughts; painters can only make them look. Abstracted reflections, or subtle conclusions in morality, can never be looked, though they may be inferred from the subjects painted; painting is therefore a more limited art in this view than poetry, in others it is more extended; but what painting does look the world can comprehend, poets speak to full effect only to their own nation. (*Annals*, 4:241–42)

This argument informs Keats's emphasis on the silence of the urn, as well as his final gesture, which has often struck critics as paradoxical, of making the urn speak. Such a turn would, even in Haydon's terms, be part of the natural province of the poet.

Haydon uses his essays in the *Annals* as a staging ground for defending the claims of painting against poetry. Haydon counters the argument, made originally by Lessing, that invention is more important in poetry, and execution in painting (*Laocoön*, 72), an observation put even more forcefully by Hazlitt: "invention is chiefly confined to poetry and words or ideas, and has little place in painting or concrete imagery" (*CW*, 20:390). Haydon, in contrast, insists that "Poets should only be called in as assistants; Painters should be ever jealous of doing nothing but realizing the conceptions of Poets: they should shew, by every subject they paint, that nature has given them the same fertility of imagination and powers of creation, the same power of exciting sympathies by the characters and the passions they display" (*Annals*, 3:249–50).

The speaker of Keats's "Urn" is at the outset of the poem a thoroughly naive believer in the mythic grandeur of Greece, and his own powers of invention are limited by his subordination to the iconic force of the Grecian sculpture. When the urn, as a "Sylvan historian," is credited "thus" with the ability to tell a "flowery tale more sweetly," its "sylvan" nature conveys not only a natural femininity but a historical privilege—that is, a Greekness—informing this greater capability. But the overdeterminations that have produced the paradoxical coding of Greece as feminine begin to dissolve the iconic value of this artifact. The distinction between Greekness and modernity quickly slides into an opposition between the urn's material presence and the arbitrary symbols of "rhyme." The word "our" initially presents a host of possibilities: does it mean we moderns (in other words, non-Greeks); we men (we who are "other" to the "sweetness" of the "sylph-an" feminine); or we poets (as opposed to the sculptor who created the urn)? It is only at the word "rhyme" that the opposition between poetry and the plastic arts is foregrounded, and "thus" becomes, metaleptically, a reference more to medium than to gender or era. This overdetermination originates not in the poem itself but in the terms of the debate as Keats receives them. The sculpture of the Laocoön, which had served as the point of departure for Lessing and Winckelmann in their argument over the relations of the visual and the verbal arts, was repeatedly cited in the Commons debate over the Elgin Marbles in 1816 as one of the reference points used in evaluating the artistic merits of the Marbles. Keats's representation of this over-determined opposition—Greek sculpture versus modern poetry—reproduces not only the paradoxical coding of Greece as natural/feminine but the asymmetry of the argument between Winckelmann and Lessing, who disagree over whether the most significant difference between the Greek statue and the Roman poem is one of historical circumstance or mode of representation.

In the speaker's attempt to fathom the meaning of the figures embellished on the urn's surface, his confusion over whether they are "deities or mortals" is based on the Golden Age mythology of the *Annals*, within which Haydon argued that the naturalism of Greek artists easily accommodated the depiction of the gods: "whether the Greeks represented gods or men, they made the forms of their gods subservient to the great laws of nature (as they knew they were obliged to represent gods by human forms)" (*Annals*, 3:70). Hazlitt also believed that the proof of the physical beauty of the ancient Greek people lay in their sculpture, in which even the gods were privileged in having their representations made in the images of Grecian mortals: "The Greek statues were copied from Greek forms. Their portraits of individuals were often superior to their personifications of their gods; the head of the Antinous, for example, to that of the Apollo" (*CW*, 18:82; *Annals*, 4:394). The very trait that demonstrates the urn's supposed superiority—namely, its ability to express a tale "more sweetly than our rhyme"—may itself be suspect, however, as a rather limited capacity. The potential irony in this dubious valorization thus opens a perspective that engages the latent contradictions in the *Annals* debates over antiquity and modernity, and over poetry and the visual arts.

While Haydon and Hazlitt deride Reynolds's beau ideal, they nevertheless attribute a natural yet perfect beauty not only to the spirit but to the physical appearance of the inhabitants of a Golden Age. The speaker in the opening lines of the "Urn" is a worthy representative of the Grecophile ideology of the *Annals*. He is thoroughly entranced by the perfection of this single artifact; his reverence for anything Greek is conveyed by his action of looking at a single vase and then trying to create a poem by communicating a knowledge of the figures carved on it. But all studies of the artistic sources of the ode's imagery indicate that this does not correspond to Keats's process of composing the "Ode on a Grecian Urn." The poem's imagery, even in the early stanzas, is not drawn from a single urn. Keats left himself free to combine images from a number of urns into the tableau suggested in the first stanza of the poem. Despite the suggestion that the persona of the poem is himself a poet, an understanding of the potential distance between Keats and that persona precludes the automatic identification of the desire of that persona with Keats's poetic, sexual, or historical "sincerity."

The flurry of questions that fills the latter half of the first stanza suggests the fervent desire of the speaker for a knowledge that would enable him to identify with the male figures on the urn, but there is very little poetry in this passage. The rhythm is choppy and monotonous, and there is none of the shading of imagery or attention to sound that characterizes the poem's opening lines. The identification of Keats with the poem's persona becomes even more problematic in the opening imagery of the second stanza:

> Heard melodies are sweet, but those unheard
>   Are sweeter; therefore, ye soft pipes, play on;
> Not to the sensual ear, but, more endear'd,
>   Pipe to the spirit ditties of no tone.

The speaker of the poem remains committed to the belief that the urn embodies a transcendent value, a value expressed in the form of melodies "sweeter" than any available to sensory representation, but this belief contradicts the naturalistic principles that Keats's circle associated with Greek art. Haydon, for example, writes in the *Annals* of 1818 of the Elgin Marbles, "you will see in these divine things, that the Greeks never sacrificed truth to an artificial 'beau ideal'" (*Annals*, 3:70). Hazlitt's attacks on the "beau ideal" of Reynolds and the Royal Academy, reprinted in installments in the *Annals* of 1818 and 1819, castigated those artists who had "carried the abstract principle of improving on nature to such a degree of refinement, that they left it out altogether" (*CW*, 18:52; *Annals*, 3:339). The persona of the "Ode on a Grecian Urn" would like to transcend material nature altogether, but the poem does not allow it. Despite the persona's professed disdain for the "sensual ear," the verse itself engages our ears, first gratifying us with the aural lilt of the repetition of "ear" and "endear'd" and then grating with its "ditties of no tone." The phonic redundancy of "no tone" is only the slightest shift from the rich melody of "slow time," but the clunkiness of "no tone" illustrates the dangers of aspiring to a beau ideal that would leave behind the "sensual ear." The semantic and phonic values of the words are in conflict; the speaker tells us that sounds do not matter, but the sensual ear says otherwise.

In the opinion of all commentators except Earl Wasserman, the poem becomes thoroughly banal as the second and third stanzas extend the speaker's desire for an imaginary ideal:

> Ah, happy, happy boughs! that cannot shed
>   Your leaves, nor ever bid the spring adieu;
> And, happy melodist, unwearied,
>   For ever piping songs for ever new;
> More happy love! more happy, happy love!

The more sympathetic commentaries excuse Keats's lapse as gently as possible. Wilson suggests that "Keats's speaker evokes an image of his own desire for naive wholeness," but he assures us that Keats soon got over such naïveté: "In his early poetry, Keats shares this bias toward the ideal as an escape from unpleasant reality, but as his poetry matures, in keeping with the reality principle, he pays more and more heed to the alienated consciousness" (833–34). Viewing the "Urn" in the context of its publication in the *Annals* makes it clear that Keats is not in fact naïve, and that the image of "More happy love! more happy, happy love!" is not sincere. This overly emphatic happiness can be compared to Hazlitt's critique of the results when a contemporary artist follows Reynolds's principle of a beau ideal: "In representing a Grecian marriage, he will refine on his favourite principle, till . . . all the women will be like the men; and all like one another, all equally young, blooming, smiling, elegant and insipid" (*CW*, 18:79; *Annals*, 4:388). This passage appears in the issue of the *Annals* immediately preceding the issue that contains Keats's "Urn." It is a tolerable paraphrase of the imagery of "Bold Lovers" and "maidens loth" finally synthesized into a "More happy love! more happy, happy love!," and there is no reason to believe that Keats is any less sarcastic in his ode than Hazlitt is in his essay.

Hazlitt's critique of the beau ideal is not confined to the level of aesthetics but also addresses the material conditions of artistic patronage in Regency England. The portrait painters of the Royal Academy invoked

Reynolds's principles that "all the arts receive their perfection from an ideal beauty, superior to what is to be found in individual nature" (24) and that "deformity is not nature, but an accidental deviation from her accustomed practice" (99) to justify the smoothing out of idiosyncrasies in individual portraits in order to bring them into conformity with a standardized ideal of personal beauty. This practice drew no objections from the patrons who commissioned the portraits, and it brought out the best in Hazlitt's considerable satiric talents: "The 'numbers without number' who pay thirty, forty, fifty, a hundred guineas for their pictures in large, expect their faces to come out of the Painter's hand smooth, rosy, round, smiling; just as they expect their hair to come out of the barber's curled and powdered. It would be a breach of contract to proceed in any other way. . . . People of fashion go to be painted because other people do, and they wish to look like other people" (CW, 18:108).

Whereas Reynolds would censure all "deformity" out of art, Hazlitt praises Hogarth, the bête noire of English art in the eyes of the Royal Academy, for his "gusto" and naturalism. In Hogarth's work, Hazlitt writes approvingly, "if the eye squints, the mouth is distorted; every feature acts, and is acted upon by the rest of the face . . . the whole is under the influence of one impulse, that of truth and nature" (CW, 6:145). Similarly, Keats's poem introduces unpleasant physical imagery that would, by the standards of a beau ideal, be deformed; the ode introduces the "deformity" when it turns from "happy, happy love" to the first imagery that is not copied directly from the urn:

> All breathing human passion far above,
> That leaves a heart high-sorrowful and cloy'd,
> A burning forehead and a parching tongue.

While the common historicist reading of the poem would identify this deviation as Keats's unconscious recognition of his postlapsarian modernity, it is more truly a mark of Keats's engagement in the contemporary debate over differences between the verbal and plastic arts. The transitional lines

> For ever warm and still to be enjoy'd,
> For ever panting, and for ever young,

which purport to describe action depicted on the urn, employ imagery more consistent with the modernity and naturalism of "A burning forehead and a parching tongue" than with the sedate grandeur of a "still unravish'd bride of quietness."

In sliding from one conceptual category (Greek and ideal) to its opposite (modern and naturalistic), the ode moves along a chain of similar imagistic vehicles ("warm," "panting," "young," "breathing," "passion," "burning," "parching") whose conceptual value changes according to their respective context. The first three terms in the series mark the ideal, the latter four the natural. The seamless transition from an idea to its opposite is, according to Lessing, a distinctive quality of poetry; its arbitrary signifiers are more easily modified than the mimetic currency of painting, which depends upon fixed and stable representations. "On canvas," Lessing writes, "every thing is visible, and visible in precisely the same way" (*Laocoön*, 77).

Keats's poem follows the path of Lessing's argument as the ode introduces unpicturesque imagery only when it departs from the imagery contained on the urn; the poem itself begins to claim the rights of the "wider sphere of poetry" to depict a range of passions that would violate the decorum of the visual arts. "There are passions and degrees of passion," Lessing writes, "whose expression produces the most hideous contortions of the face, and throws the whole body into such unnatural positions as to destroy all the beautiful lines that mark it when in a state of greater repose" (11–12); there is, however, no reason not to describe these passions in poetry: "who pauses to think that a scream necessitates an open mouth, and that an open mouth is ugly?" (20). In order to suggest the range of human passion, the poem is forced to move beyond the recycling of the imagery contained on the urn, and to offer its own antithesis.

The "Urn" thus illustrates Lessing's central argument of the formal irreconcilability of a static, visual medium and the temporal, aural form of poetry. So long as the poem attempts to reproduce the imagery contained on the urn, it can only repeat itself. The "leaf-fringe" becomes "trees," which become "happy boughs"; the men or gods and the maidens in ecstatic struggle and escape become a lover and an unfading maiden in "happy love"; the pipes and timbrels provide unheard melodies from a "happy melodist." But this is not a "tale." The repetition of "happy, happy boughs," "happy melodist," and "More happy love! more happy, happy love!" demonstrates, in its monotony, what happens when the simultaneity of the visual arts is transposed directly into poetry. When no progression occurs, the speaker is disabled to a degree that verges on stuttering; he simply repeats the same word over and over. The notion that the third stanza of the ode is a deliberate poetic failure may seem odd, but Keats's 31 December 1818 letter to George and Georgiana Keats identifies a reason for such an unusual approach. After commenting, "I can never feel certain of any truth but from a clear perception of its Beauty," Keats says:

> I find myself very young minded even in that perceptive power—which I hope will encrease—A year ago I could not understand in the slightest degree Raphael's cartoons—now I begin to read them a little—and how did I lea[r]n to do so? By seeing something done in quite an opposite spirit—I mean a picture of Guido's in which all the Saints, instead of that heroic simplicity and unaffected grandeur which they inherit from Raphael, had each of them both in countenance and gesture all the canting, solemn melo dramatic mawkishness of Mackenzie's father Nicholas. (*KL*, 2:19)

One of the resources available to poetry but not to painting, Sidmouth suggests in the *Annals*, is comparison. The effect of placing the ode's third stanza—which amounts to "canting, solemn melo dramatic mawkishness"—immediately before the dramatically more effective fourth stanza is to heighten the reader's perception of the aesthetic difference. As the poem moves toward identifying "beauty" with naturalistic truth rather than with unheard melodies, it presents a sentimental beauty whose inadequacy is clarified by contrast with a beauty that is real. The poem reclaims its poetic authority in the fourth stanza, in which it moves further away from the constraint of simply reproducing imagery borrowed from the urn. The fourth stanza begins with an implicit fiction: that the poem's speaker has moved around the urn and discovered a new scene on it. In the most evocative imagery of the stanza, the "little town" that is "emptied of its folk, this pious morn," the ode achieves its greatest poetic power precisely as it realizes the ability denied the urn itself, the ability to construct the temporal form of a "tale." The imagery not drawn from the urn (the "little town" and the "green altar") tells us where the figures of the present scene ("these" folk, this "mysterious priest," and "that heifer") have come from, and where they are going.

However, at the moment when the poem shows that the streets of the little town "for evermore / Will silent be," the straightforward progression of town-procession-altar is thrown into metalepsis by a broader temporality; the origin—the empty town—becomes an image for the final destiny of these figures who vanish into the abyss of time. The ode transforms its initial silence, which functions as the preservative amber of a Golden Age whose melodies persist, unheard by human ears, into a silence that is simply emptiness and desolation. The historical opposition, the difference between the supposed glory of Greece and our fallen modernity, mutates into a difference between visual and poetic representation.

Hazlitt suggests that Greek sculptors, in their "harmony with external nature," gave the "direct and simple imitation of nature" a "perfect form," creating a complete self-sufficiency: "Their forms are ideal, spiritual. Their beauty is power. By their beauty they are raised above the frailties of pain or passion; by their beauty they are deified" (*CW*, 4:79). But the tableau represented in Keats's fourth stanza is hardly a deified ideal; as poetic representation departs from the mimesis of the iconic forms of the sculptor, "Greece" loses its status as a transcendental signifier capable of inspiring the desire for either identification or possession. Whereas the speaker of the first stanza asked, with all the enthusiasm of a cultic believer, if he might be looking at "deities" or "gods," the speaker of the fourth stanza sees the "mysterious priest" as simply a mortal actor in a picturesque ritual. And unlike the speaker's obsessive reiteration of the few details he discovered at the poem's outset, the picture on the urn is immediately displaced in the fourth stanza by an imaginary "little town" of uncertain location ("by river or sea shore, / Or mountain-built"); such an uncertainty would be impossible in the iconic representation of the visual arts. A poet, working in the arbitrary semiotics of words, forfeits that material presence but gains in Protean suggestivity.

Hazlitt argues that this trade-off is the essential distinction between painting and poetry. Painting, he says, "embodies what a thing contains in itself," while poetry describes the "flowing, not the fixed"; it "signifies the excess of the imagination" in "that uneasy, exquisite sense of beauty or power that cannot be contained within itself" (*CW*, 5:10, 3). But as Keats empties this "little town," he carries out an implication of the temporal form of poetry that does not emerge in Hazlitt's essays. The difference between Hazlitt's "fixed" and "flowing" signs is articulated by Benjamin and brought to the study of British Romanticism by de Man in the opposition between "symbol" and "allegory"; the "symbol" is "self-contained, concentrated, and . . . steadfastly remains itself," while the allegorical sign is "a successively progressing, dramatically mobile, dynamic representation of ideas which has acquired the very fluidity of time" (Benjamin, *Origin*, 165). In the terms of this opposition, Keats's "Urn" moves beyond the realm of the symbol, defined by Benjamin as an intentional structure in which "the transfigured face of nature is fleetingly revealed in the light of redemption" (166) through "the unity of the material and the transcendental object" (160).

The representation of Attic Greece as a Golden Age asserts such an imma-nence of meaning, but as the "Urn" forsakes the idealized notion of Greece as the natural embodiment of an ideal, it moves into the realm of Benjamin's "allegory." Benjamin describes allegory as the presentation of a "truth" that is not redeemed into a human form, one that "resists being projected, by whatever means, into the realm of knowledge" (29). Keats's town, forever-more silent and desolate, is an exemplary figure of Benjaminian allegory, in which "the observer is confronted with the *facies hippocratica* [death mask] of history as a petrified, primordial landscape" (166). This "truth," Benjamin insists, "does not enter into relationships, particularly intentional ones" (35). The speaker in the first half of the poem asks repeatedly and insistently for answers and, when none are forthcoming, constructs idealized hypoth-eses; the speaker of the fourth stanza has learned enough to stop asking.

As de Man brings Benjamin's theory of allegory to bear on British Ro-manticism, he stresses the temporal nature of the allegorical sign. "In the world of allegory," de Man writes, "time is the originary constitutive cat-egory" (*Blindness*, 307). Unlike the Christian interpretation of allegory, in which the allegorical sign is a step toward a final, anagogical meaning, for de Man, as for Benjamin, allegory is forever incomplete: "It remains necessary, if there is to be allegory, that the allegorical sign refer to another sign that precedes it. . . . Whereas the symbol postulates the possibility of an identity or identification, allegory designates primarily a distance in relation to its own origin, and, renouncing the nostalgia and the desire to coincide, it establishes its language in the void of this temporal difference" (*Blindness*, 207).

In the opening stanzas of the "Urn," the poem's persona exhibits a nos-talgic "desire to coincide" with Grecian perfection, but that desire produces only an artificial sentimentality. The ode is able to establish its own poetic presence only after the speaker relinquishes that desire and contemplates the "void of temporal difference." This distance is first implied in the open-ing lines as the urn slips away from the speaker's personifications of it, into the remove of "silence and slow time." The speaker's desire to abolish this gap manifests itself in an intolerance for the temporal form of poetry, which results in the monotony and repetition of the earlier stanzas. But as the poem takes on the temporal form of allegory, it discovers a more profound problem. It is no longer the simple aesthetic or formal error committed by a mistaken persona that needs to be addressed, but the unsolicited fact of a temporality that has left an entire town without a history. The vanished town easily accepts the personifying "thou" that would not adhere to the urn. In this apostrophe,

> And, little town, thy streets for evermore
> Will silent be; and not a soul to tell
>   Why thou art desolate, can e'er return,

the anthropomorphizing "thou" does not reach toward an ideal, and the nonresponsive silence of "not a soul" simply records a human reality that is no longer human. The exemplary image of allegory, Benjamin suggests, is the ruin (177), whose presence suggests both an anteriority with which it is now impossible to coincide and the temporality that has determined its fate.

The claim of the "Ode on a Grecian Urn" to reestablish this Greek artifact as a "friend" in the closing stanza distances Keats from Benjamin's tragic vision, and it testifies to an intellectual clarity on Keats's part that eluded even Hazlitt on the mythography of a Grecian Golden Age. A year after Hazlitt "deified" Greek sculpture, he returned to that idea and registered some annoyance over the perfection of these deified beings, comparing them unfavorably with Raphael's work:

> It is for want of some such resting place for the imagination that the Greek statues are little else than specious forms. They are marble to the touch and to the heart. They have not an informing principle within them. In their faultless excellence they appear sufficient to themselves. By their beauty they are raised above the frailties of passion or suffering. By their beauty they are deified. But they are not objects of religious faith to us, and their forms are a reproach to common humanity. They seem to have no sympathy with us, and not to want our admiration. (*CW,* 5:11)

This passage has recently been cited by Martin Aske and David Bromwich as a guide to Keats's final judgment on the urn, Aske calling it "beautifully apt to the experience" (119) of the poem and Bromwich finding that this "sense of their cold self-sufficiency" is Keats's "conclusion" (391) on Greek sculptures. But this degree of disillusionment depends upon the depth of the investment in the original idealization of Greece, and the figure who holds such a thoroughly enthusiastic, naive belief is satirized by Keats in this poem. The drama of the poem registers a moment of disillusionment when the speaker refers to the urn in terms that echo Hazlitt's "marble to the touch and to the heart," but the image of "marble men and maidens overwrought" which distinguishes the Greek urn from the contemporary speaker is immediately displaced by an image that reinstates the dominance of a natural temporality, encompassing both the urn and the speaker. The imagery of "forest branches and the trodden weed" throws the desolation and the pathos of the fourth stanza over the "happy boughs! that cannot shed / Your leaves, nor ever bid the Spring adieu," and leaves the speaker temporarily unable to pronounce a summary judgment on the significance of this artifact; he is momentarily "tease[d] out of thought."

The attraction of the narrative of disillusionment for critical commentary on the "Urn" bespeaks a modern desire analogous to that which motivates Hazlitt's veneration for and consequent overreaction to the mythos of Greece. The assumption that Keats can be identified with a persona whose "naive desire for wholeness" (Wilson, 833) blinds him to the poetic insipidity of "More happy love! more happy, happy love!" depends upon the unarticulated belief that a desire for wholeness is the ineluctable mainspring of a psychic economy, despite Keats's comment that Coleridge's difference from Shakespeare was that Coleridge would "let go by a fine isolated verisimilitude . . . from being incapable of remaining content with half knowledge" (*KL*, 1:193–94). The persona of the "Ode on a Grecian Urn" spends the first half of the poem destroying the possibility of realizing "a fine isolated verisimilitude" because of his desire to identify with a transcendent wholeness. Yet the critical narrative that sympathizes with Keats's belatedness remains fixated on the image of wholeness that is finally shown by the "Urn" to be a supreme fantasy. When historicist readers lament the loss of "the cultural situation that had given purpose and meaning to the original work" (Phinney, 214) and rely on Gadamer to attest to the "similarity between the isolation of the artwork as an aesthetic object in the museum and the alienation of the artist in modern society" (Phinney, 217) as a modern aberration of that organic cultural unity, they idealize "original" culture as simply as Winckelmann, Hazlitt, and Lukacs do in their most naive moments, and they fail to credit Keats's own experience of art in makeshift museums as an alternative venue to the annual showings of the Royal Academy. Given the choice between art produced for the specific cultural situation of Regency London and art that had been fostered out to a nomadic existence, Keats and his circle came to prefer the latter.

The image of "wholeness" can be located in the future as easily as in the past, as it is in Watkins's complaint that the "Urn" "structurally excludes the feminine from history, just as it removes collective intervention from the realm of possibility," thereby making "social and therefore human wholeness impossible" (253). Yet the narrative of the "Urn" tells a story not of the exclusion of "the feminine" but of the impossibility of its "structural" exclusion. The poem's voice is most securely masculine from the middle of the first stanza to the end of the third, where the speaker clearly identifies with the male figures on the urn, but the outcome of that identification is to leave him the victim of passion. If "the feminine" is, by definition, the victim of passion (as it is in Watkins's narrative of conquest), then the speaker would have to be identified, at the poem's midpoint, as occupying the feminine position. The rigidity of Watkins's identifications of "the masculine" and "the feminine" can be undone (as they are in the "Urn") by questioning the valorization of "wholeness" upon which the stability of these identifications depends. "Wholeness" is not an essence but a signifier, and it is the central—or as Lacan calls it, the transcendental—signifier of a phallic economy. This economy originates at the moment that an infant sees an image of wholeness to which he or she can aspire; the subsequent identification of that wholeness with masculinity, and the denial of such sufficiency to women, is the basis of a patriarchal system of gender identification. As the unfolding narrative of the "Ode on a Grecian Urn" demonstrates, a masculinity that ensures the wholeness of its own subjectivity by making material nature "other" or "feminine" is as much a fantasy as is the idealized image of Greece as an age of indistinguishable deities and mortals.

From the outset of the poem, in the fissured image of Greece as both the signifier of wholeness and as feminine, the "Urn" both does and undoes the work of gender identification. The poem's first feminine image, the "still unravish'd bride," positions the feminine as the object of male possession, but as the urn becomes a "foster-child," it slips away from that positioning. The next images of women, the "maidens loth" in their "struggle to escape," are positioned by the speaker as a "goal" that "cannot fade" because it will be forever "fair," but even that fixity finally eludes him as he concludes that such perfection is "far above / human passion." The movement to the next image of the feminine, the "heifer" going to "sacrifice," could be read either as a revenge upon the ideal that has disappointed the speaker, or as a realization on his part that there is a fundamental error in the original idealization. The difference between the two readings depends upon how the speaker is identified: either as a subject whose distance from the urn is secured by the stability of his masculine identity, having rights of possession over the feminine, or as one who has moved (or has been moved) from a stance of possession to one of identification with the material world's vulnerability to time. As the imminent death of the sacrificial heifer becomes an image for the absence of the emptied little town—which in turn becomes an image for how "old age shall this generation waste"—the poem's speaker is clearly being moved in the direction of identification. The intervening image of "marble men and maidens," in which the male figures are no longer confused with gods, stands in the path of an associative chain that runs from the sacrificial heifer to the vanished town to the wasting of this generation; the coldness of the marble images functions as a reminder of the cold materiality of this personal destiny. Just as the image of becoming a sod in the "Nightingale" ode supplanted the softness of ceasing upon the midnight with no pain, so does "marble men and maidens" supplement a previous imagery of death as a simple absence (the little town's silent streets); "marble men and maidens" gives a cold and heavy feel to death, a reality distributed impartially across the divide of gender.

The final, semi-degendered image of the feminine in the poem represents the urn as a "friend to man," where the "friend" is of ambiguous gender but is still other to "man." The second half of this image reads women out of history as it uses "man" as an unmarked term, but the gender ambiguity of the image as a whole (what is the gender of this unmarked "friend"?) illustrates the impossibility of reading "the feminine," as a coding of the material, out of history. The "Urn"'s marginalizing of women in relation to "man" is consistent with the biographical Keats, who admitted, "I am certain I have not a right feeling towards Women" (*KL*, 1:341), but Keats's discomfort, sometimes bordering on hostility, toward women is not the dominant gender economy of the "Urn." The most securely stereotypical representations of women as a "goal" that "cannot fade" come from the poem's speaker in his most deluded and unpoetic moments, and his insistence that "She cannot fade" is the "Urn"'s analogue to the "Nightingale"'s "Already with thee!" The very emphases of both passages betray the speaker's suspicion that his assertion may not be true. As the repressed other to this emphatic idealization unfolds against the grain of the received narratives that the urn incorporates, poetic language narrates the instability of the raw material used in forming the cultural concepts of "the masculine" and "the feminine." The poem's representation of the instability of a patriarchal definition of the "feminine" exceeds the lack of such understanding in Keats's everyday life, and the distance between the two illustrates the potential discontinuity between the unconscious and the conscious mind, a discontinuity that is the effect, in psychoanalytic terms, of repression.

Keats's political liberalism reflects the bohemian politics of the *Annals*, in which aestheticism became a political statement for those who felt that public, political repression had come to depend upon a legitimation of private, psychological repression. Both senses of "repression" are legitimized, in

Hobbesian fashion, as a civilizing force once the irrational, or the unconscious, is identified as a repository of self-interested drives. The members of Keats's circle clearly felt that aestheticism was a means of opposing the cultural forces that were joined in what an *Annals* essayist called the "bigotted Toryism" (*Annals*, 1:49) of Johnson's literary criticism. The principles of opposition to those cultural forces are set out in Hazlitt's *Essay on the Principles of Human Action*, which contests Hobbes's idea of an irreducible personal egoism and the consequent necessity for its social control. As Hazlitt argues for a "natural disinterestedness" that occupies an even more fundamental level of consciousness than self-interest, he foreshadows Lacan's account of ego formation through anticipatory identification. In Hazlitt's words, "The imagination, by means of which alone I can anticipate future objects, or be interested in them, must carry me out of myself into the feelings of others by one and the same process by which I am thrown forward as it were into my future being, and interested in it" (*CW*, 1:1).

The trajectory of imagination, as Hazlitt describes it, can move either toward a recognition of otherness or toward speculation on one's own future, but it is only this capacity, which moves beyond the tangible faculties of sensation and memory through the "excess of the imagination" (*CW*, 5.10), that creates the possibility of interest in an "other." Such mobility of cathexis is crucial to French feminism's departures from deterministic readings of Lacan. As Cixous emphasizes, an excess of identification with the other undoes the "calculating" economy of masculine identity and produces a psychic "bisexuality" in which "*I* move into the other without destroying the other" ("Castration," 55).

As the "Urn," at the end of the fourth stanza, completes a dialectic that first idealizes the Greek urn and then comes to discover the power of temporality to negate that ideal, it falls into an affective economy whose primary force is not the calculation of gain but sheer intensity. Under the impact of the image of the silent streets, the speaker turns away from seeing the urn as a symbol of an idealized past; he is forced to confront the urn in the temporality of its history and the materiality of its form, as an "Attic shape" and a "silent form." At this moment, teased "out of thought," the speaker is unable to calculate whether the artifact signifies gain or loss, the durability of art or the all-obliviating power of time, and he cannot decide whether the question is to be asked for the self or for a world of others.

A host of contrary answers to these questions were available to Keats in the form of Hazlitt's nostalgia for the irrecoverable perfection of Greece and in Haydon's proclamations of artistic renaissance, but Keats registers the arbitrariness of either choice, and the indifference of the urn to such solutions, in the oxymoronic epithet "Cold Pastoral!" The urn embodies enough contradictory attributes to allow it to play a part in any number of narratives, and the primary interpretive challenge it poses derives from the blankness of its indifference. If we, like the poem's speaker in the opening stanzas, force the urn into a calculation of our own achievement of wholeness, the result can only be a sterile self-referentiality.

Keats's "Urn" displaces the coherence of historical narrative, which makes a clear distinction between the present and the "pastness of the past," into a structure of mere contiguity: The poem finally identifies the urn as a "friend" whose value is unaltered in changing cultural circumstances. The urn's "modernity" is that explicated by de Man as a "theoretical," rather than a "historical," concept; it does not exemplify a gregarious increase in intellect that displaces a proximity to the natural world but is a possibility that can exist at any time, one that creates "the problematical possibility of all literature's existing in the present, of being considered, or read, from a point of view that claims to share with it its own sense of a temporal present" (*Blindness*, 166). This modernity, which joins us to the past rather than dividing us from it, arises in the "Urn" as the poem crosses the temporal divide between its own modernity and the urn's antiquity. The ode makes this crossing through the exploration of the fundamental contradiction in the ideology of the *Annals*, in which Greek art is used both to exemplify a naturalism that is opposed to a beau ideal, and as proof of a Golden Age that supposedly existed in Athenian culture.

The limits of that contradiction are tested by Hazlitt's assertion that the Elgin Marbles are imitations of living models and not idealized forms; he is then forced to argue that the apparent perfection of the marble figures proves that the ancient Greeks, living in a superior climate, were much better looking than modern Britons (CW, 18:149).[6] In the grandeur of that pre-Christian age, Hazlitt alleges, there was even no fear of death: "the idea of annihilation did not impress them with the same horror and repugnance as it does the modern believer, or even infidel" (*CW*, 12:261). Keats undoes the idealization of Greece by means of a naturalistic representation of a Greek sacrifice, in which he depicts a ritual, and ultimately ineffectual, response to the mysterious forces of annihilation. Even if the cultural codes determining the actions of the figures in the ritual are mysterious to us, their motives are not. In the ensuing alliterative play on "Attic" and "attitude," the idealization of Greece is dissolved into a material signifier, and the Greeks become as mortal, and as far from deities, as we are. The "modernity" we share with ancient Greece appears in the realization of our mistake in attributing to that era an imaginary wholeness and immanence of meaning that, we wishfully believe, must exist somewhere, even if it is always outside our own experience.

The dissolution of the idealized image of Greece as a perfect totality produces what Benjamin calls the "disjunctive, atomizing principle of the allegorical approach" (208). Yet criticism of the "Urn" characteristically remains devoted to the recovery of a wholeness on the far side of the poem's own puzzlement and of its final insistence on the limitations of our knowledge. Thematic interpretations of the New Critical era, whether they identify the poem as a statement of Neoplatonism or of "robust realism," operate, as de Man argues in "The Rhetoric of Temporality," within a symbolic figural economy, where the "appeal to the infinity of a totality constitutes [its] main attraction" (*Blindness*, 188). A belief in the comprehensiveness of a conceptual totality, whether it Platonically subsumes the sensory under the intelligible, or, in the name of "realism," comprehends intelligibility in the immediacy of the sensible, leaves criticism disinclined to accept the privative "all / Ye know" of the poem's conclusion. Historicist narratives that read the poem as a failure to achieve a wholeness that existed—according to Hazlitt, Lukacs, and Gadamer—in the past, in a "cultural situation that had given purpose and meaning to the original work" (Phinney, 214), or in a future, according to Watkins, where "social and therefore human wholeness" is prevented only by "the loneliness, tension, contradictions, and struggles that characterize the bourgeois culture" (241), reinstate a Golden Age mythology that the "Urn" effectively deconstructs. Historicist narrative, even when written in a nostalgic key, distinguishes itself from the past it describes in the implicit claim of the increased scope of its own modernity; it places us within the "grand march of intellect" that both defines and is able to comprehend temporality in the totalizing form of history. Keats's urn exhibits the defamiliarizing power to "tease us out of thought / As doth eternity," then settles into a more familiar form as a "friend," no longer "far above" but "in midst of other woe / Than ours." The poem's disjunctive force resides in its ability to sever our connection to the sequentiality of historical narrative; it projects a future that, like the past, does not include us.

When Keats places the urn in the midst of the lives of later generations, he obviously envisions it playing that role in a museum setting. The ode thus implies a far more positive opinion of museums on Keats's part than is expressed in Gadamer's analogy between the "isolation of the artwork as an aesthetic object in the museum and the alienation of the artist in modern society" (Phinney, 217). The valorization of the practice of circulating artworks in decontextualized settings, based on the belief that their beauty and truth would be "instantly communicated to all eyes that behold, and all hearts that can feel them" (Hazlitt, *CW*, 4:144), was at the center of one of the most heated encounters between the Royal Academy and the emerging British Institution. When members of the Academy anonymously published a satirical *Catalog Raisonné* of an exhibit of continental painters (including Rubens, Titian, Raphael, and van Dyke) arranged by the British Institution in 1815, Hazlitt responded with a biting satire of the artistic and commercial practices of the Academy and with a defense of the principles behind the Institution's exhibit. To the Royal Academy members' protest that the importation of foreign art would hurt the trade in English art, Hazlitt responded, "Patriotism and the Fine Arts have nothing to do with one another—because patriotism relates to exclusive advantages, and the advantages of the Fine Arts are not exclusive. . . . The spirit of art is not the spirit of trade" (*CW*, 4:144).

The modern critique of the "Romantic ideology" locates the roots of Hazlitt's valorization of the unfettered individual artist in a defense of the economic free agency of the bourgeois individual. Hazlitt, however, positions himself outside the opposition between the conservative nationalism of a traditional aristocracy and the commercial interests of a transnational middle class. From Hazlitt's perspective, the Royal Academy represented a perfect harmony of patriotic and economic ideologies, while his own arguments for the asocial character of "individual genius" put him in a marginal, or bohemian, position in relation to the members and patrons of the Academy.

Hazlitt's position, that art should play a role antithetical to the binding force of culture, challenges the fundamental premise of historicist analysis, which is to describe a continuity between a cultural context and a work of art. The McGannite critique of Romantic subjectivity as a cultural rationalization of bourgeois individualism, as it is used to "historicize" Keats, reinstates Goethe's version of the classical/Romantic distinction—"Classicism is health, romanticism disease"—by placing Romantic literature in a negative relation to an ideal of wholeness that is classical in its Lukacsian derivation. But when Hazlitt argues that "the spirit of art is not the spirit of trade," he clearly wishes to separate himself from an individuality that operates in the spirit of calculated self-interest. Hazlitt's emphasis on the "originality" and "eccentricities of genius" (*CW*, 18:108–9) valorizes the deviations made by "genius" from prevailing social norms. The cultural bond valorized by Gadamer as the "roots" of a work of art—"the religious or secular function which gave it its significance" (76)—is disparaged by Hazlitt as "patriotism."

While Hazlitt's valorization of individuality makes a good deal of sense in his particular cultural situation, it is as meaningless to privilege either individual or collective identity as a matter of principle as it is to choose to describe history in either a progressive or a nostalgic narrative. The "Ode on a Grecian Urn," operating in the same cultural setting in which Hazlitt denounced both the dominant aesthetic standards of his society and the structure of patronage that upheld those standards, celebrates a deracinated beauty for its ability to communicate a power that is beyond cultural determination. The poem also claims to define, and asks us to accept, the limits of that power. The poem's persona, who at first finds the religious ritual depicted on the urn entirely mysterious, finally perceives in the urn itself a felt life that is not subsumed under any specific cultural function that this artifact could have served. Hazlitt's mimetic bias in the area of the visual arts leads him to attribute the "uneasy, exquisite sense of beauty or power that cannot be contained within itself" (*CW*, 5:3) solely to poetry, but Keats registers, both here and in the Elgin Marbles sonnet, a sense of power in sculpture that exceeds prosaic explanation. The ode's closing argument for beauty insists that only an artifact of exceptional aesthetic quality can provoke this uneasy recognition, and Hazlitt makes much the same argument when he contrasts the works of Vandyke and Titian to the portraits of the Royal Academicians: "To paint a hand like Vandyke would cost them as much time as a dozen half-lengths; and they could not do it after all. To paint an eye like Titian would cost them a whole year's labour, and they would lose their time and their labour into the bargain" (*CW*, 18:110).

Hazlitt recognizes the cost of such devotion to sheer aesthetic power. The arts cannot be progressive, and they cannot directly participate in movements of collective progress. Progress depends upon the accumulation of knowledge, as in the sciences, where "One chemical or mathematical discovery may be added to another" (*CW*, 18:8). But the power of a Titian depends upon its ability to convey the "energy," in Hazlitt's word, of the individual hand; the valorization of "genius" is the recognition of that energy. As the vehicle of the intensity of the single aesthetic effort, an artwork loses the ability to participate in the collective movement of history, but it gains the ability to communicate across cultural difference. Keats's "Urn" registers this marginal position of the artwork to the tides of history; despite the intimacy of the urn's place as a "friend," "in [the] midst" of the lives of later generations, it neither affects nor is affected by the "woe" that Keats sees as their inevitable lot. In this, Keats is more realistic than his nostalgic or utopian commentators. Changes in social structures can do away with ritual sacrifice, but they cannot eliminate either the fears that provoked those practices or the forces that generated those fears. Collective responses to such forces produce "culture," which inevitably embodies a conservative tendency to self-reproduction, and just as inevitably provokes an antithetical stance from those with a taste for novelty.

In Hazlitt's most uncompromising statement about the necessarily individual quality of art, he argues against Reynolds that "A work demonstrates genius exactly as it contains what is to be found no where else, or in proportion to what we add to the ideas of others from our own stores, and not to what we receive from them" (*CW*, 18:64). In the "Ode on a Grecian Urn," Keats's genius manifests itself not only in the intelligence of the ideas contained in the poem but also—more importantly—in the rhythmic presence of the poem itself, as an artifact whose style draws from the resources of the English language a rapid variety of effects that has been characteristic, in the canon of English poetry, of only Shakespeare and Keats. The ode manifests, seemingly at will, a linguistic density that is abundantly present in the poem's opening lines, thoroughly attenuated in the monotonous happiness of its midpoint, and restored in the increasingly evocative fourth stanza. The lingering meditation on the imaginary vanished town is abruptly terminated in an overlooked pun: the "urn" of "return," which, like the "forlorn" of "Nightingale," operates "like a bell" as its phonic excess of meaning breaks the spell of an imaginative reverie. The obtrusive wordplay of the opening lines of the final stanza (the alliteration of "Attic" and "attitude" and the pun on "brede") maintains this sense of a linguistic density in which words have attained a fully material, sonic presence. This density is reinforced by the syntactic knot of the entire initial phrase of the stanza; the double *with*s are in a disjointed parallel that could be straightened only if one of the two references of "overwrought" (that referring to the urn, and not to the men and maidens) were adopted and then applied across a comma. As Keats adopts a persona momentarily overwhelmed by the overdeterminations of the codes he seeks to interpret, his confusion is staged in a phonic and syntactic density that registers both the difficulty and the intensity of thought.

Even the style of the poem's final lines is far from declarative flatness; the lines show a subtle weave of rhythm, diction, and theme, beginning with the obvious rhetorical feature of repeated and accelerating elision. From

"Beauty is truth" to "truth beauty," the verb is elided, and in the next parallel structure ("that is all ye" / "and all ye") a larger piece, a subject-verb
combination ("that is"), drops out. Such elision is, as Geoffrey Hartman
suggests, a poetic response to the contingencies of temporality, a trope that
"speeds the mind by freeing it from overelaboration and the toil of consecu-
tiveness" ("Voice," 339). One effect of this quickening of the pace is to draw
the reader into a closer engagement with the text, in a culmination of the
poem's gradual diminishing of the initial distances that separate the speaker,
the reader, and the poem's themes. The speaker initially addresses his material and his themes from a ceremonious distance, and, in a different kind of
distancing effect, the reader is soon able to assume a position of superior
wisdom over the speaker, by means of a realization of the latter's inability to
control his own medium. But as the speaker's technical mastery returns—at
the same time that he encounters the theme of a temporality with the power
to bring an idealized Greece of "noble simplicity and sedate grandeur" down
to a naturalistic, human scale—both the poem's speaker and the reader find
themselves within the reach of that temporality.

The necessity of engaging the fact of "old age" rather than resting on the
lyrical cushion of "slow time" gives the theme of temporality an ineluctably
personal relevance that cannot be suppressed or evaded. The extension of
this theme to the reader is made explicit in the two moments of direct address to her in the final lines. It has often been argued that "Ye" cannot refer
to the reader because the poet has used the first person plural ("ours") to
refer to humanity and the second person ("thou") to address the urn only
two lines earlier; yet this argument is necessary only because the immediate
rhetorical effect of the word "ye" so clearly invokes the reader's presence.
The discrepancy between "ours" and "ye" could easily have been avoided; if
"We" had been substituted for "Ye," metrics would have been preserved. A
reading of the lines as "that is all / We know on earth, and all we need to
know," however, shows what is lacking. A phrasing that merges individuality into the first person plural does not represent the fullest extension of the
poem's themes of the ineluctably personal experiences of beauty in its immediacy and time in its inexorability. "We" do not experience beauty or
time; you do, and I do. The poem's final line joins the intimacy of apostrophe, now directed to the reader, with a thematic expansiveness that suggests
the impossibility of resistance to, or detachment from, this conclusion. Both
the thematic scope of the claims made in these lines and their inescapability
are compressed into the duplicity of the word *all*; each time it appears, it
carries both an expansive sense ("everything") and a privative sense ("the

only thing"). In a reprise of the device by which the idea of death was made more palpable in the coldness of marble, the poem's final line offers the fragmented material signifier of the urn itself as a memento mori. If "On earth" had been written "in life," that phrase would also have expressed a thematic opposition between life and art, but the sound of "on earth" triggers a phonetic recall of "urn," so that "earth" and "urn" combine to suggest the function of an urn as a receptacle for cremated ashes. Under the pressure of temporality and the densely ambiguous shadings of poetic representation, the urn, which began the poem as an icon of immortality, is transformed into a reminder of the two potential outcomes of life: to be put into an urn or to be put into the earth. The difference is barely a phoneme.

Having illustrated that the truth of a beauty drawn from "actually existing nature" is greater than that of a beau ideal "tower[ing] by degrees above the world of realities" (*CW*, 18:150), the poem can justifiably assert that "Beauty is truth, truth beauty," and can attribute that wisdom to the other, as a knowledge that belongs to the artwork itself and not to meanings that are imposed upon it. Keats's doubts about the reliability of systematic thought, or "consequitive reasoning," are registered in the letter in which he expresses doubt that any philosopher had ever come to a conclusion without arbitrarily "setting aside numerous objections." The ineluctable superiority of the ode's fourth stanza to its third illustrates a more immediate and irrefutable truth than any that could be constructed either as a beau ideal or through the coercive singlemindedness of "consequitive reasoning." In the notion that this is "all ye need to know," Keats joins in the enthusiasm of Haydon and Hazlitt when they find in art the power of giving to life what value it has, as when Haydon says of the Elgin Marbles that "I thank God daily, that I was in existence on their arrival, and will continue to do so until the end of my life" (*Autobiography*, 316), and Hazlitt that "It is worth while to have lived to have produced works like these, or even to have seen and felt their power" (*CW*, 10:111). The pantheon to which Keats aspires when he hopes to be ranked "among the English Poets after my death" (*KL*, 1:394) is not comprised solely of poets; he judged that the "three things to rejoice at in this Age" were Wordsworth's *Excursion*, Haydon's paintings, and Hazlitt's "depth of Taste" (*KL*, 1:203). This judgment confers an equal value on all artistic activity (including its reception) that produces ideas felt on our pulses. The formal differences between the arts remain, however, and readers of the *Annals* might catch, in the urn's bursting into speech, Keats's play on Haydon's observation that "abstracted reflections" can be stated only in poetry, because "Poets can make their characters speak their thoughts; painters can only make them look." At the same time, Keats's ode defers to Haydon's argument that there is a greater potential audience for the iconic representations of the plastic arts; when Keats says of the urn that "thou" has the power to embody the identity of beauty and truth, he acknowledges Haydon's point that "what painting does look the world can comprehend, poets speak to full effect only to their own nation" (*Annals*, 4:242), that is, only to those who speak their own language. The final grace note of the poem is its concession that it can only aspire to the power that the urn has achieved.

The distances we perceive between our modernity and Keats's Romanticism—or between Keats's Romanticism/modernity and the antiquity of Greece—are ultimately discrepancies of form far more than they are chronological barriers. Faced with the power of temporality to present itself as the prospect of absence, either in the cognitive void of temporal difference or as the leveling power of annihilation, both narrative (of which "history" is a form) and lyricism address that void, but they do so in antithetical ways. In historical writing, the conversion of temporality into the comprehensible form of narrative both enables the cognitive mastery of time and distances the narrator from its material reach as we join the communal grand march of intellect. Lyricism, on the other hand, manifests what de Man calls the "temptation of immediacy," the "temptation of literature to fulfill itself in a single moment" (*Blindness*, 152). Renouncing its continuity with the past or its prospects in the future, the compressed form of lyric purchases its intensity and defines its ahistorical modernity in that renunciation. De Man's definition of this literary "modernity" is based on a quintessentially "Romantic" metaphor; "The mind in creation is as a fading coal," says Shelley, and de Man takes up Shelley's metaphor of an ephemeral fire as the basis of his definition of "modernity": "Fashion (mode) can sometimes be only what remains of modernity after the impulse has subsided, as soon—and this can be almost at once—as it has changed from being an incandescent point in time into a reproducible cliché. . . . Fashion is like the ashes left behind by the uniquely shaped flames of the fire, the trace alone revealing that a fire took place" (*Blindness*, 147).

What lyric accomplishes, in its momentary modernity, is a break with history, but, as de Man observes, "the vested interest that academics have in the value of history makes it difficult to put the term seriously into question" (*Blindness*, 145). De Man's bemused comment predicts the unavoidable result of an encounter between a truly original, or modern, work and historicist analysis. Once the artwork has forged its unique departure from the "reproducible cliches" it encounters, interpreters arrive to hammer it back into conformity with its more familiar and more easily recognizable surroundings. This misreading will occur, in de Man's terms, not as a simple "mistake," a matter of contingency and competence, but as the inevitability of systematic "error." The demand for some definable continuity between the single artwork and a larger context (history, reality, truth) will result in the assimilation of the artistic part into a wholeness we already know.

The historicist narratives that distinguish moderns or postmoderns from the Romantic poets rely upon overdetermined codes, located not only in the explicit tropes of temporality in historicist discourses but also in the necessary positioning of each discourse in relation to temporality. "To prolong and repeat the emotion," Hazlitt suggests, is the "musical" purpose of poetry (*CW*, 5:12), in which the initial impulse is not subsumed into knowledge but is simply sustained. The single most common theme to emerge in the critical history of this poem has been that Keats did not, in truth, believe that

> "Beauty is truth, truth beauty,"—that is all
>   Ye know on earth, and all ye need to know.

The resistance to this emphatic aestheticism, which insists that the sustaining of the highest aesthetic impulse is the most profound human reality, has persisted from the New Critical era to the present day. Keats's critics have constructed an opposition that construes art as the immaterial shadow of a more concrete reality, called "life" or "experience" by the New Critics and "history" today. The poem's canonization then depends upon the degree to which Keats can be congratulated, either for his commitment to "the reality principle" or for articulating our alienated modernity. This opposition to aestheticism is fostered by a misrepresentation of the basis of Keats's love of art, which is rooted not in a Neoplatonic veneration of an immaterial ideal but in a powerful responsiveness to artistic imagery. For most of Keats's poetry, the imagery that is adopted and re-presented in his own work is predominantly verbal; there is less indirect allusiveness in the "Urn" than in the "Nightingale" ode, but there is some of the same oblique quotation. Fragments from Shakespeare's "The Phoenix and the Turtle" clearly inform the final conjunction of beauty and truth in Keats's funereal urn; the most obviously relevant lines from Shakespeare's poem are: "Beauty, truth and rarity . . . Here enclos'd in cinders lie"; "To eternity doth rest"; "Truth and beauty buried be; / To this urn let those repair" ("Phoenix," 53–55, 58, 64–65). Keats may have had Shakespeare's poem in mind from the outset of the "Urn," where his "still unravish'd bride" and "foster-child" are likely transformations of Shakespeare's sexless, loving figures destined to "Leaving no posterity; / 'Twas not their infirmity, / It was married chastity" ("Phoenix," 59–61).

The poetic sources of the "Urn" are not entirely so canonic; the *Annals* of 1816 printed "Original Poetry on the Fine Arts," signed "H" (not Haydon), in which an Englishman on a Mediterranean tour looked for any signs of Greek civilization "Saved from the silent lapse of wasting years" (*Annals*, 1:263); this image informs not only the "silent form" that tells how "Old age shall this generation waste," but also "the rude / Wasting of old Time" in the Elgin Marbles sonnet. Biblical associations link the most resonant and polyvalent echoes in the "Urn" from the "Nightingale" ode. The word "generation," which evoked the "ancient days" of Ruth in the "Nightingale," now informs the "old age" that "shall this generation waste." The glancing echo of "tread" and "trodden" ("No hungry generations tread thee down" and "the trodden weed") is incorporated into a simile borrowed from Ecclesiasticus; the analogy of human generations and the "trodden weed" of the "Urn" is based on a similar analogy in Ecclesiasticus: "Like flourishing leaves on a spreading tree / which sheds some and puts forth others, / so are the generations of flesh and blood: / one dies and another is born" (Ecclesiasticus, 14.18).[7] Just as imagery borne from other sources by the agency of the letter resurfaces in the "Urn," the poem itself creates a phonetic level of coherence; the "trees" with perpetual "leaves" are denuded into the "trodden weed," an assonance kept active in the "green altar." The distance between the poem's first stanza and its last is materialized in slight sonic shifts: *bride* to *brede*, *sweet* to *weed*, *slow* to *woe*.

The allusive field of the "Urn" differs from that of the "Nightingale" ode in the "Urn"'s greater reliance on visual rather than verbal imagery. In addition to drawing on Keats's familiarity with Greek urns, the imagery of the fourth stanza is particularly indebted, as Ian Jack points out, to an Elgin Marble frieze and three paintings by Claude Lorrain (219). As Jack suggests, not only the imagery but the tone of Claude's work, which is referred to in the *Annals* by a pupil of Haydon's as the "grand quiescence" (*Annals*, 4:566) of Claude, informs the "Urn" in the more stately tone that the poem acquires in the fourth stanza. The introduction into the "Urn" of details cited in Haydon's description of Raphael's cartoon *The Sacrifice at Lystra*, including the heifer and the garlanded bull, opens the poem to the sort of imbricated borrowing characteristic of the "Nightingale" ode. Raphael's *Sacrifice*, like the Elgin Marbles frieze and the Claude paintings, depicts a sacrificial procession, and the synthesis of imagery from all of these sources shows how Keats's imagination is no less active in assimilating visual source material than it is in the indiscriminate mixing of literary allusions in the "Nightingale." The depth of his aesthetic promiscuity is suggested by Keats's description of the "heroic simplicity and unaffected grandeur" (*KL*, 2:19) of Raphael's cartoons, a phrase that obliquely echoes Winckelmann's then-famous praise of the Greeks for their "noble simplicity and sedate grandeur." It is not clear whether Keats consciously echoes Fuseli's translation of Winckelmann in his letter, particularly since attributing this "Grecian" quality to Raphael would contradict Hazlitt's judgment that Michaelangelo's work was closer to Greek sculpture than was Raphael's (*CW*, 18:69); in any case, Keats clearly does not see "simplicity" and "grandeur" as the property of a single culture, "peculiar to their country," as Winckelmann claimed, which "seldom went abroad without loss." Severn claimed that Keats's praise for the "Greek spirit . . . point[ed] out to me how essentially modern that Spirit is: 'It's an immortal youth,' he would say, 'just as there is no *Now* or *Then* for the Holy Ghost'" (Sharp, 29). Keats's perception of the "modernity" of this spirit encouraged him to attempt to enter into the longrunning conversation among artists and poets, and the two *Annals* poems, the "Nightingale" and the "Urn," reflect that desire not only through direct citation of visual source material but through the imaginative synthesis of that material.

The influence of the visual arts on both the "Nightingale" and the "Urn" can be traced through the recurrence in both odes of phrases and images from Keats's "Epistle to Reynolds." Some early lines in the "Epistle" foreshadow both the perplexity of the speaker in the "Urn"'s final stanza ("Things cannot to the will / Be settled, but they tease us out of thought" ["Epistle," 76–77]) and the imagery of its fourth stanza:

> The sacrifice goes on; the pontif knife
> Gleams in the sun, the milk-white heifer lows,
> The pipes go shrilly, the libation flows. ("Epistle," 20–22)

This passage in the "Epistle" falls between an allusion to "Titian colours touch'd into real life" (19) and a reference to Claude's *Enchanted Castle* (26), yet the "Epistle" rearranges the material from these paintings as it refers to them; it takes an image found in *Bacchus and Ariadne*, "A white sail shews above the green-head cliff" (23), separates it from the poem's reference to Titian and replaces the boat on Claude's empty lake. Keats's borrowings from the visual arts in the "Epistle," like his literary allusions in the "Nightingale" ode, are not simply a matter of disjointed singulars—a heifer here, a leaf-fringe there. The mix of Titian and Claude in the "Epistle" indicates how Keats absorbs and remixes the formal repetitions of the paintings themselves. The pathos of Titian's Ariadne appears in a quieter tone in Claude's wistful, unnamed female figure in *The Enchanted Castle*, and both women inform the "Epistle"'s "beauteous woman's large blue eyes / Gone mad through olden songs and poesies" ("Epistle," 53–54).

In the "Epistle to Reynolds," the "Things" that "tease us out of thought" are tied to an intellectual overreaching that "spoils the singing of the nightingale" (lines 77, 85). When Keats returns to the images and themes of the "Epistle" in writing an ode to a nightingale, he stages an irresolvable conflict between the wild work of spontaneous fancy and the sobriety of reflective thought, while in the "Ode on a Grecian Urn" he evokes a tone of "sedate grandeur" that is able to recover from a similar moment of aporia and reclaim the possibility of the quiet contemplation of that wildness in artifacts immanent with its presence. The similarity of subject matter and polarity of tone of the two poems reflect the relations of the two artworks that are most directly cited in the poems, Titian's *Bacchus and Ariadne* in the "Nightingale" ode and Raphael's *Sacrifice at Lystra* in the "Urn," two paintings that are themselves closely bound in art history. Raphael's cartoons were an important influence on Titian, and art historians have particularly connected *Bacchus and Ariadne* to Raphael's *The Conversion of Paul* through the similarity of their designs and the certainty that Titian saw that particular cartoon shortly before composing *Bacchus and Ariadne* (Shearman, 144). The design of the *Conversion* is, however, very similar to that of several of Raphael's cartoons, and I would suggest not only that visual parallels and direct allusions make a close link between *Bacchus and Ariadne* and *The Sacrifice at Lystra*, but that Keats also made that connection. The incorporation into the "Grecian Urn" of details from Haydon's essay on the *Sacrifice at Lystra* shows that that cartoon was on Keats's mind during the composition of the "Urn," and the return to images from the "Epistle to Reynolds" suggests the associative link to the Titian painting.

Titian was a highly allusive painter, and it is reasonable to suppose, given the similarities of the two works, that the cow's head on the ground in *Bacchus* is a wry reference to Raphael's *Sacrifice*, which shows two cows, one a full body in the lower center of the painting and the second a head to the upper right whose body is blocked by the figures in the procession. If one follows from the higher to the lower cows' heads in Raphael, the severed head in *Bacchus* simply continues that line as it follows the sacrificial process

Bacchus and Ariadne, Titian. Reproduced by permission of the National Gallery, London.

to its inevitable conclusion. Raphael is not the only artistic precursor cited in *Bacchus*. The figure writhing in the grasp of snakes in *Bacchus and Ariadne* is a direct quote of the central figure in the Laocoön sculpture. It would be apparent to Keats that this sculpture, which had served both as a touchstone of comparison for the Elgin Marbles and as the central point of departure in the discussion of the merits of poetry and painting, was alluded to in one of his own favorite paintings by an Italian artist for an effect entirely opposite to the "noble simplicity and sedate grandeur" that had been attributed to the Greek sculpture. Claude's pastorals recover this serenity, which is the direct opposite of the Bacchanalian fervor pushed to its limit by Titian. *Bacchus and Ariadne*, with the cow's severed head in the dirt and its leg waved aloft, has gone through the sacrifice, and is reveling in blood and wine. In Claude, perspective is invariably removed to a distance and to the time before the sacrifice, and his processions, and even his cows, become serenely

The Sacrifice at Lystra, Raphael. Reproduced by permission of the Victoria and Albert Museum.

picturesque; they graze in the lower foreground of the *Landscape with the Father of Psyche sacrificing at the Milesian Temple of Apollo*.

Keats's comments on artworks and his incorporation of their influence into his poetry suggest that he did not see the visual arts, as did Lessing and Hazlitt, as simply mimetic, depicting only "what a thing contains in itself" (Hazlitt, 5:10). His reference to Raphael's "heroic simplicity and unaffected grandeur" shows that he saw in Raphael's "Sacrifice" not only Titian's forms but also a tonality much closer to Claude and to the statue of the Laocoön. The odes show that what Keats learned, from artists as well as from poets, is that a nearly infinite range of effects can be derived from the same material, and that the aesthetic effect in a particular case depends upon a choice that lies within a finite range of possible exploitations of form. As Keats absorbed not simply the imagery but the atmospheres of these works, their spirits are reflected in the odes. The "Nightingale," like *Bacchus and Ariadne*, goes over the edge, beginning in the deeply felt misstatement "My heart aches" and spinning itself into a wild dialectic that is irrecoverable to thought, while the "Urn," like Raphael's cartoon, goes to that edge and then withdraws to a more detached perspective, which claims the "heroic simplicity" to accept what can and what cannot be known about the confrontation between the intensive temporality of consciousness and the extensive temporality of history. The "Ode to a Nightingale" and the "Ode on a Grecian Urn" make very different aesthetic statements about similar material; their stage is the interiority of consciousness, and each poem invents an extreme situation that both demands and enables the representation of the most intensive use of the resources of consciousness.

The "Urn" is finally more decisive than the "Nightingale" ode; while the "Nightingale" does not finally know what to make of its "it" (a "vision or a waking dream"?), the "Urn," by contrast, offers a final "that" in which truth is as irrefutable and complete as it is tautological and indefinable. The scope of this aestheticism can be debated, but the principles underlying it should not be oversimplified. Its definition of the interior life as the real life does not mean that the refinement of aesthetic power is without consequences in the world of action. Ideology is reproduced through the passive repetition of clichés about oppositions like the past and the present, masculinity and femininity, or collective identity and freedom, while the critique of such clichés has been defined as a central function of "modern" art by aesthetic critics from Hazlitt to Adorno. Hazlitt's confidence in an "innate sensibility to truth and beauty," based on his assertion that "if custom is a second nature, there is another nature which ranks before it" (*CW*, 4: 68), confers on this "sensibility" and "nature" an immediately political dimension that is antithetical to the hegemonic force of "custom." The theme of "second nature" as the internal alienation of consciousness is central to Adorno's critique of ideology; in Adorno's terms, "second nature" casts the "spell of reification" as the automatic repetitions of habit erode the possibility of being affected by alterity. Those habits, Adorno argues, are more often and more effectively challenged by art than by anything we encounter in everyday life: "Reified consciousness, all-embracing in scope as it presently is, finds in aesthetic behaviour a powerful corrective that strains to work its way out from under the spell of reification in order to see the light of day" (*Aesthetic Theory*, 454).

Art "cathects the repressed," Adorno argues, breaking the "spell of reification" as it reaches to "the other side" of a "veil woven by the interaction of institutions and false needs" (27) and provokes the momentary "shudder" of "a sense of being touched by the other" (455). The "Ode on a Grecian Urn" emerges from the "spell of reification" as it deconstructs the clichés of both sides in the central aesthetic debate of its culture. Keats satirizes the lifelessness of a beau ideal that claims for art the ability to represent a truer, more harmonious nature than the one in which we live, yet produces only banal, indistinguishable portraits. He then exposes the inherent contradictions of the *Annals* critique of that beau ideal, which derided its lack of realism, yet affirmed an equally idealized and imaginary harmony in the antiquity of Greece. The poem's own moment of "shudder" clearly occurs in the contemplation of the emptied town, and if the terms of the debate, as Keats receives them, suggest that the most persistent of "false needs" is the desire to believe in the possibility of a better world than our own, then it is no wonder that it is this image that most deeply unsettles the reified narratives it confronts. Despite the threat it implies to our own existence, this vanished town easily becomes the most magnetic image in the poem; the speaker, and the reader, linger within the scope of its shadow, as its power obliterates the consideration of self-interest. It demands a disinterestedness that refuses to be assimilated into the totalizations of thought.

The desire for totalization, Lacan proposes, both begins in specularity, in the vision of phallic wholeness, and manifests itself in specularity, in the dominating power of the gaze. But Lacan also suggests, in one of his less systematic moments, that art subverts the economy of the gaze and its stereotyped positions of male voyeurism and female exhibition: "The function of the picture . . . is not, as it might at first seem, that of being a trap for the gaze. It might be thought that, like the actor, the painter wishes to be looked at. . . . I think there is a relation with the gaze of the spectator, but that it is more complex. The painter . . . gives something for the eye to feed on, but he invites the person to whom this picture is presented to lay down his gaze there as one lays down one's weapons" (*Fundamental Concepts*, 101).

These "weapons," in Lacan's linguistically structured psyche, are the symbolic identifications produced by the ego, always oriented to the transcendental signifier of its economy. The dismantling of the gaze severs the relation to the transcendental signifier; art solicits a response that would not proceed from the desire of the ego for wholeness, and that emerges outside an economy of calculation. An artwork asks its viewer to experience it as sheer contiguity, simply as a friend. As the "Urn" subjects both the artificiality of the beau ideal and the more complexly reified image of Greece to the mutability of poetic representation, it draws us into the elemental linguistic form of allegory, in Benjamin's understanding of the term, in which there is no redemption of the material and the transient into immaterial transcendence. This irredeemable mutability can be expressed in terms of the elusive Lacanian "real," but not of the Freudian "reality principle." Readings of Keats's poetry that congratulate him for the maturity of his recognition of "the reality principle" adopt, from Freud, a reality principle that is only a calculated deferral, operating within a homeostatic economy of pleasure. The economy of pleasure registered in "Beauty is truth, truth beauty" is neither homeostatic—its ahistoric "modernity" resides in the "shudder" it provokes through its violation of the habitude of custom—nor, to move to an even more fundamental level of that Freudian economy, self-interested. The commitment of this text to "truth" as something very different from a sentimentalized fantasy of a golden age is not the Freudian realism that agrees to a temporary deferral of sensory pleasure only for the sake of realizing a more significant pleasure later. The promise of a greater pleasure in the deferred, comprehensive truth of a philosophy or a history, and the experience of cognitive wholeness in envisioning that truth as a totality, is the bargain that this text rejects as illusory.

The desire to experience the "all" solely as inclusion, as everything and not as the only thing, makes the "truth" of the "Ode on a Grecian Urn" unpalatable to totalizing habits of thought. The poem's final statement, that the perception of beauty is all we need to know, is both a relinquishment of the desire to transcend temporality and an assertion by the poem of the resistance, on the part of both the aesthetic object it depicts and the aesthetic object it would become, to conversion into the iterable knowledge available to "consequitive reasoning." The indulgence of the "temptation to immediacy," and the brief lingering in the desire to "prolong and repeat the emotion" for the sake of an intensity that cannot promise melodies and legends sweeter than those of our own time on this earth, offer the reader the same rewards embraced by the poem's persona, at roughly the same cost. The density of the "Urn"'s linguistic presence can lead into the intellectual vertigo of being teased out of thought, but it offers no access to a continuity between this text and narratives that claim the power to complete the story of Keats's increasing maturity or to define a cultural epoch as "Romanticism." Such narratives demand reading against the poetry and reducing the text to a plain prose paraphrase as they confer equal measures of representative value on "Thou still unravish'd bride of quietness" and "More happy love! more happy, happy love!" As Keats suggests in his comparison of Coleridge and Shakespeare, one can have wholeness (or at least the intellectual experience of wholeness) or one can have intensity. Historicist narratives that identify Romanticism as a fragment of the larger whole of history, or that depict poetry as an incomplete representation of what McGann calls the "highest orders of knowledge" (Social, 23) make the choice for intellectual wholeness, even as the overdetermined coding of

"Romantic poetry" as an antithesis to modern critical thought reproduces the overdetermination of temporality and form that the "Ode on a Grecian Urn" deconstructs.

In our construction of a past that can be distinguished from our modernity, our "Romanticism" is Keats's "Greece," our "poetry" his "sculpture." The "Ode on a Grecian Urn" claims a proximity to antiquity that is not a projection from the self but a self-destructive empathy, and it solicits the same response from later generations. The rhetorically assertive conclusion of the poem both makes a demand on the reader and offers a promise, and it has exemplified the arguments for both the demand and the promise. The most demanding assertion in the poem's conclusion lies in the privative sense of "that is all / Ye know on earth," an assertion that everything but art—an everything represented in this text as historical knowledge, love, and religion—is subject to the mutability of time, to cultural relativity, and to the proofs and disproofs of consecutive reasoning. But anyone who says that "More happy love! more happy, happy love!" is good English poetry is simply wrong, and anyone who believes that "Thou still unravish'd bride of quietness" is not great English poetry is just as wrong. This will be true, as Haydon suggested, as long as people speak English, while a sculpture, or an urn, is not subject even to that limit. What Keats's poem offers the reader who does not insist on disbelieving it is the promise that, in return for forgoing anything so solid as an icon of immortality or a conceptual totality, the work of art, in poetry as in sculpture, offers the enrichment of some passing moments with the finest tone imaginable in an earthly interval.

the knowledge of contrast, feeling
for light and shade, all that information (primitive sense) necessary
for a poem

Letters of Keats, 2:360

ι

ι

ι

ι

ι

ι

ι

ι

ι

ι

ι

CHAPTER 3 | # The Agency

ι | # of the Pronoun

ι | ## "Ode on Melancholy"

ι

ι

ι

ι

ι

ι

ι

THE "ODE ON MELANCHOLY" is a poem so pervaded with pronominal imprecision that the reader is forced, if she is to maintain an interpretive focus on the message of the text, to supply a dramatic context that is never explicitly justified by the poem itself. The first example of this haziness occurs in the ode's opening line, where the addressee of the injunction "No, no, go not to Lethe" is not specified; the warning might be addressed to the reader, to an unnamed second person to whom the poet is supposed to be speaking or, in an internal dialogue, to the poet himself. This ambiguity is sustained throughout the second stanza in the repetitive references to a grammatical second person ("thy pale forehead," "glut thy sorrow"), and there is a further complication when a third figure, "thy mistress," is endowed with "peerless eyes." The final pronominal ambiguity in the poem is not a question of the relation between the first and second persons—the poetic persona and his interlocutor—but of the identity of the third potential person, the "She" who "dwells with Beauty," since syntax alone does not dictate whether the noun referent for "She" is the peerless mistress of line 18 or the goddess Melancholy, first introduced by name in line 26.

In considering all these moments together, it becomes clear that the "Ode on Melancholy" is persistently vague in its use of pronouns. This vagueness has not troubled critical commentary on the poem, which has focused on the ode's putative message as though these pronominal ambiguities could be overlooked or summarily resolved. The most common assumption made about the poem's beginning is that the opening line is neither an internal monologue nor a direct address to the reader, but that it stages a dialogue between a first-person speaker and another person who is present (at least imaginarily) to the speaker. It is also a working assumption in commentary on the ode that making such a distinction is not important, and that any ambiguity at the syntactic level does not impede access to the thematic level of the text. The second-person references in the poem, both implicit and explicit, are simply treated as the functional equivalent of "one," and the pronominal ambiguities of the poem are resolved in a clear and schematic fashion. The first-person speaker, the implicit interlocutor and the second-person possessives that derive from him ("thy pale forehead," "glut thy sorrow," etc.), along with the masculine third-person nominative and possessive in the third stanza ("him," "his soul") become interchangeable representations of a universal subject-position. In the case of the "She" who appears in line 21, a relatively secure critical consensus has also been reached, although at the cost of somewhat more overt editorial intervention. Not only in interpretive essays on the poem but even in textbooks prepared for undergraduate readers, Keats's critics and editors have regularly advised readers that the noun referent for "She" occurs five lines after, not three lines before, the appearance of the pronoun. Abrams, in the *Norton Anthology of English Literature*, instructs the reader that "She" is "usually taken to refer to Melancholy rather than to 'thy mistress' in line 18" (2:795); Bloom and Trilling are somewhat more flexible in *Romantic Poetry and Prose*, saying that the word "refers both to 'thy mistress,' and the goddess Melancholy" (543), but David Perkins, annotating *English Romantic Writers*, is even more emphatic than Abrams in his footnote: "She: not the 'mistress,' but Melancholy itself" (1254).

The critical tidying up of the poem's imprecise syntax has produced fairly uniform agreement about the thematic intent of the "Ode on Melancholy," but markedly less consensus about the quality of the ode. Thematic summaries of the poem from the time of the New Criticism to the present day have attempted to preserve the image of Keats as the earthiest and most commonsensical of the Romantic poets by opposing the poem's sensuousness to a visionary indulgence associated with Blake or Shelley, but the ode's melodramatic excess has complicated this image of Keats and has left the poem with an uneven critical history. While at least some of Keats's New Critical readers viewed this ode as a lapse into, in E. C. Pettet's words, "the superficial Romantic cult of melancholy" (311), most commentators have been more inclined to assimilate it to Lionel Trilling's figure of "Keats the Hero." It is difficult to believe that two such competent readers as Pettet and Helen Vendler are describing the same poem when Pettet says that

> Keats is finally caught up in a deathwards impulse, in the Romantic luxury of "half in love with easeful death." . . . Keats exults in the idea of being a sacrifice to melancholy, "among her cloudy trophies hung" (309)

and Vendler that

> Keats is turning away from passivity, spectatorship, and visionariness of a dreamy sort in order to seek some self-image more strenuous and directed. (*Odes*, 165)

Neither Pettet's nor Vendler's paraphrase can be dismissed as simply an idiosyncratic misreading of the poem. F. R. Leavis and Douglas Bush weigh in on Pettet's side of the argument, both calling the poem "decadent" (Leavis, 260; Bush, *Life*, 148) and endorsing Pettet's judgment that "Melancholy" expresses "one of the shallowest and—if the word is not too puritanical—unhealthiest parts of the Romantic attitude" (315). On the other side, there has been no shortage of critics willing to congratulate Keats for his characteristic ability, expressed in this poem, to face the most uncomfortable realities with an exemplary clarity of vision and fortitude of spirit. This reading commonly finds the poem's value in its "vivid acceptance of process" (W. J. Bate, 522), a formula that could, with little need for qualification, be said to center the interpretations of the "Ode on Melancholy" by Aileen Ward, Harold Bloom, Barbara Herrnstein Smith, Jack Stillinger, Leon Waldoff, Vendler, Anselm Haverkamp, and Hermione de Almeida.[1] In the cases of W. J. Bate, Ward, Vendler, and Waldoff, this "recognition of the transient nature of all experience" (Waldoff, 156) is explicitly connected to a biographical narrative that illustrates Keats's "rapid intellectual and emotional maturation during 1819" (Ward, 535), and any reservations about the melodramatic excesses of "Melancholy" are easily subsumed into a narrative that culminates in the achieved serenity of "To Autumn." Within this narrative, the "Ode on Melancholy" is traditionally seen as the last of the odes of May 1819, and therefore as a poem that represents "an advance over earlier odes" (Vendler, 165).

The ease with which the message of the "Ode on Melancholy" has been explicated and its value assessed (even if in contrary ways) has transcended not only its internal grammatical ambiguities but a number of mundane philological matters that are not easily resolved. Questions involving the poem's exact date of composition, its intertextual debts (particularly to Burton's *Anatomy of Melancholy*), and the relevance to the final version of the poem, published in 1820, of a canceled original first stanza raise uncertainties that are too often silently overlooked as the poem is thematized and subsumed into critical narratives in which it either plays a clearly defined, positive role in Keats's development, or, through the conceptual vehicle of "decadence," serves as an exemplary case of the immature excesses of Romanticism that have been transcended in our sober modernity. Although the "Ode on Melancholy" is usually assumed to be the last of the odes of April and May 1819 (along with "Nightingale," "Grecian Urn," "Indolence" and "Psyche"), Stillinger's recent editorial investigations have shown that there is no documentary evidence for giving any more precise date of composition for this poem than the year 1819, the date that appears on Charles Brown's transcript. Recent arguments, such as those by Vendler and Waldoff, that the odes form a sequence in which "Melancholy" serves as a transition between "Grecian Urn" and "Autumn," are based solely on the interpretations of the individual poems, and risk the circularity of finding in the odes a pattern of development that actually originates in the critical narrative itself.

The potential influence of Burton's *Anatomy* on Keats's ode is a second instance of assertions made in recent studies (e.g., "The hero's equipment comes from Petrarch and Burton" [Vendler, 157]; the "Ode draws heavily upon both Burton and 'Lycidas'" [Haverkamp, 697]) that rest on dubious philological grounds. The most extensive argument for Burton's influence on Keats was made by Robert Gittings in his biographical study *John Keats: The Living Year*, but even Gittings concluded that, despite numerous borrowings from Burton that Gittings claims began to appear in Keats's poems and letters in late 1818 and continued throughout 1819, "the 'Ode on Melancholy' takes hardly any verbal inspiration from the pages of Burton" (142). Gittings's wider argument regarding both the dates and the importance of Keats's reading of Burton was challenged first by John Middleton Murry (104–8) and then more thoroughly by Aileen Ward, who came to the conclusion that "Keats first became acquainted with Burton when Brown loaned or gave him his copy in the middle of June 1819" (543), that is, after the completion of the odes of the spring. Moreover, Ward argues in persuasive detail that except for the borrowed plot of *Lamia* (which was composed in July and August), all of the supposed echoes of Burton adduced by Gittings and others in Keats's poems and letters before September 1819 can more plausibly be traced to other sources (such as Dryden or Milton) with which Keats was certainly familiar. Since the three instances in which the *Anatomy* is explicitly cited or echoed in Keats's letters all occurred in September, and since Keats wrote in his letter of mid-September to George Keats of reading Burton "lately," Ward concludes that Keats had only skimmed the *Anatomy* in June 1819 in search of a plot for a poem—a search that would not have necessitated a very close reading on Keats's part, since the passage that serves as the basis for *Lamia* was marked by Brown before he gave the volume to Keats—and that Keats did not read Burton in any detail until September.

Ward's citations of parallels between Keats's earlier poems and the "Ode on Melancholy" effectively demonstrate that Keats did not need to read Burton in order to discover either the themes or the imagery of the "Ode on Melancholy." These same citations, however, subvert her own argument that Keats underwent a dramatic transformation in the year 1819, changing from a carefree youth who fell blissfully in love with Fanny Brawne in the spring to the more mature figure who experienced "disillusionment" over the "revelations of feminine duplicity he had found in Burton" (551–52) in the fall (a narrative that bears distinct similarities to that of the progression from the naive Greeks to the self-conscious moderns). Ward is particularly concerned to distance the Swiftian note scrawled in Keats's hand in the margin of the "Love-Melancholy" section of Burton's *Anatomy*, where Keats deplores "being one of a race of eyes nose and mouth beings in a planet call'd the earth who all from Plato to Wesley have always mingled goatish winnyish lustful love with the abstract adoration of the deity" (Forman, 268), from the initial blossoming of Keats and Fanny Brawne's love affair in the spring of 1819. But the paradoxical qualities of romantic love, in which the idealization of the romantic object is linked both to sensuality and to a mutability that Keats associates with femininity, were put in the most explicit terms in the letter draft of the poem "Fancy" in January of 1819; its imagery foreshadows the entire second half of the "Ode on Melancholy." The original draft of "Fancy" not only acknowledges that "Eve[r]y joy is spoilt by use" but also asks

> tell me who
> Has a Mistress to [for *so*?] divine
> Be the palate ne'er so fine
>   . . . She cannot sicken. (*KL*, 2:23–24)

The imagery of this "Mistress fair" is omitted from the version of "Fancy" published in 1820, from which she has been transported into the "Ode on Melancholy."

The internal evidence that has been adduced for a connection between Keats's reading of Burton and the composition of the "Ode on Melancholy" ranges from the appearance of verbal echoes to the broadest thematic correlations, but the documentary evidence of Keats's literary influences in the "Ode on Melancholy" is no more definitive than the poetic and epistolary record of his romantic attitudes in 1819. In recent criticism of the poem, Vendler has focused on particular verbal and stylistic parallels between Burton and Keats, citing the ode's description of melancholy as a "fit" and the beloved as a "mistress" as terms that appear frequently in the *Anatomy*, and noting Burton's habit of offering advice to the melancholy (as in "I may say to most melancholy men" [Vendler, 158]) as a parallel to Keats's use of admonition and exhortation in "Melancholy." Haverkamp reaches deeper into the thematics of Burton's text to suggest that both Burton and Keats grasp the idea, later and more fully explicated by Freud, that melancholy differs from other forms of mourning or sadness in that it becomes a force in itself, exceeding its causes, and so allows for no resolution.

Neither the usual assignment of the ode to May 1819 nor the assumption of Burton's influence on the poem can be ruled out if these presumptions are taken individually, but the two beliefs do not easily coexist. To group "Melancholy" with the odes of the spring, it becomes necessary either to discount Burton's influence on the ode or to account for the epistolary record, which strongly suggests that Keats's reading of Burton took place in the fall. If Burton is taken as a source for Keats's ideas about melancholy, then the dating of the poem in the spring of 1819 and the biographical narrative in which its excesses are superseded by the serenity achieved in "To Autumn" are called into doubt. If Burton's influence plays any role in Keats's decision to write an "Ode on Melancholy," Keats's receipt of the *Anatomy* from Brown in mid-June means that the poem must surely be separated from the burst of creativity in the odes of the spring. Furthermore, the repeated references to Burton in Keats's letters of the fall would seem to suggest an even later date for this poem. Despite the impossibility of absolutely disproving Ward's argument that there is no relation between Burton's *Anatomy* and Keats's ode because the "Ode on Melancholy" was supposedly written in May and Keats did not see Burton's text until June, I would suggest that two specific word choices occurring in the composition of the ode—one that is revised out of the final version of the poem, and another that appears in the canceled first stanza—are difficult to account for until they are seen in relation to Burton. This compositional history suggests at least some familiarity with the *Anatomy* on Keats's part before he wrote the "Ode on Melancholy."

In the final, published version of "Melancholy," the first two potions alluded to are "Wolf's-bane" and "nightshade." In Keats's handwritten draft of the poem, the first word of the second line starts out as "Henb," which is crossed out before the word is completed, and "Wolf's bane" is written in as the first word of the line. The first two of the herbs and roots cited by Burton for their ability to produce melancholy are "henbane, nightshade" (1:372). De Almeida has recently argued that the revision of "Henbane" to "Wolf's-bane" was made because of the different pharmaceutical properties of the two drugs, and that Keats's choice "to invoke the complex nerve poison wolfsbane over the simple debilitative henbane tells us much of the kinds of sensations and poetic inducements that the 'Ode' comes to reject" (169), but the change from "henbane" to "Wolf's-bane" clearly has poetic grounds in the differing associations of the words *hen* and *wolf* that have nothing to with the actual chemical properties of the drugs henbane and wolfsbane. Like "nightshade," "Wolf's-bane" has a slightly spooky aura that would be apparent to readers who were not as medically astute as Keats.

One explanation of Keats's choice in beginning to write the poetically inef-
fective "henbane" would be an associative linkage, originating in Burton, of
"henbane, nightshade" with melancholy.

There is a second case of a word choice that is just as poetically curious,
and that fits with Keats's markings of Burton and with the reappearance of
the same word in one of Keats's letters to Fanny Brawne in October of 1819.
The third line of the canceled first stanza to the poem reads "Stitch creeds
together for a sail," an image that is not consistent with the figurative pattern of the stanza. It is at least metaphorically possible to build a ship out of
bones—bones are solid enough to build with—a gibbet is in the general
shape of a mast; groans, were they vehement enough, could create the wind
to billow out a sail—but "creeds" have no material existence and cannot be
"stitched together" to make a sail. The oddity of this image was apparent to
at least one of Keats's friends (Stillinger suspects Woodhouse [*Poems*, 654]),
who amended two of the transcripts of the poem, penciling in "shrouds" for
"creeds." But "Religious Melancholy," the association of religious beliefs
with the madness of melancholy, is the topic of the entire last section of
Burton's *Anatomy*, in which Burton expatiates at great length (122 pages in
Keats's 1814 copy of the *Anatomy*) on the absurd religious beliefs and practices, from ancient to modern times, that show people to be "certainly far
gone with melancholy, if not quite mad" (2:540).

When Keats wrote to Fanny Brawne, "My Creed is Love and you are its
only tenet" (*KL*, 2:224) in October of 1819, he joined the themes of the two
last sections of Burton's *Anatomy*: the descriptions of love-melancholy and
of religious melancholy. The otherwise odd use of "creeds" in a poem that
includes an angry mistress but very little about religion is another small clue
that suggests an association of the "Ode on Melancholy" with Burton and
with the latter part of 1819, but the contradictions in Keats's letters
throughout the year make it impossible to construct a clear narrative of
Keats's supposed "intellectual and emotional maturation" between the
spring and fall of 1819. The worshipful declaration to Fanny Brawne that
"My Creed is Love and you are its only tenet" in October occurred a month
after Keats wrote to the George Keatses,

> Nothing strikes me so forcibly with a sense of the rediculous as
> love—A Man in love I do think cuts the sorryest figure in the
> world—Even when I know a poor fool to be really in pain about it, I
> could burst out laughing in his face. (2:187–88; September 1819)

Yet that statement of worldly cynicism appeared two months after a letter to Fanny Brawne in which Keats said

> I have two luxuries to brood over in my walks, your Loveliness and the hour of my death. O that I could have possession of them both in the same minute. I hate the world. . . . would I could take a sweet poison from your lips to send me out of it. (2:133; July 1819)

That Keats's feelings for Fanny Brawne were as intense as his rhetoric is clear from his last letters to and about her, but it is also clear from the contradictions within the letters of 1819 that there was no consistent "development" on Keats's part in that year, either from idealism to disillusionment or from immaturity to maturity. In the area of romantic love, there is instead a continual vacillation between a hyperbolic investment in a singular idealized object and a reactive amazement at the power of such an arbitrary construction. That Keats saw the imaginary formation of icons operating in a similar fashion in religion and in romantic love is clear from his repeated use of Christian religious imagery in his late poems to Fanny Brawne. It should not be surprising that Keats's skepticism about the "pious frauds of religion" reemerges in his doubts about the "rediculousness" of romantic ideals, but it is precisely in this discrepancy between the imaginary and the real, and in the power of the imaginary over the real, that melancholy acquires its uncanny force. "Imaginary grievances have always been more my torment than real ones," Keats wrote in September of 1819. "The imaginary nail a man down for a sufferer, as on a cross; the real spur him up into an agent" (*KL*, 2:181). One of the most powerful attributes of the imaginary state of melancholy is its ability to make both choice and action difficult, a difficulty that is embodied in "Melancholy" in the increasing subordination of the poem's persona to the inevitability of what "will" (9), "shall" (11, 29) and "must" (21) happen.

Given the state of the documentary evidence concerning Keats's reading of Burton, there will probably be no definitive answer to the question of the exact degree of Burton's influence on the "Ode on Melancholy." Yet there are good reasons to believe that Keats had read at least some portions of the *Anatomy* before he wrote this ode; the possibility that all of the similarities between Keats and Burton are mere coincidences is strained not only by particular verbal and thematic parallels but by Keats's broad repetition of Burton's treatment of the theme of melancholy through a heterogeneous texture of erudite parody and thematic melodrama. The most important

point about the relation between Keats and Burton is not strictly philological but thematic. Contrary to a popular current interpretation of the poem
that views its purpose as the definition and pursuit of "true melancholy,"
Keats's representation of the phenomenon of melancholy in this ode is much
closer to Burton's moody ambivalence than it is to Milton's courtship of
melancholy in "Il Penseroso." I would suggest that Keats began writing his
"Ode on Melancholy" with Milton's poem in mind but that the cancellation
of the original first stanza marks a shift away from Milton's text and toward
the spirit of Burton's.

It would hardly be a stretch for Keats, having done a turn on Milton's
"L'Allegro" in his own "Fancy," to have decided to compose a response to
Milton's companion poem on melancholy. One verbal echo of "Il Penseroso" survives in the final version of Keats's "Melancholy" in the poem's
final image, usually traced to Shakespeare's sonnet 31 ("Hung with the trophies of my lovers gone"), but which also echoes the "Trophies hung" (line
118) of "Il Penseroso." Even some of the images in Keats's original letter
draft of the poem "Fancy" but not in the final version, published in 1820,
have been transferred to the "Ode on Melancholy": the "palate . . . fine" and
the "mistress" with a "hand" to "press." But Keats's "Melancholy" is a good
deal darker than Milton's "Penseroso." Where "Il Penseroso" imagines a
final retreat into a long and serene old age of contemplation, Keats's "Ode
on Melancholy" is filled with images of abrupt intensity—"twist Wolf 's-
bane," "glut thy sorrow," "be among her cloudy trophies hung"—that would
strike a strongly dissonant note within the reflective mood of Milton's poem.

While the pleasures given by Melancholy in "Il Penseroso" are those of
philosophic knowledge, part of the gloominess of the "Ode on Melancholy"
derives from its sense of the uselessness of knowledge, since ideals, such as
Beauty, are seen as only misrepresentations of their own material origins.
By far the most extensive quotation from Burton in Keats's letters is a passage from the *Anatomy* that describes how love can transform one's perception of another person, and this passage sheds a useful light on the most
strained pronominal usage in Keats's ode, at the conclusion of the second
stanza, which advises

> Or if thy mistress some rich anger shows,
>> Emprison her soft hand, and let her rave,
>>> And feed deep, deep upon her peerless eyes.

In the lengthy passage that Keats copied nearly verbatim from the *Anatomy*
in a letter to the George Keatses in September of 1819 (*KL*, 2:191), Burton

launches a tirade that begins, "Every Lover admires his mistriss, though she be very deformed of her self, ill-favoured, wrinkled, pimpled, pale, red, yellow, tann'd, tallow-fac'd, have a swoln juglers platter face." Keats's letter incorporates nearly two-thirds of Burton's five-hundred-word tirade, in which Burton emphasizes the difference between the general assessment of a woman's appearance and her lover's perception of it, telling the reader that while "to thy judgement [she] looks like a mard in a Lanthorn, whom thou couldst not fancy for a world," yet her lover sees a paragon of beauty: "if he love her once, he admires her for all this, he takes no notice of any such errors or imperfections of body and mind" (Burton, 2:314). The dialogic division of the first-person lyric speaker in the "Ode on Melancholy" brought about by the description of "thy mistress" and "her peerless eyes" makes sense only as an oxymoronic phrasing of the paradox elaborated here by Burton. If the reference to "thy mistress" is intended to suggest an imaginary dialogue between two people, why would the first-person speaker believe that "thy" mistress has the world's most beautiful eyes? Yet even if this address is read as part of an entirely internal dialogue, "a personal poem impersonally phrased," as Vendler puts it (*Odes*, 172), the use of the second-person possessive still transforms the speaker himself from a specific individual into a universal, or stereotypical, subject-position, and so accomplishes the corresponding effect of making his mistress into a generic figure, like any other mistress, one whose eyes are just like everyone else's—the very opposite of "peerless." The shifting pronouns demand a speaker who is capable of entering into romantic idealizations while remaining fully cognizant of their arbitrary, conventional origins.

The contradiction between the idealization of a romantic other and the knowledge that this idealization is arbitrary is a contradiction that we all live with, and as Burton points out (and as Keats notes) in some of the slyest passages of the *Anatomy*, it is a contradiction at the core of religious as well as of romantic belief. In Burton's encyclopedic account of religious madness, he anatomizes the bizarre beliefs not only of ancient Greeks and Romans, modern Asians, and continental "papists" but also of heretics closer to home, such as "Anabaptists, Socinians, Brownists, Barrowists, Familists &c." (2:492); the universal sign of the follies of these groups is that "they pitty all other religions, account them damned, blind; as if they alone were the true church, they are the true heirs" (2:518). As Burton exempts only the Church of England from the vast catalog of religious follies, he takes up the position of the lover who alone cannot see the common truth about his own beloved, and Burton gives a brief glimpse of that awareness when he marvels at the bizarre practices of the natives of the Americas: "what strange Sacraments, *like ours of Baptisme and the Lord's Supper;* what goodly temples, priests, sacrifices they had in America, when the Spaniards first landed there" (2:494; my emphasis). Keats's copy of the *Anatomy* contains his marking of and comment on Burton's broadest treatment of this theme:

> In all these religions and superstitions, amongst our idolaters, <u>you shall still finde that the parties first affected, are silly, rude, ignorant people, old folkes, that are naturally prone to superstition, weak women, or some poor rude illiterate persons, that are apt to be wrought upon, . . . *for Ignorance is the mother of devotion* as all the world knowes. . . . not as our Saviour by a few silly fishermen, to confound the wisdome of the world, to save publicans and sinners but to make advantage of their ignorance, to confound them and their associates;</u> and that they may better effect what they intend, they begin, as I say, <u>with poor, stupid, illiterate persons.</u> (2:494)

The irony introduced through the near repetitions, in which the "silly, rude, ignorant people" who are the natural prey of "idolaters" could as easily be the "few silly fishermen" central to the Christian tradition as the "poor, stupid, illiterate persons" exploited by the promoters of superstition was not lost on Keats; the underlinings in the quotation are his (the italics are Burton's), and Keats expressed his appreciation of Burton's ironic jab at Christianity when he wrote, in the margin of Brown's book, "extraordinary" (Forman, 274).

While Burton's text is best known for such *jeux d'esprits*, the *Anatomy* is equally energetic in its morbidity, a note that appears repeatedly in Keats's letters of 1819 and that pervades this ode. Gittings suggests not just a parallel but an echo in the similarity of Burton's observation that

> Even in the midst of all our mirth, jollity, and laughter, is sorrow and griefe; or, if there be true happiness amongst us, 'tis but for a time . . . .a faire morning turns to a lowring afternoon (1:159)

and Keats's comment in a letter of March 1819:

> Circumstances are like Clouds continually gathering and bursting— While we are laughing the seed of some trouble is put into the wide arable land of events—while we are laughing it sprouts is [for *it*] grows and suddenly bears a poison fruit which we must pluck. (*KL,* 2:79)

Whether or not Keats gets the image of clouds sweeping in over a scene of laughter directly from Burton, this letter clearly foreshadows the development of his own floral imagery in "Melancholy"; the innocent roses and peonies of the second stanza, when touched by the drops of melancholy, bear both poison and Joy's grape in the ode's conclusion. In the darker passages of the *Anatomy*, Burton hammers away at the bleakness (if not now, then momentarily) of the human condition, citing hundreds of classical and religious authors to the effect that "All is vanity and vexation of spirit": "Our whole life is an Irish Sea, wherein there is nought to be expected, but tempestuous storms, and troublesome waves, and those infinite. . . . we bangle away our best dayes, befool out our times, we lead a contentious, discontent, tumultuous, melancholy, miserable life; insomuch, that if we could foretel what was to come, and it put to our choyce, we should rather refuse, than accept of, this painful life" (1:156–57).

This is the point from which Keats's "Ode on Melancholy" begins, as its opening words respond to a depth of despair that calculates suicide as simply a rational decision in the face of the portions of pain and pleasure that can be expected in this life. As Empson observed of the ode's opening line, "somebody, or some force in the poet's mind, must have wanted to go to Lethe very much, if it took four negatives in the first line to stop them" (205). The common reading of the ode that sees in the first two stanzas a distinction between a "false" melancholy, to be avoided, and a "true" one, to be desired, greatly underestimates the affective range of the poem. While the canceled first stanza starts out able to imagine residing, Miltonically, with "Melancholy," her location in the last line of the stanza, on "any isle of Lethe dull," holds out far less promise than does the conclusion of "Il Penseroso," but there is not much else that rhymes with "skull."

A syntactically deferred, phonetically determined adjective that changes the course of the text creates an important dramatic turn within the "Ode to a Nightingale" ("forlorn"), but in this case the assignment of Melancholy "any isle of Lethe dull" exposes the metaphor of a quest after melancholy as inadequate to the real experience of melancholy, and thus causes the entire original first stanza of the poem to be discarded. The first stanza of the final, published version of the poem begins *in medias res*, and the beginning of the second stanza finally names what precedes the temptation to suicide and the exhortation to forgo it: "when the melancholy fit shall fall." In the final version of the "Ode on Melancholy," melancholy itself never achieves the benign presence bestowed on it by Milton; there is no question of living with it as a friend. The "blue-devils" do not simply cast a "blissful cloud of summer-indolence"; they can lead, "after a day or two's melancholy," to a probable, though not a definite, belief: "yet I do not think I shall ever come to the rope or the Pistol" (*KL*, 2:32; January 1819). Vendler's contention, in response to accusations of the poem's decadence, that "Melancholy" actually offers "a therapeutic theory of aesthetic experience," which serves as a "recourse against depression" (187) through its "search for the temperate mean" (159), misrepresents Keats's stretching of the ode between two sets of extreme, even excessive verbs: the intense activity of "twist," "glut," "rave," and "burst" versus the inexorable force of what "will come," "shall fall," and "must die." Similarly, Bate's discovery of a "vivid acceptance of process" (522) is irrelevant to a text in which the final stanza is framed between what "must" and what "shall" happen, and the entire arc of which constitutes a movement from an admonition against self-destruction to an annihilation that occurs regardless of any choice or action. Neither acceptance nor refusal, which the poem attempts in its opening line ("No, no, go not to Lethe"), can affect the course of the phenomenon described by this poem as "melancholy."

When the canceled first stanza of the ode is left out of consideration, and its quest metaphor removed from critical paraphrase, it becomes increasingly clear that the older paraphrase of the poem that describes it concluding "in the idea of being a sacrifice to melancholy" (Pettet, 309) is actually more accurate than one which sees Keats looking for, and finding, a therapeutic value in "true melancholy." But to suggest, as Pettet does, that "Keats exults" in this sacrifice goes well beyond any explicit information given by the poem, and the further judgment that the very expression of such an idea is "unhealthy" or "decadent," as it cuts against the grain of Keats's text, is a valuable guide to discovering exactly where the grain of the ode lies. The poem's concluding image of self-sacrifice suggests the fulfillment of a masochistic impulse that appears in each of the previous stanza closings, in the images that "drown the wakeful anguish of the soul" and allow the "mistress" to "rave" while the persona "feed[s] upon" her "rich anger." But the ambivalence of these images disturbs the diagnostic value of psychoanalytic terms: Is it masochistic to wish to end "wakeful anguish," or to prolong it? And does the relation between the poem's speaker and someone's mistress suggest a masochistic, or a sadistic, desire on his part?

The difficulty of providing a psychoanalytic reading of the "Ode on Melancholy" that would identify not the poem's pragmatic or therapeutic purpose but the more exorbitant path of its desire is illustrated in two recent critiques of the poem, those of Waldoff and Haverkamp, both of whom consider the poem in the light of Freud's analysis of melancholy in "Mourning and Melancholia." Waldoff sees melancholy as a central theme through-

out Keats's work, and one that has been severely underestimated in importance; he argues, "Much of what Freud says about the psychology of mourning and melancholia holds important implications for any effort to understand the character and function of Keats's imagination" (23). Nevertheless,
when Waldoff turns to the "Ode on Melancholy," his conclusion echoes
that of numerous other commentators who have worked without a Freudian apparatus: "The poem concludes with a recognition of the transient
nature of all experience, and to that extent represents a will to adapt to a
world of process and change" (156). As Waldoff identifies Keats's "imagination" with "a will to adapt" to change, he converts the unconstrained force
of melancholia into the normal work of mourning. Waldoff's use of the
honorific term "imagination" to describe a willingness to relinquish the lost
object and recathect the remaining world highlights the normative bias of
Freud's distinction between mourning and melancholia, even as Waldoff
inverts Freud's own terms. Freud describes "the work which mourning performs" thus: "Reality-testing has shown that the loved object no longer
exists, and it proceeds to demand that all libido shall be withdrawn from its
attachments to that object. This demand arouses understandable opposition. . . . This opposition can be so intense that a turning away from reality
takes place and a clinging to the object through the medium of a hallucina-
tory wishful psychosis. Normally, respect for reality gains the day."[2] The
"will to adapt" to loss that Waldoff calls "imagination" is termed by Freud
"respect for reality," an attitude that Freud identifies not with melancholia
but with mourning. The single phenomenon that is valorized by the two
very different terms, Waldoff's "imagination" and Freud's "respect for reality," is the decision, in the face of loss, that what continues to exist is of
greater value—that is, it is more worthy of libidinal investment—than that
which has been lost.

The reason that Waldoff can so easily echo non-Freudian readers of the
ode is that he has adopted the most normative "Freud" as his own interpretive model, the Freud who prefers the realistic mourner to the narcissistic
melancholic. Of those who are unable to relinquish the lost object, those in
whom "the same influences produce melancholia instead of mourning,"
Freud judges, "we consequently suspect them of a morbid disposition"
("Mourning," 243),[3] a suspicion that easily cooperates with Irving Babbit's
suspicions about romanticism as a whole, and with Pettet's, Leavis's, and
Bush's charges against this poem. Keats's letters show that he was capable of
suspecting himself of such a gratuitous morbidity—"I will not spoil my love
of gloom by writing an ode to darkness" (KL, 2:43); "I shall henceforth shake

off my indolent fits" (*KL*, 2:122); "I am a Coward, I cannot bear the pain of being happy" (*KL*, 2:160); "Imaginary grievances have always been more my torment than real ones" (*KL*, 2:181)—but he could also contend, at other times, that the fault might lie not in his temperament but in his circumstances. "I am a little given to bode ill like the raven," he warned Fanny Brawne, but he pleaded that "it is my misfortune, not my fault; it has proceeded from the general tenor of the circumstances of my life, and rendered every event suspicious" (*KL*, 2:129). He also annotated Burton's observation that "almost all jewells and precious stones have excellent vertues to pacifie the affections of the minde" (Burton, 2:99) with the ironic comment, "Precious stones are certainly a remedy against Melancholy: a valuable diamond would effectually cure mine" (Forman, 267). Although it is impossible to calculate the effect of a diamond on an imaginary grievance, Waldoff rescues the "Ode on Melancholy" for inclusion in the tradition of "Keats the Hero" through a similar invocation of common sense as he identifies Keats with respect for the reality principle and distances the "Ode on Melancholy" from the morbidity associated by Freud with the melancholic temper.

Haverkamp's treatment of the ode more clearly distinguishes melancholia from mourning, as he describes the poem as an exemplary treatise on melancholy, one that, like Burton's *Anatomy*, valorizes melancholy itself as a recognition of irretrievable loss. This recognition, in Haverkamp's reading, is not a sign of morbid pathology but "the melancholy condition of subjectivity in a modern world." Layering Foucault with Benjamin, Haverkamp suggests that both Burton's *Anatomy* and Keats's ode define an epistemic break in modes of representation as their modernity moves beyond the codification of knowledge into ascending orders of significance which was characteristic of "the age of 'similitudes' and 'resemblances,' of allegory" (695). Haverkamp finds a paradigm for this historical shift in Freud's contention that melancholia differs from mourning in that the melancholic is unable to reinvest a previous cathexis into "reality," and he suggests that modernity itself becomes melancholy as it is unable to recathect its previous investment in similitude: "Reading the *new* way, that is, 'critically,' now means a structural procedure which turns melancholy in that it 'mortifies' its objects and consequently perceives them as 'dead texture'" (695; Haverkamp's emphasis). Haverkamp discovers, at one level, a therapeutic purpose in the poem's "carefully preserved detachment from experience" (700), which results from Keats's perception, following Burton, that "the antidote in dealing with melancholy, as invented in romanticism, is irony" (699). At a second, "more structural" level, Haverkamp uses the economy of the Freudian repetition compulsion described in "Beyond the Pleasure Principle" to account for the decision of reading and writing to persist in the modern era despite the knowledge of the impossibility of recovering an allegorical frame of reference: "Keats thus, until his imminent end, nourished the ambivalence at the bottom of his melancholia and followed, in a poetical 'working through,' the repetition compulsion of modern writing" (705). This repetition compulsion, which knows its own impossibility of significance, comes to serve as an evolutionary model for Haverkamp as modernity becomes the human condition, and as our modern capacity for "irony exemplifies paradigmatically the anthropomorphic condition of tropological discourse" (702).

While Haverkamp's essay conveys much of the intelligence of the "Ode on Melancholy," his use of irony as a synthetic trope and as an "antidote" to melancholy constructs a balance of forces very different from that struck by the poem. The relation between melancholy and irony is, in Haverkamp's reading, a structure of sublation through which melancholy is converted from an experiential state of loss into a true expression of the reality principle. Melancholy becomes truer to reality than the work of mourning as melancholy registers the hopelessness of a recathexis onto a new object, and so triggers a repetition that, knowing the impossibility of its own significance, takes a stance of ironic detachment. But it is in the nature of sublation to leave something behind, and a reading of the "Ode on Melancholy" focused on the antidotal properties of a "detachment from experience" leaves out the intensity, the sensuousness, and the perceived excessiveness that have led to the charges against this poem, of decadence and unhealthiness. Valuing Keats, as Haverkamp does, as a strong and sensible thinker is a comparatively modern phenomenon. His contemporary critics were more likely to find him both unlearned and pretentious—in the word so effectively revived by Marjorie Levinson, vulgar. In the "Ode on Melancholy," it is not only the energetic verbs but the sometimes fey imagery, such as the personified "Joy whose hand is ever at his lips / Bidding adieu," that suggests that this poem has not quite grown up.

Haverkamp's "structural" reading of the poem attempts to define what Freud calls the topographical and dynamic structures of Keats's ode, but it does not assay an account of what Freud terms the "metapsychological" or "economic" forces of the text, the forces that motivate the text and define its desire. In the "Ode on Melancholy," the question of desire is far more complex and oblique than the search for an "antidote." A poem that opens with such an oddly impersonal phrasing—an injunction against suicide expressed through a mythological allusion—advertises from its outset a significant gap between representational choice and motivational force. The shift that occurs in the poem's imagery from the first stanza to the second, from the mythological and the occult to the naturalistic, is easy to track, and the message expressed in these stanzas seems equally clear: avoid deadening poisons, "seize and experience the beauty of the transient natural and human world as fully as one can." Yet this sensible advice, offered as a paraphrase of the ode's second stanza by Keats's most commonsensical critic, Jack Stillinger, founders in the equally sensible explanation: "The anodynes are rejected because they shut out pleasure as well as pain: 'For shade to shade will come too drowsily, / And drown the wakeful anguish of the soul'" (8). While this advice makes unassailable good sense, its relation to Keats's poem becomes highly tenuous when, in Stillinger's paraphrastic explanation, the word "pleasure" stands in the place of Keats's "wakeful anguish." The discrepancy between these terms suggests the difficulty that the "Ode on Melancholy" presents to the formulation of a statement of its meaning that can emerge from an accurate paraphrase of it. The persistent ambivalence of this poem, which begins in the paradoxical valorization of the state of "wakeful anguish" and then both advocates and anatomizes "Pleasure," "Joy," "Delight," and "Beauty," resists paraphrases that would define it within the normative bounds of common sense.

"Mourning and Melancholia" can be usefully juxtaposed with the "Ode on Melancholy," not as a diagnostic tool that would define the unconscious subtext of Keats's poem, but as a text that itself represents one of Freud's first attempts to confront, in melancholia, a psychic economy that seems to overflow the purposive structure of the pleasure principle organized within the ego. Freud finds particularly vexing "the riddle of the tendency to suicide which makes melancholia so interesting—and so dangerous": "So immense is the ego's self-love, which we have come to recognize as the primal state from which instinctual life proceeds, and so vast is the amount of narcissistic libido which we see liberated in the fear that emerges at a threat to life, that we cannot conceive how the ego can consent to its own destruction" ("Mourning," 252). As Keats's ode contemplates suicide only through the deflected pronominal phrasing of the second-person address "No, no, go not to Lethe," the poem conforms, at least dynamically, to Freud's answer to this riddle in his hypothesis of the division of the self in melancholia, in which "one part of the ego sets itself over against the other, judges it critically, and, as it were, takes it as its object" ("Mourning," 247). Freud connects this self-division to the symptom of the self-abasing behavior that distinguishes melancholia from even the deepest mourning, and he concludes that it must be the case that the melancholic has transferred the ambivalent cathexis of a love/hate relationship with a lost object onto his own ego rather than onto another object. In its most extreme form, the resultant "sadism" (a hostility turned inward, but distinguished from masochism in that it is turned toward a part of the self viewed as an object) can manifest itself in suicidal tendencies: "The analysis of melancholia now shows that the ego can kill itself only if, owing to the return of the object-cathexis, it can treat itself as an object—if it is able to direct against itself the hostility which relates to an object" ("Mourning," 252).

But since the first-person speaker of the "Ode on Melancholy" does not seem to be particularly critical of the object-listener, Keats's ode seems to lack precisely the economic force that makes self-division so volatile as to make suicide possible. The melodrama of coming "to the rope or the Pistol" seems to have turned purely hypothetical when the avenues of self-annihilation are so occult and picturesque as wolfsbane, nightshade, or a downy owl. This indulgence in a playful pseudo-erudition may be the most powerful argument for a link between Burton and Keats, but it is often not entirely clear, in Burton or in Keats, when the playful morbidity turns serious and acknowledges the stakes for which it is playing. Is the conclusion of the ode, which leaves the melancholic "among her cloudy trophies hung," pure metaphor, or is this an aestheticized image of "the rope"? The very device that suggests the division of the ego, namely, the use of the grammatical second person, simultaneously creates a distancing effect that undercuts the potential economic force of the hostility that Freud contends is necessary to explain the suicidal tendencies of the melancholic, yet Freud's next observation about suicide and melancholia strikes directly into the most volatile part of the poem, and of Keats's writings to and about Fanny Brawne: "In the two opposed situations of being most intensely in love and of suicide the ego is overwhelmed by the object, though in totally different ways" ("Mourning," 252). In the light of this observation, the ode's opening command against suicide and the later advice "If thy mistress some rich anger shows, / Emprison her soft hand" read as precisely parallel gestures of resistance on the part of the ego to being overwhelmed, an interpretation that seems to be borne out in the initial valorization of "wakeful anguish," a state which, although it is not pleasure, at least serves as a powerful reassurance to the ego that the ego still exists. Keats's lament to Fanny Brawne, "Ask yourself my love whether you are not very cruel to have so entrammelled me, so destroyed my freedom" (*KL*, 2:123; July 1819), suggests that his passion for her threatened his sense of identity, and the response to that threat is represented in the balance of forces (rave/feed) at the end of the ode's second stanza. The paradoxes of the poem's desire do not necessarily stop there. As shown by the letter to Fanny Brawne in which Keats names, as his "two luxuries," "your Loveliness" and "the hour of my death" (2:133), such an overwhelming could be as much a temptation as a threat; Keats wrote that letter three weeks after he protested her entrammelling of his freedom.

Although the most normative of Freudian terms, *masochism*, can be used to explain away as pathological the dynamics of a desire that seems to violate the premise of the "ego's self-love" as "the primal state from which instinctual life proceeds," the vicissitudes of the death wish do not always conform to this diagnostic vocabulary. There seems to be nothing self-punishing in the image of death that appears in the conclusion to an earlier sonnet that has little, if anything, to do with Fanny Brawne: "Verse, fame and Beauty are intense indeed / But Death intenser—Deaths is Life's high mead" (*KL*, 2:81; March 1819). And it can be tricky to distinguish the real from the purely literary in even the most melodramatic moments in Keats's letters. In Rollins's annotation of the passage in which Keats imagines taking a sweet poison from Fanny Brawne's lips, Rollins notes two literary allusions— Rousseau's "C'est du poison que j'ai cueilli sur tes levres," from *La Nouvelle Heloise*, and Pope's "drink delicious poison from thy eye" ("Eloisa to Abelard")—yet he omits the most obvious literary allusion: Juliet looking to Romeo's lips for the poison to send her to her death. Given the wild rhetoric of this letter as a whole ("If ever you should feel for Man at the first sight what I did for you, I am lost" [*KL*, 2:132]), it would be presumptuous to consign even the most flamboyant expression of *liebestod* from Keats either to the realm of pure metaphoric flight or to the depths of inarticulable desire.

As the "Ode on Melancholy" is able to imagine suicide without hysteria, self-loathing, or any of the usual symptoms of an internally directed sadism, and is also able to describe, with comparable equanimity, a personal destruction brought about by impersonal, inexorable forces, the poem exceeds the economy of "Mourning and Melancholia," a text that is governed by Freud's commitment to the priority of the "life-instincts" and the ego. While the ego-centered vocabulary of "Mourning and Melancholia" would suggest that the symptom of self-loathing is only partly repressed in the "Ode on Melancholy" and that it finally emerges in the poem's closing image of annihilation, which fulfills the melancholic's "delusional expectation of punishment" (244), the more eccentric economy outlined in "Beyond the Pleasure Principle" offers terms that would categorize the ode's conclusion neither as a "punishment" nor as the idiosyncratic and aberrant desire of the masochist. If, as Freud suggests in this later essay, the "goal of all life is death," then the conclusion of the "Ode on Melancholy" would be a quintessential moment of poetic closure, where the dialectical forces of sensuous intensity and objective inexorability come to a perfect consummation. As this dialectic spans the poem as a whole, the "Ode on Melancholy" reads very well as an expression of the "oscillating rhythm" that Freud describes in "Beyond the Pleasure Principle" as operating throughout "the life of organisms": "One group of instincts rushes forward so as to reach the final aim of life as swiftly as possible . . . the other group jerks back to a certain point to make a fresh start and so prolong the journey" (41).

The ode's dialectic opposes the inevitability of what will/shall/must occur by hurling itself into the sensuality of glut/rave/feed/burst, but it also frames this oscillation within an arc that extends from the avoidance of suicide ("neither twist Wolf's-bane") to the annihilation by Melancholy ("among her cloudy trophies hung"). The narrative economy of the entire text thus corresponds to the broadest "economic" terms of "Beyond the Pleasure Principle": "The instincts of self-preservation . . . are component instincts whose function it is to assure that the organism shall follow its own path to death, and to ward off any possible ways of returning to inorganic existence other than those which are immanent in the organism itself. . . . the organism wishes to die only in its own fashion. Thus these guardians of life, too, were originally the myrmidons of death" (39). "Beyond the Pleasure Principle" suggests that one could indeed exult in the poem's final image of annihilation, and that the standard form of the paraphrase of the poem's statement of the theme of mutability—the realistic advice that transience must be accepted as a necessary condition of beauty—should be reversed so as to say that the desire to be overwhelmed by beauty is itself a subordinate form of the desire for a final consummation.

Reading the "Ode on Melancholy" through "Beyond the Pleasure Principle" thus substitutes one primal economy for another, replacing Freud's previous assumption that suicide would ordinarily be avoided out of a primary narcissism, an "immense self-love of the ego," with the premise of a homeostatic desire for quiescence so powerful that it overrides the self-interest of the ego. Yet "Beyond the Pleasure Principle" itself vacillates among forceful expressions of absolute confidence in the scientific basis of its biological thesis, moments of severe doubt about that thesis ("far-fetched speculation," Freud calls it at one point [24]), and poignant expressions of regret for what is lost under the pressure of its own analytic procedure. The moments of thematic contradiction in the essay correspond to shifts in Freud's representation of his own subject-position, as he changes from his habitual use of the clinical *wir* to the highly personal use of *ich*, then returns to *wir* in the essay's conclusion, in which *wir* becomes at least as much a plural, communal reference as it is a professional credential. In the middle of the essay, a distancing of the "I" (*ich*, *mir*) from the collective "us" (*uns*) accompanies the forceful assertion of the material irrefutability of the essay's thesis:

> It may be difficult, too, for many of us, to abandon the belief that there is an instinct to perfection at work in human beings. . . . I have no faith, however, in the existence of any such internal instinct and cannot see how this benevolent illusion is to be preserved. The present development of human beings requires, as it seems to me, no different explanation from that of animals. ("Beyond," 42)[4]

Yet Freud is also willing to confess the fallibility of this "I":

> One might ask me whether and how far I am myself convinced of the truth of the hypotheses that have been set out in these pages. My answer would be that I am not convinced myself and that I do not seek to persuade other people to believe in them. More precisely: I do not know how far I believe in them. ("Beyond," 59)[5]

The essay ends on a very different note, one that folds the caustic and agnostic *ich* within the communal and historical *wir*. "Man" is told that he "must be patient," and must find some solace for the unpredictable vicissitudes of scientific inquiry in the abiding truths of literary and religious traditions: "We may take comfort, too, for the slow advance of our scientific knowledge in the words of the poet: 'What one cannot reach flying, one must reach limping . . . / The Scripture tells us it is no sin to limp'" ("Beyond," 64).[6] As "Beyond the Pleasure Principle" concludes with the restoration of the speaking *wir*, it recoups the very themes—the teleological progress of knowledge, the wisdom of sacred books, and the consolation of belief—that had been so categorically dismissed by the *ich* in the course of the essay. The essay's close enacts the process of the repetition-compulsion it describes; its closing poetic citation from Ruckert is the same passage that Freud had quoted in a letter to Fliess twenty-five years earlier ("Beyond," 64), and its shifting pronouns put into play the problematics of subject-position that Freud describes at the outset of the essay, where he acknowledges the inadequacy of the scientific discourse of the analyst to bring about a cure. Analytic practice based upon "an art of interpreting," in which the analyst could simply "discover the unconscious material that was concealed from the patient, put it together, and, at the right moment, communicate it to him," does not, Freud admits, produce the desired result: that "what was unconscious should become conscious." It creates "no sense of conviction" in the patient, who is "obliged to repeat the repressed material as a contemporary experience instead of, as the physician would prefer to see, remembering it as something belonging to the past" ("Beyond," 18). Such a repetition occurs in "Beyond the Pleasure Principle" itself, as the text is displaced from the level of the analyst to that of the analysand. In order to so thoroughly revise his own theories, Freud acknowledges that it has become necessary to "throw oneself [einem] into a line of thought and to follow it wherever it leads" (59), a procedure that follows the lines of the "talking cure."

Freud's essay ends by asserting that it has overcome the difficulties it has discovered. It promises the hermeneutic value of a regression to a previous state, where repetition can become the means of the unveiling of truth, and where every unveiling can create a future that will be different from the past, both in analytic practice and in the history of ideas—both "therapeutic success" (19) and "slow advances of our scientific knowledge" (64) can, Freud assures us, take place. The "Ode on Melancholy" begins with its speaker in the position of the analyst, the one who is capable of offering advice to someone else suffering the effects of melancholy, yet over the course of the text, this counselor falls within the grip of the very condition that had afflicted his patient. Enacting the process of repetition, the ode enters into the melancholic state that it describes, but it offers no clear avenue of escape from either repetition or melancholy, neither through ironic detachment nor through a narrative of forward progress.

Freud's discovery that ideas, however true, come to carry "a sense of conviction" to an analysand only through the awakening of personal, associative memory echoes Keats's recognition that poetry works when it achieves a sense of repetition: "it should strike the Reader as a wording of his own highest thoughts, and appear almost a Remembrance" (KL, 1:238). Occurring repeatedly in Keats's letters is the notion that "axioms in philosophy are not axioms until they are proved upon our pulses" (1:279), an idea that acknowledges the necessary reinforcement of cognition by affect. The two most common avenues that Keats cites for turning axioms into convictions are the sense of beauty ("what the imagination seizes as Beauty must be truth—whether it existed before or not" [1.184]; "I never can feel certain of any truth but from a clear perception of its Beauty" [2.19]), and prior personal experience: "We read fine——things but never feel them to thee [*sic*] full until we have gone the same steps as the Author" (1:279).

Keats is particularly prone in the case of Wordsworth to a sense of following in a previous author's footsteps. The letter that compares "human life to a large Mansion of Many Apartments" describes Wordsworth as having come to a second stage of life, in which he explores the "dark passages" that flow from a contemplation of the "burden of the mystery," and Keats promises Reynolds, "Now if we live, and go on thinking, we too shall explore them" (1:281). A year later, Keats cited (and slightly misquoted) lines from Wordsworth's "Immortality Ode," "Nothing can bring back the hour / Of splendour in the grass and glory in the flower," in a letter to Sarah Jeffrey, adding the reflective comments that "the world has taken on a quakerish look with me, which I once thought was impossible," and, of Wordsworth's lines, "I once thought this a Melancholist's dream" (2:113; May 1819). These comments suggest that Keats, even though he fully expected to follow Wordsworth's trail, was surprised when he discovered that he could no longer distance himself from a sense of irremediable loss, nor apply the term "Melancholist" as a categorical dismissal of someone else's morbidity. In another letter to Jeffrey, Keats expanded on his better-known comment that "Shakspeare led a life of Allegory; his works are the comments on it" (2:67; February 1819): "The middle age of Shakspeare was all c[l]ouded over; his days were not more happy than Hamlet's who is perhaps more like Shakspeare himself in his common every day Life than any other of his Characters" (2:115–16; June 1819). Whether or not this observation is true about Shakespeare and Hamlet, it certainly argues a strong identification on Keats's part with the melancholy character of Hamlet (whom Freud also sees as the classic melancholic ["Mourning," 246]), and an equally strong conviction that an author's life and work are inseparable.

When Keats places the theme of the necessary connection between lived experience and thematic comprehension into the "Ode on Melancholy," he produces the poem's final strained pronominal usage:

> Ay, in the very temple of Delight
> Veil'd Melancholy has her sovran shrine,
>   Though seen of none save him whose strenuous tongue
> Can burst Joy's grape against his palate fine.

The first word of these lines, "Ay," suggests a moment of recollection on the part of the speaker, as his train of thought leads to a once familiar truth— "Ay" as "Yes, that's right." The recognition is not communicated in a dialogic division of counselor and melancholic but is reexperienced by the poem's speaker as a present reality. The ensuing statement, that the perception of Melancholy is reserved for a select few, joined to the fact that the figure making this statement is able to describe the conditions under which this perception is possible, leads to the inevitable deduction that the poem's persona, its implicit "I," possesses the requisite knowledge for this perception, and is in fact a member of this select group. The phrase "none save him" is thus not really a third-person reference but a restrictive first-person plural, meaning "those of us," and the lines should, properly, read "Though seen of none save *we* whose strenuous tongues / Can burst Joy's grape against *our* palates fine."

Critics who have condemned the "Ode on Melancholy" as "decadent" and "unhealthy" have in effect recognized, but have refused to adopt, this subject-position, and the dynamic of Freud's ambivalent pronouns in "Beyond the Pleasure Principle" indicates why they have done so. When Freud predicts that "many of us" will cling to the "benevolent illusion" that "all that is most precious in human civilization" is the result of a spiritual force, "an instinct towards perfection," yet insists that "I have no faith, however, in the existence of any such internal instinct," it is clear that *wir*, in Freud, is the representative of a subject-position with an investment in "all that is most precious in human civilization," while *ich* is a subject that has broken with the bonds of social cohesion. When Freud contends that the achievements of civilization do not demonstrate the existence of "an instinct towards perfection" but "can easily be understood as a result of [an] instinctual repression" ("Beyond," 42), this familiar Freudian principle carries an extra twist within the context of "Beyond the Pleasure Principle." In this essay, the primary instinct that is to be repressed for the sake of civil society is not sexuality or aggression, but the death instinct. One can ask—and it is a question highly pertinent to the "Ode on Melancholy"—whether it is actually a desire for death or simply a clear, unrepressed knowledge of personal mortality that interferes with a subject's identification with a social group, and with a correlative investment in the goals of a civilization that will exceed the experience of the individual.

Reading the "Ode on Melancholy" alongside the extended economy of instinct and repression offered by "Beyond the Pleasure Principle" suggests seeing the appearance of the second- and third-person pronouns *your* and *him*, rather than *my* and *we*, as symptoms of repression that, through displacement, keep the unbearable knowledge of death away from the conscious realization of the poem's speaker. The syntactic incongruities that result—the "peerless eyes" of "thy mistress," the vision of Melancholy that is "seen of none save him"—indicate the illusory quality of this displacement, and the poem's plot becomes the developing rapprochement of the first-person speaker and the inexorable forces he describes. This process of convergence reduces the speaker from the position of the analyst, the one who seemed to be capable of offering advice to someone else suffering the unfortunate effects of melancholy, to that of an analysand who, in the course of the talking cure, comes to the dual recognition of the inevitable fact of death and the ambivalent desire for it. To call this unveiling "decadent" and "unhealthy" simply reinstates the normative repression that refuses to confront this unveiling, a refusal upon which, as Freud contends, "all that is most precious in human civilization" is based.

To say that the economy of the death wish and the undoing of repression operate in the "Ode on Melancholy" still does not define the governing economy of the text, since the relation of these two structures within the poem does not seem to conform to the privilege that Freud accords to "economic" forces, which he calls "metapsychological," over the "dynamic." The unveiling of the inescapability of transience and of death in the ode appears to unfold out of its own momentum, not as a subordinate form of the expression of a true death wish. Yet even as the governing economy of the text eludes psychoanalysis, Freudian symptomatology can illuminate the affective charge of particular structures and images in this poem and can help to draw connections between the poem and the life of the poet. Freud's observation that repetitions "always have as their subject some portion of infantile sexual life" ("Beyond," 18), along with his identification of melancholia as a regression to the "oral or cannibalistic stage of libidinal development" ("Mourning," 249), suggests the specific resonance of the image of "feed deep, deep upon her peerless eyes"; the force of this entire scene becomes clearer when this decoding is coupled with Freud's suggestion that there is often a dynamic of revenge operating in repetition, such that "If a doctor looks down a child's throat or carries out some small operation on him, we may be quite sure that these frightening experiences will be the subject of the next game. . . . As the child passes over from the passivity of the experience to the activity of the game, he hands on the disagreeable experience to one of his playmates and in this way revenges himself on a substitute" ("Beyond," 17).

The "emprisoning" of the mistress's hand in "Melancholy" carries out the reversal—and the revenge—called for by Keats's "entrammelling" by Fanny Brawne. The scene should be particularly strongly motivated since Fanny Brawne was described by Keats as the cause of his original loss of autonomy, but once again the economic force that would propel the Freudian dynamic seems to be missing. The accusation of "cruelty" made, or at least suggested, in the letter does not seem to apply to the "mistress" as she is represented in the ode. Her "rich anger" is pure spectacle, and despite the hyperbolic intensity of the diction of these lines, the use of the second-person pronoun creates a partner for her who is only half participating in the scene, while the other half looks on with the alienated detachment of the melancholic. If Hamlet is for Keats (as he is for Freud) the exemplary figure of this disordered personality whose intellect distances him from the immediacy of affect, an allusion to Hamlet's visit to Ophelia, when "He took me by the wrist and held me hard" (2.1.86), may be meant to instance the alienation that this poem, through its exorbitant sensuality, is trying so hard to overcome.

While it is clear that the general economy of the "Ode on Melancholy" involves a relation of loss and value, the history of misleading paraphrase of the poem suggests the elusiveness of its calculation of that ratio. One complicating factor that has not been introduced into previous analyses of the poem is the potential relevance of the ambiguous valorization of "melancholy" in Keats's immediate cultural context. The perceived excessiveness of the ode's diction may well be a defiant response to the criticisms of *Endymion* in *Blackwood's*, the *Quarterly Review*, and the *British Critic*, which censured Keats for his use of "uncouth language" and the "gross slang of voluptuousness."[7] By placing the "uncouth" diction of "glut," "rave," and "burst" under the sign of Melancholy, Keats assimilates his social marginality to another, more legitimate position at an equal distance from the social mainstream, in the venerable disease of scholars and poets. Keats could associate melancholy not only with an English literary tradition that includes Shakespeare ("Why with Wordsworths 'Matthew with a bough of wilding in his hand' when we can have Jacques 'under an oak'" [*KL*, 1:224]), Burton ("of all other men, scholars are most subject to it" [*Anatomy*, 1:301]), Milton ("Il Penseroso"), and the eighteenth-century melancholic vogue (Porter, 96), but with Englishness itself. Melancholy had been identified, at least since George Cheyne's 1733 work *The English Malady*, as a particularly English affliction, and the phrasing of Keats's advice to the melancholic, in emphatic, monosyllabic verbs, accords with his decision to adopt the "northern" dialect of Chatterton, which he said offered the "true voice of feeling," as opposed to the Miltonic latinism which "cannot be written but i[n] the vein of art" (*KL*, 2:167, 212).

A recent study of the cultural production of the concept of melancholia suggests that this dynamic of recuperation, which distinguishes the prestigious male condition of melancholia from the common female disease of depression, has in fact been the dominant form in which the concept of melancholy has operated at least since Aristotle wondered why "all men who have become outstanding in philosophy, statesmanship, poetry or the arts are melancholic [atrabilious]?" (Schiesari, 15). Juliana Schiesari argues that "the *discourse* of melancholia legitimates that neurosis as culturally acceptable for particular men, whose eros is then defined in terms of a literary production based on the appropriation of a sense of lack" (15; Schiesari's emphasis). In Schiesari's account, the discourse of melancholia enables men to appropriate both a condition (that of lack) and an activity (that of mourning) that are conventionally assigned by patriarchy to women, and to reinvest them with a greater status as they are converted into male melancholia. To the degree that Keats's own sense of lack derived from his social marginality, indicated in his comment "My name with the literary fashionables is vulgar—I am a weaver boy to them" (2:186), and from his feeling that his freedom had been taken away by his desire for Fanny Brawne, this dynamic of recuperation is undoubtedly present in the "Ode on Melancholy."

As the ode both appropriates and valorizes the ambiguous position of the melancholic scholar/poet, it responds with some precision to the terms in which Keats is condemned by Lockhart in the *Blackwood's* review that identifies him with the "Cockney School of Poetry." Lockhart pretends to lament Keats's having fallen victim to the "melancholy effect" of a "Metromanie" (the French term for obsessive poetry writing) that has afflicted a class-based and gendered catalog of victims: "farm-servants," "unmarried ladies," "footmen," and "superannuated governess[es]." Lockhart's polemic against Keats becomes a defense not only of class and gender privileges but of the social standing of poetry and the preeminence of useful values. Contrasting these "fanciful dreaming tea-drinkers" with "*men of power*" (Lockhart's emphasis), Lockhart takes particular exception to Keats's "Sleep and Poetry" for its "long strain of foaming abuse against a certain strain of English Poets ... with Pope at their head," and he attributes Keats's invective to political motives, charging that these "men of power" were traduced by Keats because "they chose to be wits, philosophers, patriots, and poets, rather than to found the Cockney School of versification." Within his show of mock compassion for Keats, Lockhart notes his apothecary training and regrets that Keats's *metromanie* has caused him to forgo his middle-class destiny: "This young man appears to have received from nature talents of an excellent, perhaps even of a superior order—talents which, devoted to the purposes of any useful profession, must have rendered him a respectable, if not an eminent citizen."[8]

This advice to Keats to quit poetry and return to medicine has a dual political valence. It not only places poetry as an avocation above the reach of the middle class, but also restates a persistent Tory skepticism that the melancholic fashion, and the poetry that withdrew from the social world of "wits, philosophers and patriots," was an affected self-indulgence. As Johnson advised Boswell when the latter complained of feeling melancholy, "You are always complaining of melancholy, and I conclude from those complaints that you are fond of it. No man talks of that which he is desirous to conceal, and every man desires to conceal that of which he is ashamed. . . . make it an invariable and obligatory law to yourself, never to mention your own mental diseases; if you are never to speak of them you will think on them but little, and if you think little of them, they will molest you rarely" (Porter, 89). Johnson's observation that "no man talks of that which he is desirous to conceal" foreshadows Freud's suspicion that the extravagant self-loathing expressed by the melancholic is not entirely sincere. Melancholics, Freud notes, "are far from evincing towards those around them the attitude of humility and submissiveness that would alone befit such worthless people. On the contrary, they make the greatest nuisance of themselves, and always seem as though they felt slighted and had been treated with great injustice" ("Mourning," 248). Keats's response in the "Ode on Melancholy" to *Blackwood's* attempt to reassimilate him to his proper place in the middle class is not only to adopt a persona who flaunts his "uncouth language," but also to place that persona in the ambiguously aristocratic and/or demimonde circles of those with mistresses rather than wives. The relatively glamorous picture of the mistress with her "peerless eyes" is an overdetermined moment in the ongoing feud between the Keats-Hunt circle and *Blackwood's*. Keats had complained bitterly about *Blackwood's* slur that Hunt's "poetry is that of a man who has kept company with kept-mistresses" and about the further insult that "The very concubine of so impure a wretch as Leigh Hunt would be to be pitied, but alas! for the wife of such a husband!"⁹ Keats deplored what he saw as an insult not only to Leigh Hunt but also to Mrs. Hunt when he wrote to Bailey, "I never read anything so virulent—accusing him of the greatest Crimes—dep[r]eciating his Wife his Poetry" (*KL*, 1:180).

The glamorized literary valorization of the "mistress" in "Melancholy" undercuts the hypocritical prudery of *Blackwood's*, but it also exposes Keats's own guilty participation in the ambiguous valorization of "mistresses." Keats's disdain for bourgeois respectability complicated his passion for Fanny Brawne, a conflict that led him into the fantasy of dying for love: "I look not forward with any pleasure to what is call'd being settled in the world; I tremble at domestic cares—yet for you I would meet them, though if it would leave you the happier I would rather die than do so. I have two luxuries to brood over in my walks, your Loveliness and the hour of my death. O that I could take possession of them both in the same minute" (*KL*, 2:133). The flamboyant posturing of the persona in the "Ode on Melancholy" who adopts the roles of sage, lover, martyr, and rake bears out Schiesari's observation that the male melancholic "stands both in reaction to and in complicity with patriarchy" (14). When the "Ode on Melancholy" grants every personal pronoun it uses except the third-person feminine the status of a universal subject-position, it becomes complicit with patriarchy in leaving traditional gender identifications intact. But Schiesari's account of loss converted to social status, if applied straightforwardly to Keats's ode, would produce an economy of ultimate gain, a conclusion that does not accord with the poem's closing image. The most profound lack in "Melancholy" derives neither from social censure nor from the entrammelling or the overwhelming of the ego in love, but from the melancholic's sense of the instability of value—its arbitrariness and its mutability.

The "Ode on Melancholy" defiantly returns to the "gross slang of voluptuousness" that had brought scorn upon *Endymion*, but it also revises Keats's own premises in that poem. The assertion "She dwells with Beauty—Beauty that must die / And Joy whose hand is ever at his lips / Bidding Adieu" is a profound revision of the aphoristic opening of *Endymion*—A thing of beauty is a joy for ever." While Schiesari illustrates how men are enabled to convert loss into prestige precisely because there is a tradition within which they can place their angst, so that "the symbolic, or Law of the Father, indeed provides for men a discourse that ensures the positive representation of their loss" (68), Keats's resistance to the values of "men of power" leaves him in a deeply divided relation to the dominant symbolic order of his culture. The inability of the ode's persona to sustain the analyst's position and to speak, finally and definitively, as the "we" through which Freud expresses professional confidence and communal purpose marks the ambivalence of Keats's relation to patriarchal power. As de Man suggests, ideology always takes the form of a promise (*Allegories*, 146–77), and the gradual erosion, over the course of the "Ode on Melancholy," of the opening effect of authority exposes the fraudulence of the promises made by a patriarchal symbolic order to the most privileged of its citizens. As a symbolic order privileges a subject-position (such as male), it calls for a reciprocal endorsement of its value. The melancholic's willingness to consider that "if we could foretel what was to come, and it put to our choyce, we should rather refuse, than accept of, this painful life (Burton, 1:156–57) questions the reassurances of ideology at the most fundamental level—the level at which it promises that any activity is better than none at all.

A thorough understanding of the "Ode on Melancholy" needs to address all of the contradictory structures the poem encompasses: a death wish alongside the gradual dismantling of the repression of the threatening knowledge of mortality; a pose of erudition that defends the ego against its engulfment either by passion or by death, alongside a passionate sensuality that tries to overcome the loss of affect brought about by reflective detachment; and a deliberate flouting of standards of literary decorum that coexists with a stance of affiliation to a venerable literary tradition. A comprehensive reading of the poem could begin by pointing out what the ode does not contain; there is no trace of the commonsensical advice, given to Boswell by Johnson and to Keats by Tory reviewers, to turn away from melancholic self-absorption and take up the burden of social responsibility. Freud judges that the necessary precondition for melancholia is an excessive narcissism; otherwise, the disappointed cathexis would simply, and normally, be replaced onto another object rather than returning to the subject's own ego. Given the concentration of narcissistic energy in the poem's central scene ("if thy mistress some rich anger shows"), Lacanian terms would suggest that the poem remains fixated in the mirror stage, and fails to proceed to the next stage in the "normal" construction of the ego: the deflection of the specular to the social "I." Interpreting this fixation through a psychobiographical signified—the death of Keats's father when Keats was eight years old—only reinstates the supposition of the normalcy of the oedipal narrative. The ode's persistent refusal of mediation, manifested in its insistence on the most intense sensuality and on the inexorable power of forces beyond human control, points toward a position that, however male-identified, is located outside the "normal," oedipal process of subject formation.

The greatest difficulty in paraphrasing the "Ode on Melancholy" arises not simply from the multiplicity of its themes, but also from the question that in traditional literary criticism is called point of view, and that post-structuralism has come to call subject-position. The most sympathetic readings of the poem that attempt to register the melancholic depth of its sense of loss repeatedly reestablish a stable point of view on a poem that ends with the overwhelming of the subject-position that has produced the text. Although Barbara Herrnstein Smith argues strongly that the poem's persona should not be identified with John Keats, she withholds no authority from that persona as she describes the ode's initial dialogue as an address to a "novitiate knight embarking on a quest for Melancholy," in which "The speaker addresses him from a position of superior knowledge and speaks with all the authority and bitterness of his wisdom" (690). Harold Bloom grants the poem itself the full measure of "superior knowledge," although he locates that wisdom in the "it" of the text rather than in the "he" of the speaker: "The magnificence of the *Ode on Melancholy*'s final stanza is in its exactness of diction as it defines the harmony of continued apprehension of its unresolved contraries" (*Visionary*, 435). And Haverkamp's reading of the poem continues this interpretive tradition as the trope of irony is given the ability to confer the status of permanence on this "continued apprehension"; "irony," Haverkamp writes, "establishes a permanent movement that postpones indefinitely while wittingly keeping alive the dangerous impact of the postponed" (203). Using different nominal vehicles of agency (a persona, a text, a trope), these readings accomplish the same three things: they establish the source of melancholy in objective circumstances, rather than in the "morbid temperament" of the melancholic; they confer a tragic stature on the subject who confronts these "dangerous" circumstances; and they overcome the potential impact of that danger as they identify this subject with an immutable wisdom.

As Susan Wolfson has argued, there is a good deal at stake in this standard valorization of a Keats ode. When an ode is credited with the mastery of both thematic depth and formal representation through the vehicle of an impersonal poetics, the poem becomes capable of ratifying the values of "that tradition of literary criticism that views the function of poetic form as one of controlling and ordering the emotional content of poetry" ("Composition," 59). This poetics, which is as old as Plato's imagery of the chariot

driver and his recalcitrant horse in the *Phaedrus*, Wolfson sees coming undone in Keats's last lyrics to Fanny Brawne, both from the sheer force of the
passion that pushes against the constraints of poetic form and from the
effect of formal experiments that lead to "a vision of a world in which all
forms of restraint are revealed to be artificial and unstable" (73–74). While
the most sympathetically melancholic readings of the "Ode on Melancholy"
continue to reassimilate the poem to the story of the transcendence of the
human spirit, in impersonal dignity if not in person, over forces that produce transience and loss, the poetics that Wolfson discovers in the late lyrics, in which "lovers and poems alike remain vulnerable to the radical inse-
curities of experience" and to "the uncertain transformations of poetic
form" (80–81), can actually produce a more interesting and authentic "Ode
on Melancholy" than those readings that restore its impersonal authority.

The solipsistic texture of this poem describes a life that is lived in the
first-person singular and not as a role in the gregarious advance of intellect,
and it unfolds from a perspective that does not survive the processes of
discovery and consummation that constitute the text. The naming of this
introspective focus as "narcissism" can itself create a misleading origin for
analysis. Only the premise that an "I" is an irreducible epicenter, or "body-
ego," secures the premise that the poem's second- and third-person pronouns should be read as displaced representations of an ego whose narcissism is the necessary "primal state from which instinctual life proceeds"
(Freud, "Mourning," 252). When the poem begins with a second- rather
than a first-person pronoun, the superficial absence of the poem's speaker
could indicate a primary absence rather than a displacement, a lack that
opens the ode to a less ego-centered narrative of the coming into being of
the subject than can be told within an economy of instinct, ego, and repression. The confusion of the ego with a second person who has come to form
part of the ego-ideal is, as Freud suggests, a necessary element in the condition of melancholia, yet this confusion of self and other is actually a truth
about the contingency of the subject, who is more truly a bundle of
identifications than a primal unity. Keats's attempts in his letters to conceive
of a subject that is neither simply the effect of deterministic circumstances
nor an essential being is more allegorical than technical, but it is also less
circumscribed than psychoanalytic presumptions of the determinism of infantile experience would allow:

> Do you not see how necessary a World of Pains and troubles is to school
> an Intelligence and make it a soul?

... I began by seeing how man was formed by circumstances— ... what was his soul before it came into the world and had These provings and alterations and perfectionings?—An intelligence—without Identity— and how is this Identity to be made? Through the medium of the Heart? And how is the heart to become this Medium but in a world of Circum- stances?" (2:102–4; April 1819)

Keats offers this theory as an alternative to the Christian equation of iden- tity and the "arbitary [*sic*] interposition" (2:102) of a soul, but by posing the idea of an "identity" that arises from no essential origin, Keats opens up a familiar thesis, that suffering is good for building character, to the problem- atic effects of melancholy. Keats's repetitions of the word "circumstances" in his letters of 1819 link passages that unfold a confusion between inner and outer worlds, and in this confusion the attempt to discover objective laws of probability or necessity proves indistinguishable from the repeti- tions of a personal obsession. "Circumstances" can be "like Clouds continu- ally gathering and bursting," whose rain nurtures "a poison fruit which we must pluck" (2:79; March 1819), and, if one ends up a little "suspicious," "given to bode ill like the raven," it becomes impossible to tell whether this results from a victimization by "the general tenor of the circumstances of my life" (2:129; July 1819) or from a weakness for "imaginary grievances" (2:181; September 1819). "Identity," or character, may be "formed by cir- cumstances," Keats's letters suggest, but it might also be ruined by them.

This indecision appears in the "Ode on Melancholy" in the ambivalent relation between the poem's speaking subject and the knowledge that the poem unfolds. The ode is generally read as though it emanates from a uni- fied subject whose authoritative voice at the poem's outset indicates his fore- knowledge of the image of annihilation with which the text will conclude. The continuity of this subject's knowledge is, however, explicitly called into question by the gesture of recollection in line 25 ("Ay"), a gesture that indi- cates not only that the idea under recollection is familiar but also that it has been temporarily forgotten, and that the speaker is only now emerging from the state of forgetting. The authoritative effect of the opening lines can also be questioned on other grounds. Although the speaker claims to be able to offer advice to someone else suffering the effects of melancholy, throughout most of the first stanza his knowledge of melancholy seems to originate in Burton, Milton, or Shakespeare and not in actual experience. The first seven lines are a tour de force that shows off his verbal ingenuity in putting his learning to poetic effect, but this show of wit sputters out in the stanza's conclusion: "For shade to shade will come too drowsily, / And drown the wakeful anguish of the soul." The plainness and the mere repetition of "shade to shade" suggest a sudden loss of inventiveness, while the next repetition, the phonetic echo of "drowsily/drown," conveys an even deeper sense of a loss of premeditation and of the secure distance between the speaking voice and the condition for which he prescribes remedies to another. The cure itself, "wakeful anguish," seems paradoxically no more desirable than the disease, even as the hard (technically, "plosive") consonants /k/ and /g/ summon a wakening resistance against the phonetic slide into a quiescent stupor.

The convergence between the inescapable forces identified by the text and the position of the poem's speaker becomes evident in the closing line of the first stanza, in the substitution of the article *the* where anaphoric consistency would call for the possessive adjective *your*, so that "shade to shade" is said to come to "*the* soul," rather than to "*your* soul." Both the flat diction and the increasing implication of the speaker into the melancholic condition continue into the first line of the second stanza, when, again, "the," rather than "your," "melancholy fit shall fall." The growing proximity of melancholy to the poem's speaker is marked in these lines by the absence of the flamboyant figuration that fills the first stanza. Figuration returns in its simplest and most deliberate form, the simile of "like a weeping cloud," but this figure immediately reproduces the confusion of disease and cure; as a figure for melancholy itself, it produces the inevitable and appropriate rhyme "shroud," but as metaphoric vehicle it also produces the "droop-headed flowers" that, as they mutate into "globed peonies," are offered as an antithesis to the gray monotony of melancholy. When the second-person pronoun reappears just as the speaker turns from a description of melancholy itself to a new set of instructions for how to combat it, "Then glut *thy* sorrow on a morning rose," it is clear that this "second person" functions as a means of asserting both authority and immunity from danger on the part of the poem's speaking subject. The ambivalence of his relation to melancholy, marked by the show of erudition that represents melancholy as a mere literary pose and by the attribution of its dangers to someone else, suggests a speaker who has not yet learned the personal relevance of the imagery that is borrowed from the letter of March 1819, where "circumstances are like clouds continually gathering and bursting" and ultimately producing "a poison fruit which we must pluck" (2:79). The quick proliferation of potential sensuous responses to the threat of melancholic indolence, "Or on the rainbow of the salt sand-wave, / Or on the wealth of globed peonies," suggests a speaking subject who has a normal mobility of cathexis, a true nonmelancholic who is able thoroughly to forget one libidinal invest-ment in order to reinvest in another. This subject, who is still partly capable of believing that melancholy is something that occurs in books or in some-one else's life, and that the loss that provokes it can be overcome by turning to a new object of desire, is a subject who has not gone through all the "provings and alterations" that turn an "Intelligence" into an "Identity." He is comparable to the subject who could call "Nothing can bring back the hour / Of splendour in the grass, of glory in the flower" someone else's mistake, a "Melancholist's dream."

The temporary slippages from "your" to "the," and the increasing inten-sity and sensual specificity of the responses that are urged so as to combat the melancholy fit, indicate the uneasy glimmerings in the speaker's con-sciousness of the familiarity of the melancholic condition, an ambivalent recollection that situates melancholy on the unstable Freudian border of the *heimlich/unheimlich* (canny/uncanny). The pronominal ambiguities that register this ambivalence lead the speaker into the syntactic trap of attribut-ing "peerless eyes" to "thy mistress," as the discontinuity between his pre-sumption of authority and the location of a need for remediation some-where else stretches the form of his enunciation beyond paraphrasable iteration. Yet paraphrastic meaning is regularly restored in critical readings of the poem by the implicit assimilation of the two figures of this dialogue, the authoritative "I" and the lacking "you," to a single, universal subject-position. When the lacking "you" is given precedence in determining the referential status of the speaking subject, the poem is accused of decadence. When, as is more common, the speaker's stance of authority is given prior-ity in the poem and assumed in critical commentary, discursive control is reasserted over the potentially dangerous encroachments of melancholy. The cures (sensualism, realism, irony) proposed by the poem are presumed to be adequate to the disease, and the poem's theme is explicated as an asser-tion that the experience of beauty is an adequate compensation for the knowledge of transience. While this assertion is commonly offered as a holistic summary of the poem, its status as a cultural convention that pro-tects "all that is most precious in human civilization" from the morbidity of melancholy, rather than as an explication of Keats's text, can be confirmed by the fact that there is no particular passage in the poem that endorses this judgment.

The critical treatment of the poem's pronouns as functionally equivalent representations of a universal subject-position would not surprise the authors of the most recent major study of pronouns in English, who observe that it is a common practice for linguists to describe pronouns as though they were simply neutral substitutes for nouns, or, in linguistic terms, to concentrate on the anaphoric aspects of pronouns to the virtual exclusion of their deictic functions (Muhlhauser and Harré, 13). This focus, Peter Muhlhauser and Rom Harré contend, allows the pronoun forms of Standard Average European languages to perpetuate the Western sense of selfhood, Judeo-Christian in origin and codified by Descartes, which constructs an "I" formed as an internal reciprocity of individual responsibility and conceptual mastery—a subject that is, essentially, the opposite of an object (88–89). Comparing the deictic functions performed by pronouns in non-Western and in SAE languages, Muhlhauser and Harré observe that pronoun usage in many non-Western languages, such as Japanese, shows a much higher degree of overt group indexicality. They note that while "almost without exception the responsible author of a Japanese speech act is a group for which the utterer is but a spokesman or woman" (31), the most common example in SAE discourse of group indexicality occurs through the inflation of the metaphysical "I" into a voice of universal authority that Muhlhauser and Harré call the "academic 'we'." This form, which occurs in the Freudian *wir,* establishes both the authority of the speaker and the complicity of the listeners, leading Muhlhauser and Harré to argue that "in the innocent use of *we* a narrative convention rather than a purely rhetorical device is at work" (130; emphasis in original). This research is consistent with the position established by Jakobson when he contradicts those linguists who consign pronouns to the "most elementary and primitive stratum of languages." Jakobson argues that pronouns are "on the contrary, a complex category where code and message overlap," and he observes that this complexity actually puts pronouns among the latest acquisitions in child language and the earliest losses in aphasia. This complexity is exemplified in the anecdote of the child who attempts to master the overlap of code and message by issuing the edict, "'Don't dare call yourself I. Only I am I, and you are only you'" (2:132–33).

The complexity of pronouns derives from their status as indexical symbols, or shifters. An ordinary noun has its referential status fixed by linguistic code, and it refers to the same set of objects no matter which objects are present when the word is said, but the referent of "I" depends entirely on who says it. The pronoun is thus the quintessential example of Lacan's challenge to "the illusion that the signifier answers to the function of representing the signified, or better, that the signifier has to answer for its existence in the name of any signification whatever" (*Ecrits*, 150). The child who insists that "Only I am I" enacts the metaphoric crossing of the bar between the signifying pronoun and a sense of essential inner being; the fact that she does so only by imposing an arbitrary stability on the incessant sliding of signifiers and signifieds is apparent to those who have mastered the concept of indexicality, but what is less apparent to the ordinarily competent speaker of a language is that this imposition is the condition of iterable meaning. The dependence of language upon convention rather than mimesis is the basis of Lacan's revision of the Saussurean diagram that shows the signifier *tree* paired with a drawing of a tree. As Lacan points out, this pairing leaves the singularly dyadic form of the sign intact, and Lacan proposes instead to represent the relations of signifiers and signifieds by means of two identical drawings of doors, over which we find the signifiers "Ladies" and "Gentle-men." Lacan's diagram shows how the dyadic form of the sign exists only as an effect of the "punctuation" accomplished in the crossing of the bar be-tween the sliding chains of signifiers and signifieds: "What this structure of the signifying chain discloses is the possibility I have, precisely in so far as I have this language in common with other subjects, that is to say, in so far as it exists as a language, to use it in order to signify *something quite other* than what it says" (*Ecrits*, 155; Lacan's emphasis).

Language can and does signify, for another subject, something other than what it literally says, because the crossing of the bar always invokes a com-mon property, that which the speaking subject has "in common with other subjects," a linguistic resource that Lacan suggests becomes most clear when listening to poetry (154). As poetry introduces a high degree of po-lyphony into a speech act, it suspends ordinary referential signification and demands a reader who is capable of constructing coherence at a level of complexity that supersedes the dictionary definitions of individual words (such as *ladies* and *gentlemen*); polyphony plays upon the "something quite other" that is codified in the semiotic conventions of cultural usage. Saussure's premise, endorsed by Lacan, of the synchronic totality of a lan-guage offers the theoretical possibility of a mastery of the code that would amount to the mastery of all interpretive situations. As Lacan puts it, "there is no language (*langue*) in existence for which there is any question of its inability to cover the whole field of the signified, it being an effect of its existence as a language (*langue*) that it necessarily answers all needs" (*Ecrits*, 150). This closure of the "whole field of the signified" imposes no theoreti-cal limit on the authority of an "academic 'we'" to function as the spokesper-son for "all needs." But even the highest degree of linguistic competence is challenged when an entire speech act acquires the highly indexical quality of a pronoun—that is, when the "something quite other" that it speaks is no longer fully interpretable by reference to the code that "answers all needs," but takes on a particular, situational resonance that can be recognized only by those who have personal associations with the necessary contextual material.

The tension between the polyphonic and ultimately highly indexical quality of the "Ode on Melancholy" and the interpretive demand for iterative meaning has produced the history of misleading paraphrase of the poem. The language of the poem becomes literally unparaphrasable through its exploitation of pronouns as shifters, yet thematic coherence is reestablished through the critical production of a unified subject-position that purports to speak for the "whole field of the signified" that the poem represents. As Keats's critics defend the intellectual authority of his work, they assert the therapeutic value of his themes by producing a "detachment from [the] experience" (Haverkamp, 700) of the merely metonymic linearity and narcissistic self-absorption of the talking cure. When this reimposition of discursive authority becomes most overt, as in the insistence that the word "She" that opens the poem's third stanza refers "not [to] the 'mistress,' but Melancholy itself" (Perkins, *English*, 1254), the hortatory tone of the footnote indicates the problem with this authoritative assertion. Every linguistically competent English speaker initially hears, in the "She" of line 21, a reference to the "mistress" of line 18. By identifying the antecedent for the pronoun "She" as a noun that occurs five lines after, rather than one that occurs three lines before, the pronoun itself, critical commentary replaces this ordinarily competent linguistic subject, whose primary focus is on indexical clues, with a more masterful figure—an analyst whose diagnostic powers comprehend, in advance, the poem's every foray. "You" become the generic *you*, a universal subject who always already knows all you need to know about Beauty, Joy, Pleasure, Delight, and Melancholy, and who is immune from any surprise that could emerge within the temporality of the text.

The "Ode on Melancholy" reflects a different subjectivity, one that is carried along by the shift in imagery from the sensory objects of the second stanza to the allegory of sensations in the third. A transition from a scene that thoroughly absorbs the poem's speaker to a reflection upon its ephemerality is consistent with Keats's practice in other odes of 1819, and there is a consistent linguistic texture to these transitions, which leap from immediate linguistic presence to heretofore unrecognized thematic implications.

In the "Ode on a Grecian Urn," the last word of the penultimate stanza ("return"), as it triggers the reminder of the "urn," interrupts the speaker's reverie on his own imaginary scene, and in the "Ode to a Nightingale," the repetition of the word "forlorn" marks the removal of the speaker from the "faery lands" of "alien corn" and "perilous seas" back to the "near meadow" and the "still stream." In the transition from "her peerless eyes" to "She dwells with Beauty—Beauty that must die," the instigating linguistic property is not primarily phonetic presence (despite eye/die); rather, it is the recognition of the arbitrary relation between material presence ("eyes") and value ("peerless"-ness), a relation which, as it passes through a supposed instantiation ("her") that would join the material signifier to its conceptual value, instead reveals the merely conventional nature of the joining of these terms in the clichéd and fictional figure of "thy mistress." The ensuing phrase "She dwells with Beauty" was originally written "She lives in beauty," a possibly unconscious echo of Byron's "She walks in Beauty," and the revision has not entirely done away with the near echo that threatens to reduce Keats's "She" to a repetition of another "She" likewise remarkable for her eyes. The linguistic presence of a pun (peerless = sightless) must be repressed if the idealization is to be taken at all seriously, but the volume of literary associations that flock to the word "mistress" and the impossibility of an actual subject-position who could attribute a transcendent value to this particular "She," "*thy* mistress," contribute to the undoing of the iconic value that this scene tries so strenuously to construct.

The increasing self-consciousness of the poem's speaker in the final stanza as he relinquishes the iconic value of "thy mistress" seems at first to confirm Freud's most succinct observation about the difference between mourning and melancholia, that whereas in mourning "there is nothing about the loss that is unconscious," the melancholic "knows *whom* he has lost but not *what* he has lost in him" ("Mourning," 245; Freud's emphases). The content of this "what," although initially obscure to both the melancholic and the analyst, becomes clear in Freud's contention that melancholia is caused not by the actual loss of another person to death but by the loss of a part of the self that had been represented by an other who functioned as an ego-ideal. The path of hermeneutic progress seems to be clearly laid out for the subject of the ode to follow, moving from infantile dependence and illusory idealization to a more realistic and autonomous ego position, in accord with Freud's contention that melancholia is cured when the ego is able to expel the introjected figure of the other. As the internalized hostility of the initially ambivalent love/hate cathexis is recathected onto an other clearly recognized as other, Freud contends, "The ego may enjoy in this the satisfaction of knowing itself as the better of the two, as superior to the object" ("Mourning," 257). Yet this assumption of superiority never takes place in Keats's ode, and the poem never finds a cure for the condition of melancholy. Instead, the poem's early representations of inexorable forces that "will come" and "shall fall" are intensified as they pass through the female figure into "must die," an intensification that does not mark an increase in the degree of inevitability, which was never in question, but a heightening of regret regarding the inescapability of these forces. That this regret is not altruistic or focused on the fate of a female other is indicated by the immediate transferral of the status of victim from "She" to the male poetic subject, the exclusive community of the "none save him" whose "soul shall taste" this inescapable "sadness." Although the poem's final stanza constructs an implicit and valorized "we," the process through which this subject group is formed—through an analogy to the object status of the female victim—is entirely different from the construction of the "academic 'we'" through the inflation of a metaphysical nexus of individual responsibility and conceptual mastery into a figure of universal mastery, who assumes responsibility for the "whole field of the signified" of his cultural code.

The true coming into being of the subject of the "Ode on Melancholy" occurs in the drama of its pronouns as they pass from "thy" and "your" across "her" and "She" to "him" and "his." The inauthentic attribution of melancholy to someone else, a fictional second-person "you," can be discarded only after the highly theatrical scene that exposes the artificiality of the speaker's rakish pose and that delivers the poem into the dramatic, if not melodramatic, seriousness of the final stanza. The ode's closure acquires a tragic inevitability as it relinquishes the illusion of the sufficiency of homeostatic satisfaction promised in the second stanza; the poem finally acknowledges that desire is never really glutted, since even its consummation produces an unresolved excess, a byproduct, which this text names "melancholy." As the inescapability of loss is located in anticipation rather than in recollection, the "Ode on Melancholy" moves beyond even the most advanced recent psychoanalytic explorations of melancholia by Julia Kristeva, which, while they invert Freud's valorization of egoistic autonomy, continue to locate the impossibility of satisfaction in the inescapable memory of the loss of an "archaic attachment" to the first object of desire, the mother. After the dissolution of this primal bond, Kristeva writes, "the depressed person has the impression of having been deprived of an unnameable supreme good, of something unrepresentable, that perhaps only devouring might represent, or an invocation might point out, but no word could signify" (*Black Sun*, 13).

While the ode's images of devouring mark its deepest incursions into this primal economy, in the poem's final stanza neither the "what" that is lost nor the condition of loss itself seems to be at all inaccessible to the most direct and articulate representation. While Kristeva continues to represent the relation of loss and value in melancholy as a structure of exteriority, thus allowing for the possibility of a therapeutic solution in which one term would replace the other, Keats's ode suggests that value itself, "Pleasure," as opposed to a "peonie," is in not a contingent but an identitarian relation to loss; not only does the possibility of loss produce the differential out of which value emerges, but value is what produces both the possibility and the necessity of loss. This anticipatory perspective emerges in the change in the representative quality of the female figure in the poem. In the second stanza, she appears as a material, present object, introduced into the series of naturalistic figures in the stanza, and the degree of her objectification is marked by the fact that the stanza's closing metaphor continues the metaphor of consumption (glut/feed) that makes her available to the male poetic subject. The attempt to absorb this object into a controlled, predatory economy of idealization never quite takes hold, however, and "She" becomes, in the third stanza, not the embodiment of a consumable value but an exemplary representation of the principle of mutability. This latter objectification, although it falls short of the recognition of the other as a subject, is very different from a material objectification. The problem posed in the final stanza of the "Ode on Melancholy" is not the inability to represent an irretrievably lost object but the impossibility of evading the consequences of the economy of consumption that pervades the poem.

When this transitional scene, which marks a shift from a material economy of need to a symbolic economy of desire, is decoded as a regressive fantasy, even the most advanced psychoanalytic procedures eliminate the excessive productivity of imagination. Kristeva's translation of Freud's "who" and "what" into, respectively, "Object" and "Thing" makes melancholy explicable in terms of a straightforward referentiality: "The depressed narcissist mourns not an Object but the Thing. Let me posit the 'Thing' as the real that does not lend itself to signification, the center of attraction and repulsion, seat of the sexuality from which the object of desire will become separated" (13). In Freud's "what" and Kristeva's "Thing," psychoanalysis continues to look for the referent that causes melancholy, but if melancholy, like passion, exists precisely in the exceeding of any natural cause, then the genetic economy of psychoanalysis, far from providing the possibility of a cure or an antidote for melancholy, does not even accurately represent the reason for the melancholic condition. As Keats's ode shifts from naturalism and homeostatic closure to an allegorical level of figuration that describes the transience of the natural, the poem unfolds the replacement of presence by value characterized by Derrida, in his reading of Rousseau, as the economy of supplementarity. This supplementary movement beyond a state of nature, a state characterized by an "equilibrium between reserve and desire" (*Grammatology*, 185), produces both the need for representation and its inescapable artificiality. The gap between the material, natural world and the realm of representation determines Rousseau's decision to withdraw from the world in order to write and so present his "real value," while the same logic of the supplement also furnishes the terms for Rousseau's polemic against women for transforming "natural" sexual promiscuity into what Rousseau calls, in a rhetoric of hostility and with no acknowledgment of irony, "moral love" (183). Out of this profound ambivalence, Derrida identifies "two series working themselves out" throughout Rousseau's texts, series that refine Lacan's distinction between the level of need and the realm of desire. The first series progresses from the sensible to the intelligible through a clearly regulated, homeostatic pattern in which needs are identified and addressed: "(1) animality, need, interest, gesture, sensibility, understanding, reason, etc." As the second, supplementary series comes into existence, it, like melancholy, builds on itself, creates its own momentum, and continually pushes out of reach its own goals: "(2) humanity, passion, imagination, speech, liberty, perfectibility, etc." (183).

While this account of the shift from the materiality of need to the representative level of desire would be characterized by Freud as a regression to a dynamic, rather than an economic, account of the formation of melancholy, Derrida bridges the opposition between the material and the symbolic in his contention that the "master-name" of this latter series is "death" (183). Death determines the operation of this supplementary series both literally and figuratively: literally, since, as Rousseau contends, humans have become the only animals who anticipate their own deaths, this knowledge determines their temporal imaginations; and figuratively, since, as the supplement institutes both value and the subject through the imagining of difference, it also demands the forfeiture of presence in an unmediated, or fully natural, state, and it replaces material presences with representative substitutions. When sexuality becomes passion, it becomes entirely different from the animal satisfaction of a need.

This difference is, however, literally nothing, and when Rousseau tries to understand how "natural" sexuality becomes singularly focused under the sway of human passion, he comes to the perplexed realization that, in Derrida's terms, "One can never explain, in terms of nature and natural force, the fact that something like the difference of a *preference* might, without any force of its own, force force" (178; Derrida's emphasis). Keats flips from side to side of this alchemic transformation of sex into love; he writes, half-believing, of "her peerless eyes" even though he knows of nothing so "rediculous." Keats knows that his long quotation from Burton ("Every Lover admires his Mistress, though she be . . .") is true to the fact that peerlessness is as pure a shifter as any pronoun, even though as a perception it can punctuate the signifying chain with an intensity, as when Fanny Brawne walks into the room, that exceeds ordinary material sensations. While the second stanza of the "Ode on Melancholy" valorizes that intensity, it makes the mistake of imagining a position from which the "life-instincts" of sensuality could be endlessly gratified. This error is encouraged by a cultural order that provides identities, such as "men of power" and the "academic 'we'," through an identification with the culture itself as a universal subject. The second stanza of "Melancholy" ends by adopting for a moment such a stereotypical, fully interpellated identity, one that closely mirrors the pose of *Blackwood's* "wits, philosophers and patriots" for whom mistresses would be a status symbol of masculinity.

The recognition of the artificiality of that identity opens the gap between material need, which is satiable, and desire, which always points beyond itself in anticipation. De Man emphasizes Rousseau's use of a theatrical metaphor to describe the imaginary relations of those who have passed beyond the natural level of need. "What is here called language," de Man contends, "differs entirely from an instrumental means of communication: for that purpose, a mere gesture, a mere cry, would suffice" (*Blindness*, 131). While gestures and cries are, as de Man points out, highly efficient instruments of communication, their mimetic quality has nothing in common with the artificial and systematic representations of beings who have broken with the forces of natural determination. The imaginary relations of desire move, for better or worse, beyond the "entire field of the signified" of every *langue* or symbolic order, the function of which is to provide the illusion of its ability to "answer all needs." The liberal humanist conception of an antagonistic relation between autonomous egos and social cohesion is a fiction that the "Ode on Melancholy" never quite enters. Its inability to say either "I" or "we" is not a Freudian but a Lacanian version of the talking cure, in which discourse uncovers no secret trauma; rather, in its metonymic slide beneath both social censure and the ego, discourse brings to the surface what is furthest from the common knowledge of the social "we," yet is vastly oversimplified as the "drive."

The theatrical space of representation, which precludes direct communication, is also the improvisatory space of identity formation. The "Ode on Melancholy" plays at roles—counselor, rake, philosopher—that it sheds as it gropes toward something more real than such identities can offer. The single role that it is finally unable to surpass is that of the melancholic. The melancholic temper undoes the artificiality of each of the poem's socially authoritative identities, and the narcissistic melodrama of the third stanza gives the melancholic's sadness a theological significance even as it depicts melancholics as deeply antisocial and highly theatrical beings. Their inability to forget the difference that death will make leaves them incapable of moderating their desires to social norms, and their knowledge of the artificiality of social identities puts them always at a distance from the roles they play, even if they know that these roles are the only identities. In the assumption of identities, as the "Ode on Melancholy" shows, not even pronouns are innocent. The emergence of the "him" in the third stanza of the ode displaces the inauthentic "you" through an effect of analogy between "him" and the objectified "She," an analogy that subverts the speaker's imaginary relation of identification and competition with "men of power." This newly constructed universal subject acquires "his" tragic destiny after a double transference: When the metaphorical nothing that makes her "peerless" is said not to fade or pass but "die," the existential finality of the word "die" brings out the material difference that separates subjects from their social bonds and from each other. Derrida suggests that this inability to forget difference has an ethical value, providing the necessary ground of the recognition of the other as other, rather than leaving recognition to depend upon an economy of pity that operates through perceived likeness. As ethics passes not through natural "pity" but through the formal law of analogy of discrete objects that makes it universal, it is not restricted to those whom the subject feels "like." The "Ode on Melancholy," however, never returns the subject position to "her," and the poem's ethical immaturity lies not in its exorbitant sensuality but in its forgetting of "thy mistress," and in its inability to imagine an intersubjectivity on the other side of its theatrical space. But at least the poem does not ultimately assume the most common authorial identity, the pose of omniscience with which it began, nor succumb to the most common and debased form of intersubjectivity, that which takes place in the fiction of pure communication among equal and indistinguishable subjects contained within a closed field of the social signified.

Those who see the world from a melancholic half-distance of theatrical specularity, the "Ode on Melancholy" suggests, paradoxically live more intensely than the fully interpellated subjects, the "men of power" who live simply and wholeheartedly within the symbolic order. But it would be a great oversimplification to say that the poem valorizes or "exults in" melancholy, or that it concludes with the same confidence in its advisory ability with which it began. Its final perspective is neither comparative nor intersubjective but personal, and from the subjective center of its being it describes, in lyrical precision and rhythmic regularity, the noose tightening around its existential options. Those options are presented in the poem's consuming verbs, which imagine, in the second stanza, meeting force with force: "glut thy sorrow" and "feed deep, deep." The image of the "hand" of Joy, "ever at his lips / Bidding adieu," suggests, however, in the delicacy of its motion, an adversary who will win this match without any exertion at all. The rhyme *lips/sips*, and the analogy it conveys with Joy and Pleasure, recognizes that every act is a collaboration in this consumptive narrative, which can come to only one end. Comparatively, the poem contends, those who confront this fate head on, without the evasive adoption of a group identity, will get the most of Joy before his departure, but it also acknowledges that even those who "burst Joy's grape against his palate fine," an image that returns the poem to the intensity of "glut thy sorrow," cannot have pleasure as a pure and homeostatic consummation. There is always the hangover registered in the drop from "burst Joy's grape" to the flat, figureless "taste the sadness." The poem's melancholic subject is not finally consumed, but he is as fully objectified as "She" could ever be, when he is turned into a trophy and hanged. His demise is brought to a rhythmic closure in the gradual tightening of the poem's rhyme scheme. In the first stanza, the entire closing sestet is made up of weak or slant rhymes: *berries/mysteries, be/drowsily, owl/soul*. The sestet of the second stanza leaves only the last rhyme slant: *peonies/eyes*. But the final sestet registers the force of what will, shall, and must happen to the poem's subject in a relentless rhythmic closure: *Delight/might, shrine/fine, tongue/hung*. The closing rhyme also incorporates an internal rhyme in the last line, *among/hung*, which brings the hard consonants ("wakeful anguish") that had initially stood for the resistance of the ego into the service of the forces that sweep it away. Having thoroughly deconstructed the authority of that consoling fiction of pure intellectual and group identity, the "academic 'we'," the "Ode on Melancholy" cannot finally pretend that the imaginary distance between its persona and some other "you" or "her" or "him" protects its speaking subject from the annihilation it describes. The fullest attainment of knowledge or identity has no effect on the fact of mortality, and the subject of the "Ode on Melancholy" does not, in the end, claim that it is possible to defer indefinitely the knowledge of his own impending nonexistence.

No poem is intended for the reader, no picture for the beholder, no symphony for the listener.

Benjamin, "Task of the Translator"

To night I am all in a mist.

Letters of Keats, 2:167

ℓ

ℓ

ℓ

ℓ

ℓ

ℓ

ℓ

ℓ

ℓ

ℓ

CHAPTER 4 # Negative Dialectics and

ℓ # Negative Capability

ℓ ## "To Autumn"

ℓ

ℓ

ℓ

ℓ

ℓ

ℓ

ℓ

FEW POEMS IN English literary history have proved so satisfying to modern readers as Keats's ode "To Autumn." The iconic density of the poem projects a sense of self-sufficiency that has inspired panegyric and deflected critique. Allen Tate's judgment that the ode "is a very nearly perfect piece of style but it has little to say" (264) was echoed in midcentury by a chorus of commentators who celebrated the poem's immersion in "sensation, or sensuous impression" (Finney, 2:707), its "escape into the luxury of pure . . . sensation" (Bush, "Keats," 242), and its willingness to rest "almost content with the pure phenomena" (Muir, 73). Proceeding beyond the point of impressionistic appreciation, and diverging from the second half of Tate's judgment, has proved to be a decidedly slippery enterprise. Even those readers who have noted that the poem "nowhere mentions man and admits no generalized reflections into its catalog of observed particulars" (Bush, *Life*, 178) and that there is "no suggestion of the discursive language that we find in the other odes" (W. J. Bate, 581) have found it difficult to resist the temptation to supply the explicit summary statement that the poem abjures. In 1970 Herbert Lindenberger compiled a survey of interpretations of "To Autumn" and discovered a wide range of thematic paraphrases of the poem encompassing, as he put it, "a spectrum that moves from a pessimistic view stressing the imminent death of nature at the end of the poem to an optimistic view affirming the future rebirth of life in the spring" (130). Surprisingly enough, the poles of this spectrum were set out by Douglas Bush and Walter Jackson Bate, the very critics who note the absence of "generalized reflections" and "discursive language," and whose views of Keats otherwise accord on nearly every point. In this case, though, Bush finds a funereal tone in the poem's close, in which Keats achieves "the power to see and accept life as it is, a perpetual process of ripening, decay, and death" (*Life*, 178), while Bate feels that the poem evinces Keats's "inability to conceive fulfillment without a spring of promise still implicit within it" (584).

Recent commentary on this poem has more often focused on the ode's ability to gratify its readers' desire for poetic sensation than on finding fault with an absence of determinable thematic statement. The perceived richness of the poem has been attributed to its intrinsic rhetorical density; its ability "to create an equivalence to Autumn" flows, according to Virgil Nemoianu, from "the multitude, the excess even, of processes functioning inside the poem, their superimposition, their apparent contradictions" (208), which frustrate thematic summary and leave a reader with nothing but the presence of "Nature . . . questioning itself and answering itself by movements and objects" (210). Other readers have contextualized the ode's the-

matic reticence within a literary history. Geoffrey Hartman connects Keats's
report of the genesis of the poem in his view of "stubble fields" on a
"sunday's walk" to his ensuing praise of Chatterton for being "the purest
writer in the English Language," one who wrote "genuine English Idiom in
English words" (*KL*, 2:167), and Hartman concludes that the ode reflects
Keats's nativist satisfaction with the English landscape and language in its
"hesperian" distance from an "eastern" classical poetry written in an
epiphanic mode ("Ideology," 126). Paul Fry has suggested that "To Autumn" may actually represent a return to the classical tradition in an archaic
mode of the ritual hymn. Fry offers as the model for the serenity of Keats's
ode Horace's "Hymn to Mercury," which, after narrating a series of epi-
sodes that prove the god's powers, surprisingly asks nothing from him. Fry
proposes that the eloquence of the hymn proves that the poet has already
received what the god has to offer; the poem is a thanksgiving, not an en-
treaty. Similarly, Fry sees Keats choosing to view autumn as an emblem of
fullness rather than of loss, and he commends Keats's ability to sustain "the
impression that a single season, and indeed only one mood among many
even within that season, may represent the essence and wholeness of being"
(269). Keats's seeming contentment with the "wholeness of being" found in
the season elicits from Fry an essay of elegant paraphrase that aims at nothing more than mirroring the sense of sufficiency found in the poem itself.

Even this relatively uniform critical history produces two significantly
unresolved issues. The vocabulary used to describe the poem's perfectness
shifts easily from the rhetorical to the ontological, yet even an entirely perfect piece of style is not exactly the equivalent of pure sensation or natural
phenomena. The more obvious question that arises from the wide spectrum
of impressions of the poem's final tone can only be addressed after the first,
more technical question about the ode's mode of representation is clarified.
Such a brief technical excursion can also help to contextualize the two most
influential recent readings of "To Autumn," those of Helen Vendler and
Jerome McGann. While Vendler's analysis serves as a capstone to the tradition of critical tribute to the poem and McGann's essay is a critique of both
that tradition and the putative politics of the ode, Vendler's and McGann's
treatments of "To Autumn" often mirror each other, even as they both di-
verge from the most significant structures of the poem itself. I would like to
illustrate in this essay what is lost when the New Historicism, as exemplified
in Romantic studies in the work of McGann and Marjorie Levinson, tries to
bypass poststructuralism in order to launch a direct attack on a formalist
criticism whose investment in a unified cultural tradition makes it a fairly

easy target for Althusserian critique. McGann's argument with the politics of "To Autumn" depends upon an initial agreement with the most common New Critical reading of the poem, as a self-fulfilling formal structure; McGann is then able to subject the meaning that emerges from that reading to the terms of Althusserian critique. The process that Althusser describes as interpellation, however, is less uniform than Althusser's unproblematic use of the term "imaginary" would suggest. I propose that "To Autumn" is a far more self-conscious poem than either its votaries or its critics have acknowledged; it ponders and unsettles the process of identity formation that Althusser describes as happening so automatically.

Tate's contention that "To Autumn" "has little to say" bears looking at. A poem whose subject is one of the most pathos-laden topoi in Western literature—the season that represents the end of a cycle of vegetative growth— can hardly avoid "saying" something, in the sense of conveying some affective content to the reader. The evident affection that this poem has inspired in so many commentators suggests that it communicates more than a pure description of natural phenomena. The difficulty of paraphrasing its content is located by Tate as an absence within the poem itself, whereas it would be more accurate to see the problem residing in the relation between the poetic text and the critical discourse on that text. The peculiar difficulty of paraphrasing "To Autumn," when seen as an effect of the poem's style, can be explained through Jakobson's distinction between metaphoric and metonymic language and his account of the interpretive implications of the two styles. In the case of metaphoric language, Jakobson contends, the critic possesses a "homogeneous means" of access; as poetic symbols stand in for ideas, the critic can simply substitute other terms for the same concepts. If a "lamb" is a substitutive term for the idea of hope, then Bate's term "spring of promise" can be a perfectly adequate restatement of the same concept. But metonymy, according to Jakobson, "based on a different principle, easily defies interpretation" (Jakobson and Halle, *Fundamentals*, 95). The differing emphases of Bate's and Bush's readings of "To Autumn" originate in the different points at which they center the poem's metonymic field. Bate's optimistic reading is more consistent with the satisfied tone that pervades the ode's reception history, but the impression of the poem's serene richness is in fact more unproblematically located in the ode's first stanza than in its last. In order to stretch the theme of natural fullness to the very end of the text, Bate needs to explain away the repeated references to death in the poem's final stanza ("the soft-dying day," "a wailful choir," "gnats mourn," and "wind lives or dies"); to argue that the swallows in the last line "are not necessarily gathering for migration" (583); and to restore the presence of "spring" to a text that has explicitly refused to turn in that direction for solace.

When the relative absence in "To Autumn" of discursive statement is supplemented by its surfeit of physical detail, it becomes clear that, in Jakobson's terms, the coherence of the poem depends more on contiguity than on a substitutive relation between presence and concept. As "To Autumn" traces its simultaneous passage through both a diurnal movement from dawn to dusk and a seasonal span from the peak of natural fruition in early autumn to the postharvest gleaned fields, the poem's imagery changes from the predominantly visual imagery of the first stanza to chiefly aural imagery in the final stanza. The initial, spatial model of contiguity is thus supplanted by a temporal model in the course of the text, as the relations among images change in structure: initially one-thing-next-to-another, finally one-thing-after-another. The final stanza deploys a series of temporal markers ("While," "then," "now"), which construct a regular temporal progression. The refusal to recur to thoughts of spring at the outset of the final stanza is an acknowledgment that this second, temporal model of contiguity runs in only one direction. Autumn is scattered, in a random omnipresence, throughout the second stanza; the inversion in the stanza, by which an image of winnowing precedes images of reaping and gleaning, conveys a disregard for an accurate representation of temporal progress. At the stanza's close, however, the inexorable "oozings hours by hours" instate a forward motion whose force arranges the choral movement of the final stanza.

Emphasizing the temporality of autumn would seem inevitably to foreground the conventional topos in which autumn represents the death of the year, or, in a different but no less familiar or depressing theme, the cyclicity of the seasons illustrates the contrast between nature's capacity for perennial renewal and the human progression through only one cycle of growth, "ripening, decay and death." An analysis that presents the poem's temporal development as its central narrative would seem to suggest that the persistent critical complacency toward "To Autumn" is mostly a mistake, perhaps the result of some sort of anesthetic effect brought about by the bounty of the first stanza, which Hartman calls a "drunk sentence" ("Ideology," 143). But that complacency could also be ascribed to the predominance of metonymy over metaphor in the style of "To Autumn," a rhetorical feature that allows the poem to acquire its opulence of naturalistic detail without the interference of an evaluative thought. Moving beyond the purely technical level of Jakobson's observation that "metonymy defies interpretation," we can begin to describe the hermeneutic effects of this resistance by comparing it to Erich Auerbach's claim that, in contrast to a biblical text, "Homer can be analyzed, as we have essayed to do here, but he cannot be interpreted" (11). As Auerbach outlines the difference between Homeric and biblical modes of representation, he attributes Homer's resistance to interpretation to a style that creates only a uniform foreground. The appeal of Homer's text then resides, according to Auerbach, not in any meaning that it makes available through the substitution of word for concept, but in the plurality and clarity of its contiguous relations. "To represent phenomena in a fully externalized form, visible and palpable in all their parts, and completely fixed in their spatial and temporal relations," Auerbach tells us, is "the basic impulse of the Homeric style" (4).

As Auerbach describes the very different mode of coherence of the biblical text, he draws upon the structuralist topography of two axes of speech. Biblical coherence is said to overcome the "horizontal disconnection of the stories and groups of stories in relation to one another" by means of "their general vertical connection" to "one concept of universal history and its interpretation" (14). The "horizontal" coherence of a Homeric story is, in contrast, capable of containing a wide variety of discursive, logical, and material relations without referring beyond itself to a conceptual whole, and Auerbach's highest praise for the sophistication of the Homeric style addresses both the variety of its methods and the seamlessness of its effect. The world created by the Homeric poems, Auerbach contends, "exists only for itself, contains nothing but itself" (11), and it constructs this self-sufficiency through metonymic profusion:

> The separate elements of a phenomenon are most clearly placed in relation to one another; a large number of conjunctions, adverbs, particles, and other syntactical tools, all clearly circumscribed and delicately differentiated in meaning, delimit persons, things, and portions of incidents in respect to one another, and at the same time bring them together in a continuous and ever flexible connection; like the separate phenomena themselves, their relationships—their temporal, local, causal, final, consecutive, comparative, concessive, antithetical, and conditional limitations—are brought to light in perfect fullness; so that a continuous rhythmic procession of phenomena passes by, and never is there a form left fragmentary or half-illuminated, never a lacuna, never a gap, never a glimpse of unplumbed depths. (4)

The effect of Keats's decision in "To Autumn" to adopt a metonymic style, which presents an exceptionally dense naturalistic foreground while avoiding suggestive symbolic depths, can be illuminated by contrasting the ode's opening imagery with Thomson's use of similar imagery. The stylistic understatement of Keats's "Season of mists" contains no hint of the apocalyptic possibilities suggested by Thomson's use of the "roving mists" of autumn as the tenor of an epic simile in "The Seasons":

> A formless grey confusion covers all.
> As when of old (so sung the Hebrew bard)
> Light, uncollected, through the Chaos urged
> Its infant way, nor order yet had drawn
> His lovely train from out the dubious gloom. (731–35)

While Thomson, like Milton (*PL*, 7:243–46), echoes the account in Genesis of Light piercing Chaos to reach the earth and create the first day, the first stanza of "To Autumn" offers only precise and unemphatic description of an ordinary day, unaccompanied by any suggestion of universal-historical significance. As the first stanza of the ode begins to distinguish individually perceptible objects, such as vines, thatch-eaves, and trees, from the generally atmospheric "mellow fruitfulness" of the opening line, its style of understated naturalism reflects the unobtrusive process of the sun's burning off the morning mist. This flatness, Auerbach tells us, is characteristic of Homeric representation, where the richness of sensory foreground is accompanied by an absence of evaluative commentary: "The general considerations which occasionally occur," Auerbach writes, "(for example . . . that in misfortune, men age quickly) reveal a calm acceptance of the basic facts of human existence, but with no compulsion to brood over them, still less any passionate impulse either to rebel against them or to embrace them in an ecstasy of submission" (11). The seeming neutrality of the opening of "To Autumn" reflects the thematic ascesis of the metonymic style, but the ode does not entirely maintain the inhuman detachment that Auerbach finds in the Homeric texts when they describe terrible violence with fluent impassivity. In particular, the affective and anthropomorphic qualities of the verbs that describe animal sounds in the last stanza of "To Autumn" ("mourn," "bleat," "whistle," and "sing") suggest some shadowy margins around the picturesque scenery.

Placing "To Autumn" in the context of the two sonnets in which Keats explores two poles of affective response to seasonal change can help to show

how Keats trimmed the symbolic range of the imagery of this ode, and it also illuminates some of the possibilities that lie at the very border of the text. The first of these sonnets was written on 30 December 1816 and printed in the 1817 volume of Keats's poems:

> On the Grasshopper and the Cricket
> The poetry of earth is never dead:
>   When all the birds are faint with the hot sun,
>   And hide in cooling trees, a voice will run
> From hedge to hedge about the new-mown mead;
> That is the Grasshopper's—he takes the lead
>   In summer luxury,—he has never done
>   With his delights; for when tired out with fun
> He rests at ease beneath some pleasant weed.
> The poetry of earth is ceasing never:
>   On a lone winter evening, when the frost
>   Has wrought a silence, from the stove there shrills
> The Cricket's song, in warmth increasing ever,
>   And seems to one in drowsiness half lost,
>   The Grasshopper's among some grassy hills.

While the "Grasshopper and the Cricket" celebrates a "poetry of earth" by sustaining the presence of summer in the midst of winter, a second sonnet, written in early March of 1818 and published, with some revision, under the title "The Human Seasons" in Hunt's *Literary Pocket-Book* for 1819, closes with a wintry perspective on the march of all four seasons:

> The Human Seasons
> Four seasons fill the measure of the year;
>   Four seasons are there in the mind of man.
> He hath his lusty spring, when fancy clear
>   Takes in all beauty with an easy span:
>   He hath his summer, when luxuriously
> He chews the honied cud of fair spring thoughts,
>   Till, in his soul dissolv'd, they come to be
> Part of himself. He hath his autumn ports
>   And havens of repose, when his tired wings
> Are folded up, and he content to look
>   On mists in idleness: to let fair things
> Pass by unheeded as a threshold brook.

He hath his winter too of pale misfeature,
Or else he would forget his mortal nature.

"To Autumn" takes winter's cricket from the "Grasshopper and Cricket" sonnet and moves it outdoors to the summer hedge, thereby making "Hedge-crickets." The ode also takes from "Grasshopper" both the idea of animal sounds as a natural poetry of earth and the device of an onomatopoeic representation of those sounds: "shrills" in the sonnet, "twitter" in the ode. From "The Human Seasons," the ode adopts the imagery of autumn "mists," an image that carries a great deal of resonance in Keats's poems and letters. The central conceit of "The Human Seasons," that of consciousness moving through progressive stages, is the basis of Keats's comments on Wordsworth's genius in "Tintern Abbey," which Keats associates phonetically with the imagery of mists: "We are in a Mist—*We* are now in that state—We feel the 'burden of the Mystery'" (*KL*, 1:281). The image recurs in a letter that Keats sent from Winchester in August of 1819 to Fanny Brawne ("I see you through a Mist"), and a simile in that letter refers to "my unguess'd fate—all sp[r]ead as a veil between me and you" (2:140). In the letter to Reynolds that describes the genesis of "To Autumn," Keats writes, "To night I am all in a mist" (2:167). Mists also represent a sense of mystery in a sonnet written, according to Brown, a few feet from a precipice near the peak of Ben Nevis on 2 August 1818, when Keats described the mists surrounding him as obscuring the knowledge of hell, heaven, and ourselves:

Read me a lesson, Muse, and speak it loud
  Upon the top of Nevis, blind in mist!
I look into the chasms, and a shroud
  Vaprous doth hide them; just so much I wist
Mankind do know of hell: I look o'erhead,
  And there is sullen mist; even so much
Mankind can tell of heaven: mist is spread
  Before the earth beneath me; even such,
Even so vague is man's sight of himself.
  Here are the craggy stones beneath my feet;
Thus much I know, that, a poor witless elf,
  I tread on them; that all my eye doth meet
Is mist and crag—not only on this height,
But in the world of thought and mental might.

Juxtaposing "To Autumn" with the Ben Nevis sonnet highlights a significant omission in the ode that severs it from one of the most common strains
in the literary representation of autumn. While the sonnet looks down for
some knowledge of "hell," "To Autumn" takes place entirely between the
earth and the sky; there is no mention in the ode of the underworld to which
Proserpine is consigned, with the consequent mourning of Ceres and the
withdrawal of her fertility from the earth. When this omission is coupled
with the fact that the only season not explicitly mentioned in "To Autumn"
is winter, despite the declared centrality of winter to the human perception
of time in "The Human Seasons," we see just how deliberately Keats declined to make explicit one of the most familiar avenues for the representation of the autumnal in "To Autumn."

While the first two stanzas of "To Autumn" present the uniform foreground of Homeric representation, the third stanza contains numerous sug-
gestions of, if not unplumbed depths, at least some shadowy distances. One
way of looking at the poem's final image, as it removes itself from the earthly
activities celebrated in the earlier stanzas, is described by de Man in "The
Intentional Structure of the Romantic Image": "images of levitation . . .
uncover a fundamentally new kind of relationship between nature and consciousness" (75). De Man sees such "images of levitation" departing from a
pantheist poetics as they disclose the unbridgeable gap between the natural,
material, predictable world and the unmoored activity of consciousness, by
means of the principle that "The word is always a free presence to the mind"
(69). Language thus becomes the basis for "a possibility for consciousness to
exist entirely by and for itself, independently of all relationship with the
outside world, without being moved by an intent aimed at a part of that
world" (76–77). This stage of poetic consciousness is described by de Man
as a surpassing and demystifying of an immediately prior stage in which
"Poetic language seems to originate in the desire to draw closer and closer
to the ontological status of the object" (70). The argument that "To Autumn" remains within a poetics based on organic principles has been made
most recently and most explicitly by Vendler, who contends that the ode is
engaged in "bringing symbol as close to mimetic appearance as possible"
(268). The degree of the poem's success in suggesting an ontological equivalence to the natural world is borne out by its critical history, but de Man's
contention that images of levitation in fact represent an incommensurability between consciousness and nature implies that the poem itself is not
nearly so confident of the stability of its own being.

As the emphasis on intentionality in its title suggests, "The Intentional

Structure of the Romantic Image" is a direct challenge to the terms of the
New Critical reception of the Romantic poets. When William Wimsatt
argued in "The Structure of Romantic Nature Imagery" that Romantic
poetry was as historically important and as poetically valid as the work of the
metaphysicals, he identified its significance in the ability of Romantic poets
"to read meanings into the landscape" by "discerning the design which is
latent in the multiform sensuous picture," and he offered "To Autumn" as
"a brilliant romantic instance" of this ability (83). In contrast to the Metaphysical preference for explicit simile, "To Autumn" embodies, for Wimsatt, the Romantic tendency to make "less use of the central overt statement
of similitude" (82). Through the adoption of "a structure which favors implication rather than direct statement" (88), Wimsatt argues, Romantic
poetry "tends to achieve iconicity by a more direct sensory imitation" (87).
The celebration of the supposed pure sensuousness of "To Autumn" in the
New Critical era indicates the ability of the poem to satisfy the desire for a
natural iconicity that transcends nonpoetic meanings, but de Man's contention that the Romantics were in fact the first writers to "put into question,
in the language of poetry, the ontological priority of the sensory object"
(77), looks at the same phenomenon—the pervasive representation of nature in early nineteenth-century British poetry—and comes to an opposite
conclusion. Romantic writers, de Man contends, find no implicit or latent
design in the sensory landscape, but discover instead the gap between the
human desire for design and the blank materiality of the natural world.

Vendler's analysis of "To Autumn," which attributes the success of the
ode to Keats's ability finally to "enact" the "truth he had so far been able
only to assert" (233), shares with Wimsatt a valorization of Romanticism for
its ability to embody meaning without overt statement, but Vendler's praise
of the poem's sensory richness only partly echoes Wimsatt's description of
the iconic style of the Romantic poets. Vendler's assertions that "To Autumn" "uses sense to speak of spirit" and employs "things as the vehicle of
spirituality" (274) adopt the central argument of Wimsatt's valorization of
nature poetry for its implicit sensory representation of an immanence of
meaning. Contrary to de Man's contention that images of levitation represent an alienation from nature in which "language has itself become a celestial entity, an inhabitant of the sky" (75–76), divorced from natural process,
Vendler finds in the ode's final image a music of the spheres: "the nearly
invisible last choir seems to suggest the participation of life in the rhythms
of a third realm . . . a polyphony in the skies" (264). But when Vendler
summarizes the style of the poem with the formula that "Keats's central

effort in the language of 'To Autumn' is to have thoughts and emotions embodied by sensuous things" (275), she departs from Wimsatt's praise of the natural iconicity of Romantic poetry and exposes the gap that de Man comes to define as the central insight of that poetry. Vendler's allowance that it takes an "effort" to show thoughts embodied by things implies not a natural mirroring—in which thought merely reveals a design implicit in nature, and so finds an image of itself—but the separate existences of two disparate realms that need deliberate suturing. The joining of these realms is the central narrative of Vendler's reading of "To Autumn."

Vendler's conclusion, that "To Autumn" becomes the discursive site "where the tragedy of necessity cannot tell itself apart from the current of desire" (288), is based on a single term, *work*, which operates as the central valorization of her account of the ode and which expresses equally the two poles of the dialectic, "necessity" and "desire," that require synthesis. Yet the preeminent value of work is better embodied by Vendler's essay than in Keats's ode; there could be no more thorough single account of Keats's craftsmanship in "To Autumn" than Vendler's meticulous tracing of the weave of the poem's multiple, overlapping structures, and Vendler's extensive analyses of the ode's intertextual borrowings are always, if not definitive, at least suggestive. But the central narrative that Vendler discovers in the ode moves in a direction precisely opposite that of the poem itself. Vendler describes "To Autumn" as originating in the "stubble-plains" that appear in both Keats's letter about the poem and in the ode's third stanza; in Vendler's view, the ode overcomes an implicit "absence at the center of the world" (260) represented in that image by means of "reparatory motions of replenishing the landscape" (258). But the poem itself unfolds with the forward motion of time, passing from the burgeoning fullness of late summer in the first stanza to the far more precarious balance between autumnal ripeness and its encroaching dissolution in the final verse. Vendler converts the poem's temporal progression into spatial form at the close of her essay, when she focuses on the multiplicity of patterns in "To Autumn" and the "stern perfection of its structure" (288), rather than on the poem's own ending in its most evanescent image.

Although Jerome McGann's discussion of "To Autumn" in "Keats and the Historical Method in Literary Criticism" sets itself in polemical opposition to precisely the sort of work that Vendler's essay does, McGann's account of what Keats intends and accomplishes in the poem is virtually identical to Vendler's at both the formal and the thematic levels. McGann's condemnation of both intrinsic, or "text-centered," approaches and the "pseudo-historical criticism," in which the "historical focus is upon literary history" (1014), pretty much covers Vendler's case, but McGann's account of "To Autumn" nevertheless constructs a similar narrative (the reparation of a lack), and comes to a similar conclusion about Keats's pursuit and eventual achievement of a kind of solace in "To Autumn." In McGann's story, "To Autumn" helps Keats to overcome multiple kinds of lack or absence. At a personal level, "To Autumn" functions as a wish-fulfillment; it creates an "ideal autumn" of "perfect harvests and luxurious agricultural abundance" (1021), which is "the dream of a mind that recalls the lost promise of the spring" (1023). The desire behind this dream is, for McGann, transparent and straightforward: "Keats imagines such an autumn—he writes this ode— because he needs to develop some means for silencing that melancholy question: 'Where are the songs of spring?'" (1023).

In a more public context, as part of the 1820 volume of Keats's poetry, the conformity of "To Autumn" to poetic decorum and the taste of conventional readers becomes, according to McGann, part of a plan hatched by Keats and his publishers, Taylor and Hessey, to rehabilitate their reputations after the damage done by their publication of *Endymion* in 1818. In addition, where Vendler locates the lack that provokes the poem's narrative of reparation in the literary image of "stubble-plains," McGann materializes this lack in historical fact: "1819 brought in a good harvest in England, and the year was notable for its abundance precisely because of the series of disastrous harvests which characterized many of the years immediately preceding" (1021). This "series of disastrous harvests" and Keats's injured poetic reputation thus fill the same role in McGann's historicist narrative that the image of bare stubble-fields plays in Vendler's biographical and literary-historical account.

The vicissitudes of temporality are overcome in McGann's essay, as in Vendler's, through the imposition of spatial form. McGann contends that the words of "To Autumn" "seem aspiring to the condition of pictorial silence, where images present themselves in arranged groupings and sequences" (1022), a state that is presented as a summary of the entire poem, when it more truly describes only the first stanza. If McGann and Vendler are in agreement over what happens in the ode, they nonetheless disagree entirely over its significance. For McGann, "To Autumn" is "illusive" and an "attempt to 'escape' the period which provides the poem with its context" (1023–24), while for Vendler, "the resolve to enter the open fields of the reaped furrow" represents a "heroic compositional choice" (14).

McGann's argument, which casts "To Autumn" as an exemplary instance of the "Romantic ideology," relies heavily upon two significant misrepresentations of the immediate circumstances surrounding the original production of the poem. In the first case, McGann insists upon making clear distinctions among a "private poem," such as "This Living Hand," which is "never deliberately communicated to anyone else"; a "personal poem," such as "To Fanny," meant as a communication to a single other person; and public poems, written for publication. Crossing categories, by interpreting poems belonging to one category in terms that belong to another, McGann warns, involves "introducing a special bias into the critical act" (1012). McGann then treats "To Autumn" as a "public" poem, and he argues that the defining questions to be asked about its "initial historical moment" are "when and where and by whom was this poem originally published?" (1015). These questions allow McGann to introduce the narrative of Keats, Taylor, and Hessey constructing the 1820 volume with a distinct ideological agenda in mind: "The whole point of Keats's great and (politically) reactionary book was not to enlist poetry in the service of social and political causes—which is what Byron and Shelley were doing—but to dissolve social and political conflicts in the mediations of art and beauty" (1017). There is a perfect symmetry, in McGann's story, between Keats's public and private motives. In McGann's Althusserian terms, not only is the relation between Keats's desire for respectability and his need to silence melancholy questions analogous, but the achievement of a respectable reputation is also in fact the means by which Keats could acquire a satisfying identity and live, as Althusser puts it, "naturally" and "spontaneously."

The first flaw in this story is that before "To Autumn" became, in McGann's terms, a "public poem," it was a personal poem, and, before that, the letter to J. H. Reynolds on the evening of its composition suggests, it was a private poem. The letter written to Reynolds on 21 September 1819 describes the genesis of "To Autumn"; this is the well-known account of "stubble-fields," "chaste weather," and "Dian skies." But the first version of "To Autumn," which changed very little by the time of the poem's publication nine months later, appears in a different letter written the same day and sent to Richard Woodhouse. In the Woodhouse letter, Keats wrote, "You like Poetry better—so you shall have some I was going to give Reynolds," and he then put on paper the original text of "To Autumn." At the close of the ode, Keats added in the letter, "I will give you a few lines from Hyperion on account of a word in the last line of a fine sound," and he then wrote out five lines from *Hyperion*, underlining the word *legend-laden* (*KL*, 2:170–72). McGann's argument that a poem changes meaning as it enters a new public environment does not answer the objection that he has used events occurring in March and April of 1820 (Keats's discussions with Taylor and Hessey) as the "initial historical moment" that explains events occurring on 21 September of the previous year: the stylistic choices made in the composition of "To Autumn" and the consequent decision to send it to Woodhouse "because you like Poetry better." Considering Keats's expression, in the subsequent comment about *Hyperion*, of the criterion for liking poetry— namely, the ability to appreciate "a word in the last line of a fine sound"— the "personal" motives that went into the writing of "To Autumn" were far more clearly present at the poem's conception than were Keats's converging desires, hypothesized by McGann, for personal escapism and public respectability.

The desire of this poem in its "private" existence is far more opaque than that discovered by McGann in its "public" version. "To Autumn" presents, quite explicitly, the illusory nature of perpetual fullness (which McGann casts as its desired telos); "the bees" may "think warm days will never cease," but the absence of emotional tone in these lines does not mean that the poem itself has unconsciously entered into that illusion. When Keats wrote to Reynolds on 21 September, "To night I am all in a mist," one point about which he confessed confusion was an inability to distinguish, in the draft of *Hyperion*, the "false beauty proceeding from art" from the "true voice of feeling" (2:167). If "To Autumn" seems not to know the meaning of the progression from fruitfulness to stubble-plains, its quest for the beauty or true feeling in the scene, and the "unguess'd fate" behind the mists, was not, on 21 September 1819, directed toward public consumption.

The second crucial misrepresentation in McGann's shoehorning of "To Autumn" into the "Romantic ideology" is his marshaling of biographical evidence from Keats's letters from Winchester in the fall of 1819 in support of the argument that Keats found Winchester a "wonderful refuge" that was "magical in [its] ability to carry him away to a charmed world far removed from the quotidian press of his money affairs and the dangerous political tensions of his society" (1021). Citing Keats's appreciative letters about the beauty of Winchester as a "respectable, ancient aristocratical place" (*KL*, 2:189), McGann argues for Keats's apolitical/reactionary desire to find a "respite" from "the contemporary social scene," but this is a highly selective, even gerrymandered, account of Keats's letters from Winchester. It is in the letters from Winchester that Keats makes the most explicit declarations of his political allegiances and his intention to participate in the political life of England: "I will write, on the liberal side of the question, for whoever will pay me" (2:176), and "I hope sincerely I shall be able to put a Mite of help to the Liberal side of the Question before I die" (2:180). Both passages, from letters to Brown and Dilke, were written on 22 September, one day after the composition of "To Autumn." Keats's letters from Winchester also contain his long disquisition to the George Keatses on the three phases of modern English history, in which "changes for the better" consist of gains in popular freedom from royal or aristocratic power. In this letter, written in the same week as "To Autumn," Keats characterizes the central issue of contemporary English politics as the clash between populist strivings and the illegitimate defense of traditional privileges, and he sets progressive writers on the side of "the people." The "Court," Keats writes, has "spread a horrid superstition against all inovation and improvement— The present struggle in England of the people is to destroy this superstition." The censorship of "Tom Payne" and of "deistical pamphlets" is cited as part of the government's fomenting of "superstitious horror" (2:193–94). This epistolary record does not suggest someone who has retreated into an apolitical fairyland.

De Man's account of the ontological stakes of the movement from representations of landscape invested with symbolic meaning to images of levitation that break with the "poetry of earth" can be supplemented with the historical observation that the ode "To Autumn" in fact contains, but is not limited to, a reactionary political formation far more specific than the vague accusation of escapism lodged against it by McGann. As Raymond Williams's study *The Country and the City* amply documents, the nostalgia of the pastoral has the specific political valence of glorifying a fictional Englishness, an "earlier and happier rural England," which actually existed in "no place" and "no period" (35). The defense of Goldsmith's "rural Virtues" is connected, in a Tory literary tradition, to the privileging of a land-based aristocratic order over the newer wealth associated with money, trade, and the growth of cities. This mythology persists in the writings of Tory cultural critics to the present day; one such statement, produced as recently as 1993, is that "England is of its essence a rural place, and by losing contact with their rural roots the English have, in effect, ceased to exist as a people" (A. N. Wilson, 6). Whatever it could mean for the hub of an empire to be "of its essence a rural place," the celebration of pastoral continues to appeal today, as it did in 1819, to the desire for rootedness, or a sense of belonging to an organic order of universal-historical significance.

conservative desire for transparent access to a natural immanence of meaning, and that he recognized its congeniality to his own "aristocratic temper."
But both his letters and the ode register a countermovement to such immersion in a sense of universal-historical belonging. De Man's analysis of the
significance of images of levitation in destabilizing this supposed organic
immanence restores to the poem the possibility of self-critique; the ode is
not simply a blind reflection of its own cultural moment, waiting to be
demystified by our "socio-historical" insights, as McGann contends (1025),
but is itself a moment of powerful insight into desires that, the critical history of the poem suggests, are still operative today. Whether one construes
this internal critique as the questioning of an ideology or as a departure
from the structure of ideology which stands behind particular ideologies is
less relevant, for the moment, than the realization that "To Autumn" enters
a reactionary ideology and then, gently and without denouncing the un-
truth of that ideology, glides into a very different representation of the organic order that has been made so attractive by that imaginary formation.

In its movement away from an uncritical absorption in a pastoral ideal,
"To Autumn" becomes far more enigmatic in its conclusion than in its opening. The disparate, even contradictory, paraphrases that emerge in the treatment of its final stanza testify not only to an inscrutability that has often
been characterized as "impersonal," but also to an affective force that is
entirely opposite to impersonality. The formal rhetorical balances of the
poem's final stanza present a range of images that carry a good deal more
emotional force than does the imagery of the first stanza, even though the
poem itself seems to commit itself to no particular response. The difference
becomes clear in a comparison of anthropomorphic images from the first
and the third stanzas: the third stanza's image of "gnats mourn," versus the
first stanza's "bees" who "think warm days will never cease." While the bees'
error is so obvious as to preclude our entering into their delusion, the difference between their mistaken belief and our greater knowledge does not
seem very significant; not much would seem to be at stake in the difference.
When "the small gnats mourn," however, the structure of cognitive difference and emotional indifference is reversed. The pathetic and anthropomorphic verb "mourn" activates, in a logically disjunctive but emotionally
consistent pattern, the two traditionally negative representations of autumn,
as the death of the year, and as an integral part of a cyclic process that is
"never dead," but whose capacity for infinite renewal emphasizes the finity
of those who are unable to return to their "lusty spring, where fancy clear /
Takes in all beauty with an easy span." The image of the gnats is particularly

effective in conspiring with the temporal motion of the stanza to construct the analogy between the year's death and our own. This analogy presses home the question of the significance of the difference between our linear relation to temporality and nature's cyclic character, but it does not even begin to answer that question.

The inscrutability of the conclusion of "To Autumn" is due at least partly to the inadequacy of the resources that exist for imagining the future, a temporal problem that was available to Keats in the terms set out by Hazlitt in *Essay on the Principles of Human Action*, and that is apt to be familiar to a modern reader as the instigating paradox of Benjamin's "Theses on the Philosophy of History." As Hazlitt ponders our means of conceptualizing the future, he theorizes that we are tied to the present by sensation and to the past by memory, but are connected to the future only by imagination, a faculty that is much less tangibly linked to our own identities; this faculty is as capable of imagining the future of another as it is our own (*CW*, 1.22–23). For Benjamin, our ability to imagine the past so much more powerfully than the future explains the backward view of the "angel of history" (257) and the terrible paradox at the heart of human history: People are far more willing to go to war over "the image of enslaved ancestors rather than that of liberated grandchildren" (260). In his second "Thesis," Benjamin attributes this paradox to the retrospective bias of our temporal imaginations; after citing Lotze on "the freedom from envy which the present displays toward the future," Benjamin reflects that "The kind of happiness that could arouse envy in us exists only in the air we have breathed, among people we could have talked to, women who could have given themselves to us" (253–54). Benjamin's exhortations to read "against the grain" of history are meant to break the considerable power that the spell of nostalgia has in producing the reification of "a people." If the sensations and the memories that "To Autumn" provokes seem far more real than the "unguess'd fate" hinted at in the poem's conclusion, this difference is a measure not of the greater significance of sensations and memories but of their greater availability as analogies to our own palpable memories.

In the tenuous imagining of the future in "To Autumn," fear is, if only slightly, more apparent than desire, and a fear, as de Man has pointed out in his explication of Rousseau's giant, may be only a hypothesis, not a reality (*Allegories*, 151). Such a formation of the hypothetical, as an imagining of a difference from the real, becomes for de Man the peculiarly human means by which, through fictions, we become different from the blind predictability of nature. De Man's contention that most literary criticism goes against the grain of this imaginary activity, operating instead under the presumption of a "tyranny of reference" that is "anti-poetic" (47), is borne out, in exemplary forms, in McGann's and Vendler's readings of "To Autumn." Both of their readings of the ode negate the poem's fictive activities through the dispelling of its fears. McGann argues that "The poem's special effort is to remove the fearful aspects of [its] themes" as it forms a contract with the reader: "The reader agrees to look at autumn, and to contemplate change and death, under certain precise and explicitly fictional guises. The reader accepts the invitation because these mediations, though recognizably fictional, nevertheless promise a real, human benefit: the beauty of the mediations can transform one's felt response to the ideas of change, death, decay" (1019). Thus for McGann, "fiction" stands in a clearly oppositional relation to truth and to fear—not, as for de Man, in an indeterminate or hypothetical relation that reflects both an attempt at truth and an inability to know whether it has been reached.

Vendler specifies fears in the poem that are slightly different from those usually connected to the contemplation of autumnal decline; she sees "To Autumn" confronting the fear only partly acknowledged in the sonnet that begins "When I have fears that I may cease to be," and finally overcoming this "fear of dissolution (connected in his mind with sexuality)" (234–35). Vendler's account of how Keats conquers this fear through work outlines, in an uncritical form, the poetic social contract that McGann looks at more skeptically. The ode "To Autumn," Vendler believes, shows that "in the last analysis [Keats] thinks of the poet as a worker, one who does socially productive labor" (284), while McGann argues that the poem's "message is that the fine arts, and by extension imagination generally, are more humanly productive than any of the other more practical sciences of the artificial" (1023). At a descriptive level, there is very little difference between these two statements, yet both are far removed from Keats's leisurely epistolary observation that the scene of stubble-fields "struck me so much in my sunday's walk that I composed upon it. I hope you are better employed than in gaping after weather" (2:167). Vendler contends that "To Autumn," like Milton's Eden, *Paradise Lost*, represents "nature tamed, not nature wild; agriculture and gardening, not indolence" (239), and she infers from this an analogy to the poet's own activity. Keats's response to the biblical parable of the grain of wheat sent into the earth to die, Vendler finds, takes the form of a counterteaching: "Untransmuted, life drops back into the earth and into the endless biological cycle. . . . Keats's parable recommends that it be taken away from nature and transmuted into 'store'" (258–59). Vendler makes

Keats out to be a worker rather than a gaper, but this Miltonic analogy does not illustrate how the poet actually "*does* socially productive labor." Depicting labor is, after all, not exactly the same as doing it.

Vendler's work in the Romantic period, which reaches its fullest expression in her essay on "To Autumn," itself does the "socially productive labor" that she attributes to Keats, and she does this work in conformity with the principles of the New Criticism as elaborated by Cleanth Brooks when he proposed that the value of a poem depends upon whether the attitude it expresses "seem[s] to be that which the mind of the reader can accept as coherent, mature, and founded on the facts of experience" ("Irony," 1043). The unusually explicit appearance of "the reader" in a New Critical text, at this crucial moment in the formulation of founding principles, suggests the extratextual, social grounding of New Critical practice. Given the cultural relativity not only of the concept of maturity but of the determination of what counts as "the facts"—let alone "the facts of experience"—the work of the New Criticism, as it follows Brooks's principles, can legitimately be seen as the interpellation of individuals as subjects, by way of their recognition of phenomena that become "facts" in a consensual experience of reading. Vendler argues of Keats that "he admires without stint both nature and intelligence, but he admires even more culture's teleological aim toward store, and the soul's aim toward identity" (294); the reciprocity of the two processes—achieving "identity" and creating a socially productive "store"— makes it clear that Vendler, like Krieger, places a preeminent value on the social construction of a determinate *someone*, even as both Vendler and Krieger would like to present that "someone" as a natural given.

Vendler's commitment to the value of interpellation becomes most transparent when she castigates Marjorie Levinson and John Barrell for their materialist readings of "Tintern Abbey"; Levinson and Barrell misunderstand, Vendler rails, that "a lyric is *a role offered to a reader*" (Vendler's emphasis) in which the "generalized and abstracted . . . emotions therein" transcend barriers of time, space, and gender ("Tintern Abbey," 184). The particular "generalized and abstracted" emotions offered in "Tintern Abbey," Vendler specifies, are "the ability to hear the sad music and the visitation of elevated thoughts [which] spring from the speaker's acquisition of social maturity through social suffering" (185). The theme of this sentence—which reads as if it might have been lifted from Vendler's chapter on "To Autumn"—is virtually identical to the central principles of her study of Keats; the marked sameness shows how deeply committed is Vendler's work, and that of the New Criticism in general, to the production of a determinate range of subjects. In an odd argumentative gesture in her polemic against Levinson and Barrell, Vendler gives away the game when she asserts that the premise that "Lyric reposes on a presumed resemblance between readers" is grounded on a "quite reasonable assumption until rather recently, given the size and social coherence of the historical audience for written lyric" (184).

If it is simply the historical fact of "social coherence" that makes a poem meaningful for a reader, then Vendler essentially agrees with McGann: "Poetry is written, and read, within the determinate limits of specific social structures" (*Ideology*, 157). Its "socially productive labor" is the most fundamentally social work of all: It performs the interpellative act that produces the identities of its readers. Synthesizing the principles of the American New Criticism and the Harvard Keatsians, Vendler presents the central ideas of her study as experiential facts that should be recognizable to any properly mature reader. The basic disagreement between Vendler and McGann is that Vendler is satisfied enough with these principles to wish to grant them the status of facts, while McGann is dissatisfied with the same principles and calls them ideology. But neither Vendler's New Critical reading nor McGann's New Historicist analysis can give a poem an indeterminate or hypothetical relation to a determinate context of "facts" or "ideology."

In Vendler's account, "To Autumn" dispels the hypothetical fear that "I may cease to be" by subsuming personal, mortal identity under the socially productive role of the worker, but the ode "To Autumn" produces no such determinate identity for our mirroring. Its progression from an imagery of rooted presence to a culminating image of flight is persistently reversed in critical readings of the poem that restore the poem's stability; such persistent reversal testifies to the difficulty that the ode presents to a subject expecting to read a communication from another subject within a shared universal-historical framework. The ode's imagistic culmination in flight, together with its initial circulation as a gift, puts it on a conceptual terrain that has been most extensively theorized, in contemporary terms, by Helene Cixous. Lest this turn to Cixous seem gratuitous, let me immediately point out the precise coherence that Cixous' celebration of an ambiguous, nonmasculine sexuality imposes on the otherwise unintelligible personifications of "To Autumn." Virtually all commentators on the poem presume that the personified "autumn" represented in the ode is female, an "earth-goddess," as Vendler puts it, conspiring with a "sun-god" (*Odes*, 248). This presumption, which allows Vendler to identify Keats's autumn as Ceres, generally goes unquestioned even though the poem never uses a feminine pronoun. In a single glancing break with the critical habit of assuming the femininity of "Autumn," Paul Fry, who generally adheres to the convention of identifying autumn as female, once refers to the reaper in the second stanza as male, and he is severely chastised by Vendler for this "error" (Fry, 269; Vendler, *Odes*, 324). Yet neither "To Autumn" itself nor the literary tradition upon which it draws is as unambiguous about the gender of autumn or of nature as the consensual commentary on the poem would suggest. The word *friend*, which contributes to the gender ambiguity of subject/object relation in the "Ode on a Grecian Urn" ("a friend to man"), blurs gender identification from the outset of "To Autumn." The general usage of the term "bosom-friend" would, according to the *Oxford English Dictionary*, suggest, though it would not demand, a male figure. The seemingly most feminine image of the personified "thee" of the second stanza is the suggestion of long hair in "Thy hair soft-lifted by the winnowing wind," but here McGann contributes perhaps his most interesting observation on the poem. McGann suggests that this personification "is suggestively related" not only to Ceres but to Bacchus, since "that divinity's history in art and poetry shows him frequently represented as a handsome youth with fine, long-flowing hair" ("Keats," 1018, 1032). McGann does not argue that this personified figure must be Bacchus rather than Ceres, but simply that the ode's imagery is equally "suggestive" of these two figures from the classical tradition.

The presumption that Keats's autumn is necessarily female is eroded not only by the pictorial tradition of representations of Bacchus but also by a significant crack in the uniformity of the literary-historical tradition upon which Keats drew for his representation of the season. Vendler acknowledges that "To Autumn" is influenced by Spenser's "Mutability Cantos," but she insists that Keats's autumn "is not, as in Spenser, a masculine figure" (243). Keats's borrowing from Spenser is, however, far more detailed and complicated than Vendler acknowledges. Spenser's depiction of autumn, in which the season is always represented as a time of abundance, is clearly a central influence on Keats's ode. In Spenser's pageant of the seasons, autumn is "Laden with fruits that made him laugh, full glad" (canto 7, st. 30), and in the pageant of months, both the early autumn of September and the later autumn of November are depicted as emblems of fullness, and as male; September is "heavy laden with the spoyle / Of harvests riches" (7.38), and November is overstuffed, "full grosse and fat, / As fed with lard . . . For, he had been a fatting hogs of late." Even in November, a prospective temporality is redeemed as time becomes cyclic rather than linear; November looks through winter and toward spring: "In planting eeke he took no small delight" (7.40).

The most important legacy in "To Autumn" from Spenser's poem comes from the depiction of "great dame Nature":

> Yet certes by her face and physnomy
> Whether she man or woman inly were,
> That could not any creature well descry:
> For, with a veile that wimpled every where,
> Her head and face was hid, that mote to none appeare. (7.5)

For Spenser, the ambiguity of whether Nature "man or woman inly were" is a means of describing Elizabeth's politically functional sexual ambiguity; Keats finds the principle of Nature's indeterminacy interesting in itself, and he inverts Spenser's terms. Where Spenser suggests that Nature's true character is hidden by an obscuring veil, Keats asserts that Nature, as autumn, is easily found: "Who hath not seen thee oft amid thy store?" But where Spenser overrides the impossibility of making a true determination of the gender of this elusive figure by simply calling Nature "she," Keats gives no such minimally determinate form to this omnipresence; throughout "To Autumn," he uses only the genderless second-person pronoun for autumn. The persistent critical identification of Keats's autumn as female, despite the lack of explicit information to that effect in the text of "To Autumn," repeats Spenser's arbitrary identification of Nature as "she." The basis for this assumption is that, under a signifying system in which "he" designates a subjectivity unmarked by gender, the indeterminate but necessarily marked material opposite to that subject is, by differential default, a "she."

As the imagery of "To Autumn" continually falls short of the conventional identification of autumn as a female figure who would be the natural complement to the male sun, the poem never quite enters into the system of binary polarity that forms the founding signifying structure of phallologocentrism. The invisibility, the seeming naturalness, of binary thought is the repeatedly transgressed boundary of "To Autumn." The existence of "autumn," and of four seasons, is an idea, a secondary formation born out of a binary polarity—warm and cold—in which the moments of transition from one state to the other are further differentiated and given distinct identities and names. The simple binary form of the polarity is found in the sonnet "On the Grasshopper and the Cricket," in which the year moves directly from summer to winter; when the next level of differentiation, involving spring and autumn, is presented in "The Human Seasons," the interior landscape becomes far more meditative than that of the earlier sonnet. In the construction of literary history, as exemplified by Vendler's work, the construction of an identity for the intermediate state of "autumn," as it moves along the vertical pole of substitution, takes the form of a personification. Vendler joins "To Autumn" to the timeless presence of a universal (that is, Western) literary history by pushing the poem's images up the vertical axis of substitution so that the ode's initial scene of a conspiracy between the sun and autumn becomes an encounter between Apollo the sky-god and Ceres the earth-goddess (248). As Keats's "Autumn" glides through the preformative stage of the personification, giving us only the pure shifter of the second-person pronoun as the referent for autumn, it undoes the stability of that identity formation and more closely approximates the material nature that precedes the construction of arbitrary and consensual signs such as "autumn." Nature, embodied in the poem's first stanza by the bees, sees only the continuity of "warm days"; the bees do not know that it is no longer "summer." Only the creature with the temporal imagination to know his "mortal nature" can recognize the signs of stubble-plains in swollen gourds.

To the degree that the final image of "To Autumn" suggests the inability to "forget his mortal nature," De Man's contention—that images of levitation come to signify a gap between the human and the natural world—operates here, not in the power of the "free presence" of language to move beyond the confines of natural process, but in nature gathering itself and departing from the earthbound human viewer. Yet even such a reading of the poem's conclusion depends upon one last personification: the inference, as de Man puts it, of a subject from a predicate, of a determinate someone who speaks the text. This personification appears in its most emphatic form in Vendler's assertion about the poem's close: "In this stanza of the creatures, the most discreet and yet most constitutive element is the unmoving center from which all is seen and heard" (254). But no such "unmoving center" is ever named in the poem; there is neither first-person pronoun nor Wordsworthian deictic, no "here" that would mark the speaker's presence. What in fact appears in the poem's final nine lines is the stylistic effect of a pendulum-like swing. In five lines there are four sets of a rising/falling imagery that gives the stanza its pervasive mobility:

> While barred clouds bloom the soft-dying day
> And touch the stubble-plains with rosy hue;

>Then in a wailful choir the small gnats mourn
>   Among the river sallows, borne aloft
>   Or sinking as the light wind lives or dies.

The pattern is set in the initial panoramic sweep that frames the entire landscape of the ode; the expansive movement toward the skies, "While barred clouds bloom the soft-dying day," is followed by a unifying of the entire scope of the poem's imaginative vision in the descent to earth: "And touch the stubble-plains with rosy hue." The expansive upward movement is repeated, in a diminished arc, in the choir of gnats, who are then dropped into the "river sallows." The ascent/descent oscillation is then quickly repeated, twice—"aloft / Or sinking" and "light wind lives or dies"—and the rising movement is alliteratively bound, as "light" and "lives" pick up the sound of the up-stroke, "aloft." Although this line introduces the poem's final new rhyming word, "dies," the clause nevertheless achieves its own phonic closure at the completion of the down-stroke. At that point the word "dies" gathers and repeats the most prominent phonemes (aside from the already alliterated /l/) of the phrase "light wind lives or dies": the plosive /d/ of "wind" (virtually identical to the /t/ of "light"), the broad vowel /ai/ of "light," and the /s/ of "lives," which is also the phonemic alternate for /d/ (as in *defend/defense*).

The breadth of the pendular swing diminishes through its four repetitions, but in the new syntactic beginning of line 30, an effect of greater scope is recreated out of an imagery of magnitude; the size of the lambs ("full-grown"), the volume of their sound ("loud bleat"), and the distance covered by that sound ("from hilly bourn") all enlarge the spatial perspective of the scene, and form the counterpoint for "Hedge-crickets sing." Such tiny creatures, and such a small sound, described in such clipped tones, can be heard only from very nearby, a necessity that forms the contracting movement that alternates with the expansive, diphthong-laden "And full-grown lambs loud bleat from hilly bourn." The reader is prepared, by "Hedge-crickets sing," for a new expansive movement, which then appears. The brevity of the image of the crickets and its consequent sense of sudden termination create a suspended poise, from which the poem's final images unfold in a leisurely rhythm, finally carrying out a stunning, yet well-prepared, departure from the regularly pendular movement of the stanza. A creature of the sky, a "red-breast," capable of a louder sound than a hedge-cricket, "whistles," and it whistles "from," the preposition that, as in the case of the lambs, conveys distance. The couplet rhyme *soft/croft* helps to effect closure on the sixth instance in this stanza of an expansive or upward movement, which had been followed, in each previous case, by a downward, diminishing, or retractive return: barred clouds/stubble-plains; small gnats/river sallows; borne aloft/sinking; light wind lives/or dies; full-grown lambs/hedge-crickets. "The red-breast whistles from a garden-croft" should then, in the stanza's pattern, be followed by a return to earth, but instead the ode produces its most unexpected and destabilizing effect. The single bird (the only lone creature in the stanza) is multiplied ("swallows") and dispersed into a prepositional and plural distance that affords no relation: "gathering swallows twitter," not *from*, but "*in* the skies." This final plurality, "skies" rather than *sky*, is phonetically rather than semantically determined, both as a rhyme for "dies" and as an alliterative continuation of "swallows"; the sibilance of "skies," furthermore, repeats and revives the poem's opening stylistic gesture, the plural identification of autumn as a "Season of mists" rather than of "mist." The "Conspiring" of autumn and the sun is a pun (to *con/spire* means, in its Latin roots, "to breathe with"), and the tenor of "Conspiring"—the sense of a pervasive suspiration in the landscape—is instantiated in the recurring breathiness of the poem's language.

De Man has taught us to feel our separation from this life force. When we encounter such nonrelational skies, an "uncertain Heaven" or a sky that "seem'd / Not a sky of earth," the familiar perception of a sheltering dome can open into a gap that marks our difference from Nature and confronts us with "the real terror of death" ("Time," 9), that it is beyond our power to control by an act of representation. De Man's paradigm for Romantic poetry, that it repeatedly arrives at such vertiginous moments of impasse, conforms more closely, at least at a descriptive level, to the metonymic action of "To Autumn" than do most essays that purport to be readings of the poem. However, de Man's habitual use of images of a fall to exemplify the self-conscious moment of recognition of this gap (as in "The Rhetoric of Temporality," "The Resistance to Theory," and "Aesthetic Formalization in Kleist") indicates a judgment that this moment is ultimately to be seen as a loss. Converting this moment of vertigo into a fall, and a fear, transforms a pure hypothesis into a slightly more determinate form, and it is not at all clear that this is a judgment that can be applied to the final vertiginous moment of "To Autumn," in which there is no return to a poetry of earth.

Cixous weighs the image of flight differently, seeing no imminent fall within it but finding it a "woman's gesture" that evades the endless reappropriation of a masculine economy. "Making language fly" separates desire from the homeostatic path of Ulysses returning to himself, as the act of flying carries out the desire of a libido that goes further, since "she is how-far-being-reaches" ("Sorties," 87). When language becomes, in de Man's term, this "free presence," the possibility of "dissolution (connected in his mind with sexuality)" (Vendler, *Odes*, 234–35) becomes not a fear to be dispelled, but a drive that takes "To Autumn" beyond the appropriative economy that imposes second nature everywhere. At the poem's outset, this expansive drive is bound to a specific, nativist ideology; at its close, the drive is divested of content. In his letters, Keats schematizes the difference between these cathexes, one that restores personal identity in a mirroring relation to a greater whole and another that loses itself in undifferentiated otherness, when he describes the opposition between the appropriative, Wordsworthian "egotistical sublime" and his own camelionic "poetical character." Cixous' description of the feminine libido echoes Keats's account of "infor[ming] other bodies" (*KL*, 1:387); in Cixous' terms, this libido moves "within the hims and hers whom she inhabits just long enough to watch them" (88).

What happens in the final stanza of "To Autumn" is, as Cixous writes, "what happens to the subject, the personal pronoun" when "she is in a pervasive relationship of desire with every being," namely, "she makes another way of knowing circulate" (96). There is no "constitutive center," not even a pronoun, in the final scene of "To Autumn." The swallows are not seen from somewhere else; the poem simply picks up and goes. The second stanza at least allowed for the agency of seeking for autumnal presences, but the last stanza invites the annihilation of identity described in Keats's letter to Woodhouse about the "camelion poet"; it allows for a "relationship of desire" with a plethora of beings without the interference of an interpretive agent. Critical paraphrases that reintroduce the Wordsworthian subject into the landscape flatten out the poem's final effect by preventing it from completing its last gesture of levitation.

McGann entirely reabsorbs the ode's representation of "change and death" into a Freudian, homeostatic economy when he contends that "the reader agrees" to entertain the poem's "explicitly fictional guises" because of their "real, human benefit," their ability to "transform one's felt response" to this final absence (1019). Both "the reader" and the "human" are defined here within the economy of the Freudian "pleasure principle"; a little reality is admitted, so long as the ultimate outcome is a gain of pleasure. Cixous characterizes this economy of calculation, which McGann assumes is the natural mode of "human" thought, as the male libidinal economy: "Man is strategy, is reckoning . . . 'how to win' with the least possible loss, at the

lowest possible cost" ("Castration," 47). This economy of calculation un-
derwrites McGann's account of the economic agenda behind the publication of the 1820 *Lamia* volume, but the initial circulation of "To Autumn" as
a gift to Woodhouse because "You like Poetry better" reflects a more gratuitous economy that operates outside such considerations. McGann's focus
on the poem's publication history, which places Keats in a public space and
defines his interest as the production of a respectable poem and the recap-
turing of a respectable audience, conforms to the stereotypical structure of
male desire as Cixous describes it, which puts its gifts into circulation only
for the sake of return; this economy demands a return of "more masculinity:
plus-value of virility, authority, power, money, or pleasure" ("Sorties," 87).
While the anticipation of a return of "plus-value" of cultural authority is
clear in the arrangements for the publication of the 1820 *Poems*, the return
on the bond constructed between Keats and Woodhouse by means of a
passage from *Hyperion* with "a word in the last line of a fine sound" is not so
obvious, at least in terms of a "masculine" economy that objectifies its other.
But neither is this gift entirely inexplicable; Cixous characterizes both the
economy of the gift and a writing that possesses a "tactility," a "touch that
passes through the ear" ("Castration," 54) as acts of personal de-propriation
that come about through the "failures" of "the machine" to produce a
proper male subject ("Sorties," 98).

This machine is the machine of ideology, and its failures should not be
surprising to a poststructuralist era. Althusser acknowledges an "organic
link" between his own postulate that "*ideology is eternal*"—that it is "an *omni-
historical* reality, in the sense in which [its] structure and functioning are
immutable"—and Freud's postulate that "the *unconscious is eternal*, i.e, that it
has no history" (161; Althusser's emphases). What post-Freudian psychoanalysis has shown us is how mutable and fragmented are the forms of the
unconscious. Althusser posits a single "structure of all ideology" that is
"*speculary*, i.e., a mirror-structure" (180), a structure of perfect reciprocity,
with no excess and no lack. This is a fine description of how ideology works,
but as Adorno tells us, it never works perfectly: "It is one of the basic char-
acteristics of ideology that nobody ever believes it entirely" (*Aesthetic*, 334).
Even when ideology works, it doesn't cover everything, and those who are
tempted to peek beyond the veil sometimes end up far outside culturally
determined discursive ground. For a male subject, such drifting has an inevitable effect on the stability of identity formation, and the repeated accusations of the insufficient masculinity of Keats's poetry that formed a critical
majority, if not an orthodoxy, throughout the nineteenth century indicate

both the fragility of the construction of sexual difference and the transgressive potential of Keats's most purely "aesthetic" work. Behind the coding of "masculine" and "feminine" identities lies the Freudian opposition of "active" and "passive," an opposition that can only assign a poetry written in the passive condition of negative capability to the feminine side of the ledger, or else reinterpret it into a more recognizable and usable form. In the case of "To Autumn," the latter has been the dominant critical response; the poem has been cast as something picturesque or even "socially productive" rather than being confronted as a text that fades into an "unguess'd fate." Levinson's transposition, throughout *Keats's Life of Allegory*, of the nineteenth-century suspicion of Keats's masculinity into a metaphor for his ambiguous class position is an unnecessary and misleading move. One of the most fundamental ideological investments of any patriarchal society is the protection of the position of intellectual mastery that has been coded "male," and a discourse that demonstrates enormous technical skill, yet declines to assume the cognitive authority that accrues to that position, carries plenty of potential for disturbance at the immediate level of sexual identity.

In a recent essay titled "Romantic Poetry: The State of the Art," Levinson has set out to forge a new "rhetoric of romanticism" that would address an incommensurability between Romanticism's reaction to Enlightenment thinking and the Enlightenment premises of the New Historicist study of Romanticism.[1] In contemplating the question of what happens to the concept of value when one abandons an Enlightenment narrative that joins it, through knowledge and power, to progress, Levinson comes to identify the canonicity of Romantic poetry with a concept she calls "romantic indifference." She argues that the unique ability of Romantic poetry to project a "fantasy of quiet being" (203) is finally, historically present in our postmodern era: "For the first time, the objective core of romanticism's subjective themes emerges: its attachment to matter over mind, suffering over doing, unreadability over generation" (201). Levinson maintains the hegemony of historicist analysis while forgoing the Enlightenment premise of a progressive historical narrative; she does so by embracing and extending McGann's principle of the metaleptic determination of poetic value. The ability of Romantic poetry to negate Enlightenment premises is not, she insists, something "there from the start" in "myriad-minded works that anticipate every critical future," but is truly present "for the first time" only as a result of the critical histories of these works: "The reach of the poetry is not the cause of its canonicity but the effect: a result of the social processes in which the poems have participated" (200).

The withdrawal of "To Autumn" from socially progressive narratives thus "emerges," in Levinson's argument, only in the present, only in a criticism that responds to a history of Enlightenment impositions on Romantic poetry. Its negative capability was never "there," in Keats's mind or in his words on 21 September 1819; that effect is only a dialectical precipitate of the questions and answers that have been imposed on the poem in its reception history. Canonicity becomes pure historical contingency rather than a recognition of transcendent, ahistorical, or transhistorical value; any poem that happens to have been endlessly written about is historically significant. The rest are silent.

The subtlety of Levinson's thesis, which allows for an equation between value and indifference by means of the construction of a "radically nonopportunistic modeling of mind-matter relations" (204), offers a far better match for the flatness of "To Autumn's" portrayal of its final vanishing point, which is uninflected by self-centered lament or "ecstasy of submission," than is available in either New Critical or socially progressive New Historicist narratives. Yet the notion that this resistance to the imperialism of identitarian habits of thought is only there now, "for the first time," as an effect of our postmodern removal from dialectics of persuasion, greatly underestimates the reflexive capacities that can accompany "representational nonviolence." Levinson casts the meeting of a Romantic poem and modern critics as a historical matter, when a text that not only describes but is itself "a probability effect rather than a distinct entity" (209) encounters "professional readers who are also, as they write, vectors of the present" (189). Identifying Wordsworth's barely sensible "Old Man Travelling" and "Old Cumberland Beggar" as exemplary figures of a Romantic indifference to Enlightenment values, Levinson urges us to see in the "nonstrategic indifference" (202) of such figures that "ours is an agency unavailable to any reflexive or reproductive purposes" (209).

This equation of reflexivity with reproduction ends up valorizing a mindlessness that "To Autumn" specifically critiques through its overdetermined image of the unceasing and unthinking activity of the bees. Keats's bees are not only an embodiment of nature in its indifference to the distinction between "summer" and "autumn"; they are also, in their literary-historical legacy, the exemplary figure for organized labor. The most extensive use of the image of bees as perfectly industrious and interchangeable "little Citizens" occurs in the fourth book of Virgil's *Georgics:* "Their Toyl is common, common is their Sleep" and "All, with united Force, combine to drive / The lazy Drones from the laborious Hive" (lines 270, 241–42; Dryden's translation). Using the bees as the basis for political allegory, Virgil and Dryden offer no political options beyond factional warfare, leading to chaos and ruin, or the complete absorption of each individual into a collective identity bound by "servile Awe" to an Absolute Subject, a Queen-Bee, transformed by Dryden, for his own political purposes, into an "Idol King" (line 307).

As the hive becomes an image for a perfectly functioning ideological machine, second nature is embodied in the stupid predictability of insect life, which happily dedicates itself to sheer reproduction. Virgil makes explicit the theme that "To Autumn" handles more obliquely; bees are oblivious to their temporal destiny because they are only part of an endless process in which they participate without reflection:

> tho' the race of Life they quickly run,
> Which in the space of sev'n short Years is done;
> Th' immortal Line in sure Succession reigns,
> The Fortune of the Family remains:
> And Grandsires, Grandsons the long List contains. (lines 301–5)

In Keats's text, this obliviousness is simply a mistake; "they think," wrongly, that "warm days will never cease," participating in an illusion of continuity that is reproduced within a fully interpellated subject who does not gape after weather because, fully absorbed in a second nature that sees no difference between old buildings and trees, he does not know his difference from nature itself. Keats did not forget his mortal nature between the writing of "The Human Seasons" and "To Autumn," but the ode does not, as does the sonnet, state its knowledge. The closest it comes to naming "mortal nature" is its revision, in its closing image, of Virgil's description of a bee swarm that makes "a swarming Cloud arise, / That sweeps aloft, and darkens all the Skies" (lines 83–84). As Keats displaces the representation of mortality from the bees to the swallows, the latter become an unsurpassable point, a final resistance to appropriation within a larger intelligibility. The final ambiguity posed by "To Autumn" is its last moment of defiance of a machinelike reproductive order: Are we to give this a tragic de Manian inflection, or, like Cixous, see in it a refusal to mourn, an "oblivion of *acceptance*" ("Castration," 54; Cixous' emphasis). Indifference does not necessarily depend upon an absence of reflection; as Socrates the midwife told his friends, "The hour of departure has arrived, and we go our ways—I to die and you to live. Which is better God only knows" (Plato, "Apology," 134).

Althusser contends that the real question to be asked about ideology is not who is responsible for it, but why it is necessary: "Why do men 'need' this imaginary transposition of their real conditions of existence in order to 'represent to themselves' their real conditions of existence?" (163). Althusser's answer—that not only is ideology necessary for the formation of social practices but that without it, subjects could not live "'spontaneously' or 'naturally'" (171)—cannot be overturned by a return to Romantic nature poetry as a site of the spontaneous overflow of powerful feelings. "To Autumn" is not a spontaneous or a natural phenomenon but the result of an act of exorbitant concentration that does not collapse or condense into a message. The poem never quite produces what McGann calls a publicly coherent "communication-event" (1015), and Vendler's valorization of the "social coherence of the historical audience for lyric" is as jeopardized by Keats's act of giving the poem to Woodhouse, rather than to Reynolds, as is McGann's placement of poetry in the public sphere of reputation. Keats's perception that this poem would really only matter to the odd subject, and would else be caviar to the general, makes "social coherence" irrelevant to the possibility of a meeting of minds when the subject is not entirely within the terms of a shared ideology. Levinson asks for immanence and critique, together, as the condition of an authentic poetry or a criticism, and she postulates that only this combination raises either discourse above pragmatically or sociologically defined categories ("Romantic Poetry," 186). "To Autumn" conveys immanence in its sense of an oceanic oneness in being, yet as that feeling shifts from the rootedness of an organic ideology to the unbounded space of open skies, the text gives the barely deferred feeling of the impermanence of this state. Both the immanence and the critical power of the poem emerge from different kinds of negativity: its immanence from its negative capability, its ability to belong to an otherness; its capacity for critique from a negative dialectic that posits an ideological position and then glides away to a very different space from which one can only gape, like the angel of history, at what has been left behind.

Levinson's intensely scrupulous attempt to discover an ethics in Romanticism does not remedy, and in fact intensifies, the most significant problem of the first wave of the New Historicist study of Romanticism; the "fantasy of quiet being" comes to apply only to the poems, which are driven into even deeper silences, made even more incapable of questioning their own natures. Despite the repeated invocation of Adorno's work in both McGann's and Levinson's essays, their own dialectics and the work they have inspired remain focused on the recognition of dominant historical tendencies; such work cannot capture Adorno's sense of the value of negativity, or his focus on the power of those agents that deconstruct hegemony at its margins. A greater emphasis on the recovery of historical context should not entail a regression to an uncritical discourse of "facts" that emerge from a totalizing "truth."

This regression is nowhere more clearly accomplished than in McGann's essay "Plato and the Dialectic of Criticism," which is addressed, with Blakean irony, "To the Deconstructionists." McGann offers Socrates as the model literary critic, based upon his ability to "provide a structure within which we are to understand the 'truth' of those realities" that "are obscure to the poets themselves," and McGann suggests that the *Ion* is only the "most famous" of these demonstrations (*Social*, 30, 23). De Man is of a very different opinion: "Socrates," he contends, "had it coming to him" (*Rhetoric*, 279). While McGann's defense of Socrates involves a thorough elucidation of his own fundamental critical principles, de Man's prosecution of Socrates appears simply as a digressive moment in a broader discussion of the relations of power that lie between writers and readers. Yet de Man's indictment opens up a significant question that is bypassed in McGann's essay: Why does Socrates always win? Adorno addresses this question somewhat less cryptically than de Man when he argues that "Plato's pedagogy cultivated martial values" in its defense of the "prejudice that the imperishable must be the good—which is to say no more than that in permanent warfare the stronger is always right" (*Dialectics*, 131). When historicist analysis sets out to register the significance of the most powerful forces within a cultural moment, it runs the risk of entering hegemonic warfare on its own terms and of reenacting the martial values that it purports to critique. A critical subject who becomes a self-defined "vector of the present" (Levinson, "Romantic Poetry," 189) constructs critical identity as historical necessity, but reading historically should not entail fostering the illusion that seeing the material world as humanly and historically constructed gives thought the representative power to define either "the present" or "the romantic ideology" as monolithic entities. No reader of Keats should be as secure as McGann is in believing Socrates to be the unambiguous victor of the *Ion*. The structural similarity between that text and Keats's *Lamia* is too obvious (Apollonius as Socrates, Lysius as Ion, Lamia as poetry), and the history of critical identification with Apollonius is too blatant in exposing the habitual privilege granted to thought to repudiate its material, "female" other. Carrying the ambiguity of Keats's *Lamia* back to Plato's *Ion* would let us see the *Ion* itself as a standoff, in which it is impossible to tell whether Socrates' interrogation has demonstrated Ion's lack of understanding of his art or the insufficiency of Socrates' own interpretive categories.

When McGann says of "To Autumn" that it fools us into thinking that all autumns are the same, he implies that the truth is that they are not the same. Well, they are and they aren't. Those of us who are likely to form the audience for Keats's poetry may no longer be subject to disastrous harvests, but every year comes to the end of its cycle of growth, the same now as for Keats in 1819; the analogy between such an ending and our personal histories is the same; and the contrast between the perennial renewal of nature and the nonrenewal of our own existential contract is the same for us as it was for Keats. Hazlitt, as the ode "To Autumn" shows, was wrong about our relation to historically removed texts; they do say something about us. The reception history of "To Autumn," which is filled with a great love for this poem and a lack of concern over its existential doubts, tells us of our desire to belong to something larger than the self, something that ideally, seamlessly, joins the human and the natural. This desire is manifest in readings of "To Autumn" that do not so much critique this poem as acclaim it, without dwelling on the fears that provoke that desire, or, in Vendler's case, by strenuously dispelling those fears through the assertion of the value of work in making one a part of a social whole. In its final stanza, this poem says something else to us about what the world looks like from outside that sense of belonging. In the end, "To Autumn" is not a working poem, and its greatest value does not lie in its craftsmanship, extraordinary as that is. The poem is not an integral part of either an ontological or a historical whole; it is neither a piece of nature nor of second nature. Its final image of an imminent vanishing reflects the immeasurable economy of the gift; a trace of the other, a trace left to cover their departure.

NOTES

Preface

1. *The Letters of John Keats, 1814–1821*, vol. 1, p. 387. All quotations from Keats's letters are from this edition, which is cited in the text as *KL*.

2. *The Poems of John Keats*, ed. Jack Stillinger. All quotations from Keats's poetry are from this edition and are cited by line number.

Chapter 1

1. All quotations from Shakespeare's plays and poetry are based on *The Complete Works of Shakespeare*, ed. David Bevington, and are cited by line number. I have sometimes restored original spelling and punctuation.

2. *John Milton: Complete Poems and Major Prose*, ed. Merritt Y. Hughes. All quotations from Milton's poetry are from this edition and are cited by line number.

3. Bloom contends that the "spirit" of Milton "haunts" the poem in "Keats and the Embarrassments of the Poetic Tradition," (516), and cites Milton's lines

Then feed on thoughts, that voluntary move
Harmonious numbers; as the wakeful Bird
Sings darkling, and in shadiest Covert hid
Tunes her nocturnal note (*PL*, 3.37–40)

as a foreshadowing of Keats's use of the word "darkling" that "contains the whole kernel of the 'Ode'" (*Visionary Company*, 430); Leslie Brisman sees "the poem's relationship to death . . . bound to Keats's relationship with Milton" (*Milton's Poetry of Choice and Its Romantic Heirs*, 100); Paul Fry extends Bloom's quotation to include Milton's invocation of Urania and the tradition of blind bards, and argues that "the Miltonic passage . . . covers the whole territory of Keats's ode" (*The Poet's Calling in the English Ode*, 243); and John Hollander suggests of "forlorn" that "The word is . . . Miltonic," as "Keats's 'forlorn' is like a very echo from within his text, but it reaches back to another voice behind it" (*The Figure of Echo*, 37).

4. Besides the full versions of these stories in Catullus's *Marriage of Peleus and Thetis* and in Ovid's *Heroides*, synopses appear in several compilations of classical mythology with which Keats was familiar: Lempriere's *Dictionary*, Tooke's *Pantheon*, Baldwin's *Pantheon*, and Spence's *Polymetis*. Tooke and "Baldwin" (actually William Godwin) have Ariadne herself becoming the constellation, although that does not occur in either Catullus or Ovid.

5. Biblical quotations are taken from the King James Bible. Keats's *Universal Family Bible* is based on the King James.

6. The woodcut of Ariadne that appears on page 35 of *Ovid's Epistles* is very reminiscent of Titian's Ariadne. Dryden is listed among the translators in an advertisement for the publisher, Tonson, on the last page of the volume. I have not been able to determine whether Keats in fact saw this book.

Chapter 2

1. The differing versions of the poem and the questions raised by the variants are outlined in Robert Gittings's *The Odes of Keats and Their Earliest Known Manuscripts* and in Jack Stillinger's appendix to *Twentieth Century Interpretations of Keats's Odes*.

2. Wolfson hears in "Beauty is truth, truth beauty" a "final, desperate surmise of a reader not happy with an absent legend" (*The Questioning Presence*, 326–27); Paul Fry finds the poem's last lines "unequivocally ironic" as they reveal "an urn of decidedly limited insight" (*The Poet's Calling in the English Ode*, 256–57); Michael Hinden argues that "the context of the message is restricted to the speaker's experience of the urn," as the poem makes an "important distinction between art and life" ("Reading the Painting, Seeing the Poem: Vermeer and Keats," 30); Douglas Wilson declares, "First we must concede that this loaded equation is not all we need to know in this world" in order to achieve "the reader's superior consciousness" of the "speaker's final inability to 'complete the picture'" due to "a dialectic between his [the speaker's] own alienated condition and his ideal longing for the naive songs of the piper" ("Reading the Urn: Death in Keats's Arcadia," 840, 823, 829); and Theresa Kelley contends that the word "ye" in the final line refers to the urn rather than to the reader, and hence that "the speaker replies to the urn's aphorism 'Beauty is truth, truth beauty' by indicating this is the urn's truth, not his and, presumably, not ours" ("Keats, Ekphrasis and History," 230).

3. The dedication to the "Select Committee" follows the title page of vol. 1 of the *Annals*. Richardson's epigraph appears on the title page for each year's collection of the individual volumes of the *Annals*, beginning with vol. 2 (1817), and is also used to open several of Hazlitt's essays on Reynolds (*Annals*, 3:337 [July 1818]; 4:165 [July 1819]; 4:357 [October 1819]). The "Ode to a Nightingale" appeared in the *Annals* in July 1819 and the "Ode on a Grecian Urn" in January 1820.

4. This essay first appeared in the *London Magazine* issues of February and May of 1822, and is found in Hazlitt's *Complete Works*, vol. 18.

5. Hazlitt's essays on Reynolds's *Discourses* first appeared in the *Champion* of November and December of 1814 and January of 1815. They were reprinted in the *Annals of the Fine Arts* of April, July, and October of 1819, and are found in the *Complete Works*, 18:62–84.

6. Hazlitt gets this idea from Winckelmann: "The most beautiful body of ours would perhaps be as much inferior to the most beautiful Greek one, as Iphicles was to his brother Hercules" (*Reflections*, 4).

7. The "apocryphal" Book of Ecclesiasticus is contained in Keats's *Universal Family Bible*, which is based on the King James translation. This image from Ecclesiasticus is imported into the *Iliad* by Pope (but not by Chapman): "Like leaves on trees the race of man is found; now green in youth, now withering on the ground. . . . So generations in their course decay" (*The Iliad of Homer*, trans. Alexander Pope [London: George Bell, 1898], 6:181–86).

Chapter 3

1. Aileen Ward, "Keats and Burton: A Reappraisal"; Harold Bloom, *The Visionary Company*, 432–36; Barbara Herrnstein Smith, "'Sorrow's Mysteries': Keats's 'Ode on Melancholy'"; Jack Stillinger, "Imagination and Reality in the Odes of Keats"; Leon Waldoff, *Keats and the Silent Work of Imagination*; Vendler, *The Odes of John Keats*; Anselm Haverkamp, "Mourning Becomes Melancholia—A Muse Deconstructed: Keats's 'Ode on Melancholy'"; Hermione de Almeida, *Romantic Medicine and John Keats*.

2. "Mourning and Melancholia," in *The Standard Edition of the Complete Psychological Works of Sigmund Freud*, vol. 14, trans. James Strachey (London: Hogarth Press, 1955), 244. All quotations in English from Freud's work are based on this edition. When Freud's precise wording is significant, I have amended Strachey's translation in order to provide a more literal rendering of Freud's words and have then included the German passage in the endnotes.

3. I have amended this translation; "krankhaften" suggests "morbid" in addition to Strachey's more clinical term "pathological": "die wir darum unter den Verdacht einer krankhaften Disposition setzen" ("Trauer und Melancholie," in *Zur Technik der Psychoanalyse und zur Metapsychologie*, 258).

4. "Vielen von uns mag es auch schwer werden, auf den Glauben zu verzichten, daß im Menschen selbst ein Trieb zur Verkollkommung wohnt. . . . Allein ich glaube

nicht an einen solchen inneren Trieb und sehe keinen Weg, diese wohltuende Illusion zu schonen. Die bisherige Entwicklung des Menschen scheint mir keiner
anderen Erklarung zu bedurfen als die der Tiere" (Freud, *Gesammelte Werke*, 13:44).

5. "Man konnte mich fragen, ob und inwieweit ich selbst von den hier entwicklten
Annahmen uberzeugt bin. Meine Antwort wurde lauten, dab ich weder selbst
uberzeugt bin, noch bei anderen um Glauben fur sie werbe. Richtiger: ich weib
nicht, wie weit ich an sie glaube" (Freud, *Gesammelte Werke*, 13:63–64).

6. "Im ubrigen mag uns ein Dichter (Ruckert in den Makamen des Hariri) uber
die langsamen Fortschritte unserer wissenschaftlichen Erkenntis trosten:

'Was man nicht erfliegen kann, mub man erhinken . . .

Die Schrift sagt, es ist keine Sunde zu hinken'." (Freud, *Gesammelte Werke*, 13:69)

7. John Gibson Lockhart, "Cockney School of Poetry, No. 4," in *Blackwood's
Edinburgh Magazine*, August 1818; John Wilson Croker, review of *Endymion* in the
Quarterly Review 1818; and an anonymous review of *Endymion* in the *British Critic*
are all similar in tone and are conveniently reprinted in *Keats: The Critical Heritage*,
ed. G. M. Matthews, and *Keats Reviewed by His Contemporaries*, ed. Lewis M.
Schwartz. The phrase "uncouth language" comes from the *Quarterly* (Matthews,
111) and the "gross slang of voluptuousness" from the *British Critic* (Matthews, 94).

8. Lockhart, *Blackwood's*, from *Keats Reviewed*, 120. I have not seen any mention of
the curious echo in this review of Keats's reference to "Men of Power" in a letter to
Bailey in November of 1817, in which he distinguishes them from "Men of Genius"
(*KL*, 1:184), and Lockhart's pointed revalorization of the term in a review written
after a conversation with Bailey about Keats.

9. "On the Cockney School of Poetry, No. 1," *Blackwood's Edinburgh Magazine*,
October 1817 (2:38–41).

Chapter 4

1. Marjorie Levinson, "Romantic Poetry." Despite Levinson's explicit distancing
of her argument in this essay from the study of Keats's odes (206), her attempt to
theorize a "fantasy of quiet being" actually brings this essay closer to the approach to
materiality in "To Autumn" than anything in *Keats's Life of Allegory*. I see this essay as
a significant advance beyond the historicist paradigms previously offered by
Levinson and McGann, and that is the primary reason I have wanted to engage its
argument here.

BIBLIOGRAPHY

Abrams, M. H., ed. *The Norton Anthology of English Literature*. New York: Norton, 1993.

Adorno, Theodor. *Aesthetic Theory*. Trans. C. Lenhardt. London: Routledge and Kegan Paul, 1984.

——. *Negative Dialectics*. Trans. E. B. Ashton. New York: Continuum, 1973.

Almeida, Hermione de. *Romantic Medicine and John Keats*. New York: Oxford University Press, 1991.

Althusser, Louis. "Ideology and Ideological State Apparatuses (Notes Towards an Investigation)." In *Lenin and Philosophy and Other Essays*. Trans. Ben Brewster. New York: Monthly Review Press, 1971.

Aske, Martin. *Keats and Hellenism*. Cambridge: Cambridge University Press, 1985.

Auerbach, Erich. *Mimesis: The Representation of Reality in Western Literature*. Garden City, N.Y.: Doubleday, 1957.

Bate, Jonathan. *Shakespeare and the English Romantic Imagination*. Oxford: Clarendon Press, 1986.

Bate, Walter Jackson. *John Keats*. Cambridge, Mass.: Harvard University Press, 1963.

Benjamin, Walter. *Origin of German Tragic Drama*. Trans. John Osborne. London: NLB, 1977.

―――. "Theses on the Philosophy of History." In *Illuminations*. Ed. Hannah Arendt, trans. Harry Zohn. New York: Schocken Books, 1969.

Bloom, Harold. "Keats and the Embarrassments of the Poetic Tradition." In *From Sensibility to Romanticism*. Ed. Frederick W. Hilles and Harold Bloom. New York: Oxford University Press, 1965.

―――. *The Visionary Company: A Reading of English Romantic Poetry*. Garden City, N.Y.: Anchor Books, 1961.

Bloom, Harold, and Lionel Trilling, eds. *Romantic Poetry and Prose*. New York: Oxford University Press, 1973.

Bridges, Robert. *John Keats: A Critical Essay*. Lawrence and Bullen, 1895; repr. London: Oxford University Press, 1929.

Brisman, Leslie. *Milton's Poetry of Choice and Its Romantic Heirs*. Ithaca: Cornell University Press, 1973.

Bromwich, David. *Hazlitt: The Mind of a Critic*. Oxford: Oxford University Press, 1983.

Brooks, Cleanth. "Irony as a Principle of Structure." In *Critical Theory Since Plato*. Ed. Hazard Adams. New York: Harcourt, Brace, Jovanovich, 1971.

―――. *Modern Poetry and the Tradition*. Chapel Hill: University of North Carolina Press, 1939.

―――. *The Well-Wrought Urn*. New York: Harcourt, Brace, and World, 1947.

Burton, Robert. *Anatomy of Melancholy*. 11th ed. London: J. Walker and R. Lea, 1813.

Bush, Douglas. *John Keats: His Life and Writings*. New York: Macmillan, 1966.

―――. "Keats and His Ideas." In *The Major English Romantic Poets: A Symposium in Reappraisal*. Ed. C. D. Thorpe and Carlos Baker. Carbondale: Southern Illinois University Press, 1957.

―――, ed. *John Keats: Selected Poems and Letters*. Boston: Houghton Mifflin, 1958.

Chase, Cynthia. "'Viewless Wings': Intertextual Interpretation of Keats's 'Ode to a Nightingale'." In *Lyric Poetry: Beyond New Criticism*. Ed. Chaviva Hosek and Patricia Parker. Ithaca: Cornell University Press, 1985.

Cixous, Helene. "Castration or Decapitation." *Signs* 7, no. 1 (1981): 41–55.

―――. "Sorties." In *The Newly Born Woman*, Cixous and Catherine Clement. Trans. Betsy Wing. Minneapolis: University of Minnesota Press, 1986.

Cluysenaar, Anne. *Aspects of Literary Stylistics: A Discussion of Dominant Structures in Verse and Prose*. New York: St. Martin's Press, 1976.

Cook, Eleanor. "Birds in Paradise: Uses of Allusion in Milton, Keats, Whitman, Stevens and Ammons." *Studies in Romanticism* 26 (1987): 421–43.

De Man, Paul. *Allegories of Reading*. New Haven: Yale University Press, 1979.

―――. *Blindness and Insight*. 2nd ed. Minneapolis: University of Minnesota Press, 1983.

―――. "The Intentional Structure of the Romantic Image." In *Romanticism and Consciousness*. Ed. Harold Bloom. New York: Norton, 1970.

―――. *The Rhetoric of Romanticism*. New York: Columbia University Press, 1984.

———. *Romanticism and Contemporary Criticism*. Baltimore: Johns Hopkins University Press, 1993.

———. "Time and History in Wordsworth." *Diacritics* 17 (1987): 4–17.

Derrida, Jacques. *Of Grammatology*. Trans. Gayatri Spivak. Baltimore: Johns Hopkins University Press, 1970.

Dryden, John. "The Fourth Book of the Georgics." In *The Poems of John Dryden*. Vol. 2. Ed. James Kinsley. Oxford: Clarendon Press, 1958.

———. "Ovid's Art of Love, Book 1." In *The Poems of John Dryden*. Vol. 4. Ed. James Kinsley. Oxford: Clarendon Press, 1958.

Eliot, T. S. *Selected Essays: 1917–1932*. London: Faber and Faber, 1932.

Empson, William. *Seven Types of Ambiguity*. New York: New Directions, 1966.

Finney, Claude. *The Evolution of Keats's Poetry*. Cambridge, Mass.: Harvard University Press, 1936.

Fisher, Philip. "A Museum with One Work Inside: Keats and the Finality of Art." *Keats-Shelley Journal* 33 (1984): 123–34.

Fitzgerald, F. Scott. *The Letters of F. Scott Fitzgerald*. Ed. Andrew Turnbull. New York: Scribner's, 1963.

Fogle, Richard Harter. "Keats's 'Ode to a Nightingale'." *PMLA* 68 (1953): 211–22.

Forman, H. B, ed. *The Complete Works of John Keats*. New York: Thomas Crowell, 1900.

Freud, Sigmund. "Beyond the Pleasure Principle." In *The Standard Edition of the Complete Psychological Works of Sigmund Freud*. Vol. 18. Ed. and trans. James Strachey. London: Hogarth Press, 1955.

———. "Jenseits des Lust-Prinzips." In *Gesammelte Werke*. Vol. 13. Ed. Anna Freud et al. London: Imago, 1940.

———. "Mourning and Melancholia." In *The Standard Edition of the Complete Psychological Works of Sigmund Freud*. Vol. 14.

———. "Trauer und Melancholie." In *Zur Technik der Psychoanalyse und zur Metapsychologie*. Leipzig: Internationaler Psychoanalytischer Verlag, 1924.

Friedman, Geraldine. "The Erotics of Interpretation in Keats's 'Ode on a Grecian Urn': Pursuing the Feminine." *Studies in Romanticism* 32 (1993): 225–43.

Fry, Paul. *The Poet's Calling in the English Ode*. New Haven: Yale University Press, 1980.

Fuseli, Henry. *Lectures on Painting*. New York: Garland, 1979.

———. *The Mind of Henry Fuseli: Selections From His Writings with an Introductory Study*. Ed. Eudo C. Mason. London: Routledge & Kegan Paul, 1951.

Gadamer, Hans-Georg. *Truth and Method*. Trans. and ed. Garrett Borden and John Cumming. New York: Seabury, 1975.

Garrod, H. W. *Keats*. Oxford: Clarendon Press, 1926.

Gerard, Albert. "Prometheus and the Aeolian Lyre." *Yale Review* 33 (1944): 482–97.

Gittings, Robert. *John Keats: The Living Year*. Boston: Little Brown, 1968.

———. *The Odes of Keats and Their Earliest Known Manuscripts*. Kent, Ohio: Kent State University Press, 1970.

Gradman, Barry. "*King Lear* and the Image of Ruth in Keats's 'Nightingale' Ode." *Keats-Shelley Journal* 25 (1979): 21–22.

Grennan, Eamon. "Keats's *Contemptus Mundi:* A Shakespearean Influence on the 'Ode to a Nightingale'." *Modern Language Quarterly* 36 (1975): 272–92.

Hartman, Geoffrey. "Poem and Ideology: A Study of Keats's 'To Autumn'." In *The Fate of Reading*. Chicago: University of Chicago Press, 1975.

———. "The Voice of the Shuttle." In *Beyond Formalism*. New Haven: Yale University Press, 1970.

Haverkamp, Anselm. "Mourning Becomes Melancholia—A Muse Deconstructed: Keats's 'Ode on Melancholy'." *New Literary History* 21 (1990): 697–706.

Haydon, Benjamin. *Autobiography*. Ed. Edmund Blunden. Oxford: Oxford University Press, 1927.

———. *The Autobiography and Memoirs of Benjamin Robert Haydon*. Ed. Alexander P. D. Penrose. New York: Minton Balch, 1929.

———. "Cartoon of Delivering the Keys." *Annals of the Fine Arts* 3 (1818): 249–59.

———. "On the Cartoon of the Sacrifice of Lystra." *Annals of the Fine Arts* 4 (1819): 226–47.

Hazlitt, William. *Complete Works*. Ed. P. P. Howe. New York: AMS Press, 1967.

Hinden, Michael. "Reading the Painting, Seeing the Poem: Vermeer and Keats." *Mosaic* 17 (1984): 17–34.

Hollander, John. *The Figure of Echo: A Mode of Allusion in Milton and After*. Berkeley: University of California Press, 1981.

Jack, Ian. *Keats and the Mirror of Art*. Oxford: Clarendon Press, 1967.

Jakobson, Roman. "Shifters, Verbal Categories and the Russian Verb." *Selected Writings*, Vol. 2, *Word and Language*. The Hague: Mouton, 1971.

Jakobson, Roman, and Morris Halle. *Fundamentals of Language*. The Hague: Mouton, 1956.

Keats, John. *The Letters of John Keats, 1814–1821*. Ed. Hyder Edward Rollins. Cambridge, Mass.: Harvard University Press, 1958.

———. *The Poems of John Keats*. Ed. Jack Stillinger. Cambridge, Mass.: Harvard University Press, 1978.

Kelley, Theresa. "Keats, Ekphrasis and History." In *Keats and History*. Ed. Nicholas Roe. Cambridge: Cambridge University Press, 1995.

Krieger, Murray. "The Ekphrastic Principle and the Still Movement of Poetry." In *The Play and Place of Criticism*. Baltimore: Johns Hopkins University Press, 1959.

———. "'A Waking Dream': The Symbolic Alternative to Allegory." In *Words about Words about Words*. Baltimore: Johns Hopkins University Press, 1988.

Kristeva, Julia. *Black Sun: Depression and Melancholia*. Trans. Leon S. Roudiez. New York: Columbia University Press, 1989.

———. "From One Identity to an Other." In *Desire in Language: A Semiotic Approach to Literature and Art*. Trans. Thomas Gora, Alice Jardine, and Leon S. Roudiez. New York: Columbia University Press, 1980.

———. *Revolution in Poetic Language.* Trans. Margaret Waller. New York: Columbia University Press, 1984.

———. "Within the Microcosm of the Talking Cure." Trans. Thomas Gora and Margaret Waller. In *Interpreting Lacan.* Ed. Joseph H. Smith and William Kerrigan. New Haven: Yale University Press, 1983.

Lacan, Jacques. *Ecrits: A Selection.* Trans. Alan Sheridan. New York: Norton, 1977.

———. *The Four Fundamental Concepts of Psychoanalysis.* Ed. Jacques-Alain Miller. Trans. Alan Sheridan. New York: Norton, 1981.

———. "Position de l'inconscient." In *Ecrits.* Paris: Editions du Seuil, 1966.

Leavis, F. R. *Revaluation: Tradition and Development in English Poetry.* New York: Norton, 1963.

Lessing, Gotthold Ephraim. *Laocoön: An Essay Upon the Limits of Poetry and Painting.* Trans. Ellen Frothingham. New York: Noonday Press, 1965.

Levinson, Marjorie. *Keats's Life of Allegory: The Origins of a Style.* Oxford: Basil Blackwell, 1988.

———. "Romantic Poetry: The State of the Art." *MLQ* 54 (1993): 183–214.

Lindenberger, Herbert. "Keats's 'To Autumn' and Our Knowledge of a Poem." *College English* 32 (1970): 123–34.

Lukacs, George. *The Theory of the Novel.* Trans. Anna Bostock. Cambridge, Mass.: MIT Press, 1971.

Matthews, G. M., ed. *Keats: The Critical Heritage.* London: Routledge, 1971.

McGann, Jerome. "Keats and the Historical Method in Literary Criticism." *MLN* 94 (1979): 988–1032.

———. *The Romantic Ideology.* Chicago: University of Chicago Press, 1983.

———. *Social Values and Poetic Acts.* Cambridge, Mass.: Harvard University Press, 1988.

Milton, John. *Complete Poems and Major Prose.* Ed. Merritt Y. Hughes. Indianapolis: Odyssey Press, 1957.

Muhlhauser, Peter, and Rom Harré. *Pronouns and People.* London: Basil Blackwell, 1990.

Muir, Kenneth. "The Meaning of the Odes." In *John Keats: A Reassessment.* Ed. Muir. Liverpool: Liverpool University Press, 1958.

Murry, John Middleton. *Keats.* New York: Noonday Press, 1955.

Nemoianu, Virgil. "The Dialectics of Movement in Keats's 'To Autumn'." *PMLA* 93 (1978): 205–14.

Ovid. *Heroides and Amores, with an English Translation.* Trans. Grant Showerman. Cambridge, Mass.: Harvard University Press, 1977.

———. *Ovid's Epistles, Translated by Several Hands.* London: Jacob Tonson, 1701.

Perkins, David. *The Quest for Permanence.* Cambridge, Mass.: Harvard University Press, 1959.

———, ed. *English Romantic Writers.* New York: Harcourt, Brace and World, 1995.

Peterfreund, Stuart. "The Truth about 'Beauty' and 'Truth': Keats's 'Ode on a Grecian Urn,' Milton, Shakespeare and the Uses of Paradox." *Keats-Shelley Journal* 34 (1985): 62–82.

Pettet, E. C. *On the Poetry of Keats.* Cambridge: Cambridge University Press, 1957.

Phinney, A. W. "Keats in the Museum: Between Aesthetics and History." *Journal of English and Germanic Philology* 90 (1991): 217–24.

Plato. "Apology." In *Works of Plato.* Vol. 3. Trans. B. Jowett. New York: Tudor, n.d.

Porter, Roy. *Mind-Forg'd Manacles: A History of Madness in England from the Restoration to the Regency.* Cambridge, Mass.: Harvard University Press, 1987.

Ransom, John Crowe. "Criticism as Pure Speculation." In *Critical Theory since Plato.* Ed. Hazard Adams. New York: Harcourt, Brace Jovanovich, 1971.

Reynolds, Joshua. *The Discourses of Sir Joshua Reynolds.* London: Oxford University Press, 1907.

Rollins, Hyder Edward, ed. *The Keats Circle.* Cambridge, Mass.: Harvard University Press, 1965.

Saussure, Ferdinand de. *Course in General Linguistics.* Ed. Charles Bally and Albert Sechehaye, with Albert Reidlinger. Trans. Wade Baskin. New York: McGraw-Hill, 1966.

Schiesari, Juliana. *The Gendering of Melancholia: Feminism, Psychoanalysis and the Symbolics of Loss in Renaissance Literature.* Ithaca: Cornell University Press, 1992.

Schwartz, Lewis M., ed. *Keats Reviewed by His Contemporaries.* Metuchen, N.J.: Scarecrow, 1973.

Shakespeare, William. *The Complete Works of Shakespeare.* Ed. David Bevington. New York: HarperCollins, 1992.

Sharp, William. *The Life and Letters of Joseph Severn.* New York: Scribner's, 1892.

Shearman, John. *Raphael's Cartoons in the Collection of Her Majesty the Queen, and the Tapestries for the Sistine Chapel.* London: Phaidon, 1972.

Sidmouth, Lord Viscount. "On the Affinity between Painting and Writing, in point of Composition." *Annals of the Fine Arts* 1 (1816): 1–20.

Smith, Barbara Herrnstein. "'Sorrow's Mysteries': Keats's 'Ode on Melancholy'." *Studies in English Literature* 6 (1966): 679–91.

Spence, Joseph. *Polymetis: or, An Enquiry concerning the Agreement Between the Works of the Roman Poets, And the Remains of the Antient Artists.* London: R. Dodsley, 1747; repr. New York: Garland, 1976.

Spenser, Edmund. "Two Cantos of Mutabilitie." In *Edmund Spenser's Poetry.* Ed. Hugh Maclean. New York: Norton, 1968.

Spiegelman, Willard. "Keats's 'Coming Muskrose' and Shakespeare's "Profound Verdure'." *ELH* 50 (1983): 347–62.

Spitzer, Leo. "'Ode on a Grecian Urn'; or, Content vs. Metagrammar." In *Essays on English and American Literature.* Ed. Anne Hatcher. Princeton: Princeton University Press, 1962.

Stillinger, Jack. "Imagination and Reality in the Odes of Keats" and Appendix. In *Twentieth-Century Interpretations of Keats's Odes.* Ed. Stillinger. Englewood Cliffs, N.J.: Prentice-Hall, 1968.

Tate, Allen. *Essays of Four Decades.* Chicago: Swallow Press, 1968.

Taylor, Mark. "Keats' 'Ode to a Nightingale'." *Explicator* 36 (1978): 25.

Thomson, James. *The Poetical Works of James Thomson*. Ed. J. Logie Robertson. London: Oxford University Press, 1961.

Trilling, Lionel. "The Poet as Hero: Keats in His Letters." In *The Opposing Self: Nine Essays in Criticism*. New York: Viking Press, 1955.

Universal Family Bible. London: J. Cooke, 1773.

Vendler, Helen. *The Odes of John Keats*. Cambridge, Mass.: Harvard University Press, 1983.

———. "'Tintern Abbey': Two Assaults." In *Wordsworth in Context*. Ed. Pauline Fletcher and John Murphy. London: Bucknell University Press, 1992.

Waldoff, Leon. *Keats and the Silent Work of Imagination*. Urbana: University of Illinois Press, 1985.

Ward, Aileen. "Keats and Burton: A Reappraisal." *Philological Quarterly* 40 (1961): 535–52.

Wasserman, Earl. *The Finer Tone: Keats' Major Poems*. Baltimore: Johns Hopkins University Press, 1953.

Watkins, Daniel. "Historical Amnesia and Patriarchal Morality in Keats's 'Ode on a Grecian Urn'." In *Spirits of Fire*. Ed. G. A. Rosso and Watkins. Rutherford, N.J.: Associated University Presses, 1990.

White, R. S. "Shakespearean Music in Keats's 'Ode to a Nightingale'." *English* 30 (1981): 217–29.

Williams, Raymond. *The Country and the City*. New York: Oxford University Press, 1973.

Wilson, A. N. "Everything England Used to Be." *New York Times Book Review*. 30 May 1993, 6.

Wilson, Douglas. "Reading the Urn: Death in Keats's Arcadia." *Studies in English Literature* 25 (1985): 823–44.

Wimsatt, William. "The Structure of Romantic Nature Imagery." In *Romanticism and Consciousness*. Ed. Harold Bloom. New York: Norton, 1970.

Winckelmann, Johann Joachim. *Reflections on the Painting and Sculpture of the Greeks*. Trans. Henry Fuseli. London: A. Millar, 1765; repr. Menston, Yorkshire: Scolar Press, 1972.

Wolfson, Susan. "Composition and 'Unrest': The Dynamics of Form in Keats's Last Lyrics." *Keats-Shelley Journal* 34 (1985): 53–82.

———. *The Questioning Presence: Wordsworth, Keats and the Interrogative Mode in Romantic Poetry*. Ithaca: Cornell University Press, 1986.

Zeitlin, Froma. "On Ravishing Urns: Keats in His Tradition." In *Rape and Representation*. Ed. Lynn A. Higgins and Brenda R. Silver. New York: Columbia University Press, 1991.

INDEX